AF905081

Interest and Capital

Interest and Capital

The Monetary Economics of Michał Kalecki

JAN TOPOROWSKI

OXFORD
UNIVERSITY PRESS

OXFORD
UNIVERSITY PRESS

Great Clarendon Street, Oxford, OX2 6DP,
United Kingdom

Oxford University Press is a department of the University of Oxford. It furthers the University's objective of excellence in research, scholarship, and education by publishing worldwide. Oxford is a registered trade mark of Oxford University Press in the UK and in certain other countries

© Jan Toporowski 2022

The moral rights of the author have been asserted

First Edition published in 2022

Impression: 1

All rights reserved. No part of this publication may be reproduced, stored in a retrieval system, or transmitted, in any form or by any means, without the prior permission in writing of Oxford University Press, or as expressly permitted by law, by licence or under terms agreed with the appropriate reprographics rights organization. Enquiries concerning reproduction outside the scope of the above should be sent to the Rights Department, Oxford University Press, at the address above

You must not circulate this work in any other form
and you must impose this same condition on any acquirer

Published in the United States of America by Oxford University Press
198 Madison Avenue, New York, NY 10016, United States of America

British Library Cataloguing in Publication Data
Data available

Library of Congress Control Number: 2021949541

ISBN 978–0–19–881623–2

DOI: 10.1093/oso/9780198816232.001.0001

Printed and bound by
CPI Group (UK) Ltd, Croydon, CR0 4YY

Links to third party websites are provided by Oxford in good faith and for information only. Oxford disclaims any responsibility for the materials contained in any third party website referenced in this work.

Acknowledgements

The ideas in this book are the distillation of many years of reflection, even before this book was conceived. While the intellectual biography of Kalecki took up nearly three decades of my career as an economist, these ideas go back to my earliest serious work in banking and finance, the work that caused me to pick out Kalecki as a guide when I started on my systematic study of Economics. Along the way, I have heaped up intellectual debts that, in the way of these debts, have always exceeded my comprehension and the use that I have been able to make of the credit advanced. Early on I was able to make the acquaintance of Victoria Chick and Jerzy Osiatyński. The first introduced me to monetary economics proper, and the second to the work of Kalecki in general. I later benefitted greatly from discussions with Joseph Halevi, Geoff Harcourt, Charles Goodhart, Riccardo Bellofiore, and Kazimierz Łaski; and, along the way, Bruno Bonizzi, Jennifer Churchill, Sheila Dow, Guglielmo Forges Davanzati, John Grahl, Robert Calvert Jump, Ewa Karwowski, Tadeusz Kowalik, David Laidler, Marc Lavoie, Noemi Levy-Orlik, Julio López, Photis Lysandrou, Douglas Mair, Maria Cristina Marcuzzo, Clara Mattei, Jo Michell, Tracy Mott, Anastasia Nesvetailova, Arturo O'Connell, Luigi Pasinetti, Malcolm Sawyer, Mimoza Shabani, Anwar Shaikh, Henryk Szlajfer, Hanna Szymborska, and Alessandro Vercelli. What is of value in these chapters is in great measure due to their influence. I retain sole responsibility for obstinate vestiges of my ignorance.

Building a book on the fragments of Kalecki's monetary thinking is also an opportunity to put together in more systematic form the previously published pieces of my interpretation of that thinking. Accordingly, the chapters in this book draw largely on material published before, that I have been able to re-write for this larger project. The first part of the book draws on my two volumes of Kalecki's biography. Chapter 5, containing Kalecki's fable on credit and debt, has been through various versions, as I tried to make sense of the fable. Latterly it appeared in the Fifth Accademia Lincei Guggenheim Conference in the History of Economic Thought on 'Financial Instability, Market Disruptions and Macroeconomics Lessons from History and the History of Economic Thought', Rome, 17–18 December 2019, as 'Debt and Debt Management: Lessons from History'; Chapter 7 appeared in an earlier incarnation as 'Anwar

Shaikh and the Classical Theory of Interest: A Critical Note' in the *Cambridge Journal of Economics* (vol. 44 no. 2, March 2020); an expanded version of Chapter 8 appears in the *Annals of the Fondazione Luigi Einaudi*; Chapter 9 is an extended version of 'The Transfer Theory of Government Debt: What Keynes Learned from Kalecki', my contribution to the festschrift for Sheila Dow, edited by Penelope Hawkins and Ioana Negru; Chapters 10 and 11 use material from 'Open Market Operations' in D. G. Mayes, P. L. Siklos, and J-E. Sturm (eds), *The Oxford Handbook of the Economics of Central Banking* (Oxford University Press, 2019); and finally Chapter 12 draws on my entry on 'Monetary Policy' in Nikolaos Karagiannis and John E. King, *A Modern Guide to State Intervention* (Edward Elgar, 2019). The editors of these publications and their reviewers are due thanks for their contributions to these chapters.

Contents

Introduction

The Understated Monetary Considerations of Kalecki

There is a common view that there is not much in the way of monetary analysis in the work of Kalecki. Even perhaps his closest associate from the time when Kalecki was developing his monetary ideas, Josef Steindl, in considering Kalecki's analysis of economic dynamics, was moved to write that

> ...the influence of money...in Kalecki's theory plays a very subordinate role, partly for historical reasons. At his time, the long-term rate of interest did not change very much, and he could rightly argue that its influence on investment was not important. The times have changed in this respect, and also the situation on the continent [of Europe—JT] has always been rather different from the British institutional background. Generally speaking you do not find in Kalecki very much about the topics which are Professor Minsky's subject: finance, debt, credit cycles. I don't think that Kalecki denied the importance of these factors in any way. But for him they were secondary to, and in a sense derived from, the events in the 'real' sphere of production, investment, overcapacity, and so on.[1]

That impression is certainly confirmed by any comparison between his writings on money and finance, and the extensive writings on money of the economist with whom Kalecki is most commonly compared, John Maynard Keynes. A result of this comparison is the tendency that may be found in the Post-Keynesian literature, to 'fit' Kalecki's into the lacunae in Keynes's analysis, combining Kalecki's theories of distribution and the trade cycle with Keynes's monetary analysis and theories of aggregate demand as, for example, in Reynolds *Political Economy A Synthesis of Kaleckian and Post-Keynesian Economics* (1987), in effect dropping Kalecki's monetary analysis. The present

[1] Steindl, 'Reflections on Kalecki's Dynamics', 1989b, pp. 312–13. Steindl's view is shared even by students of Kalecki's monetary analysis. In a chapter on 'Kalecki's Monetary Economics' Gary Dymski concluded: 'Scholars are in broad agreement that Kalecki's monetary approach is underdeveloped' (1996, p. 116).

Interest and Capital: The Monetary Economics of Michał Kalecki. Jan Toporowski, Oxford University Press.
© Jan Toporowski 2022. DOI: 10.1093/oso/9780198816232.003.0001

work arises out of a sense that this view not only unfairly neglects a vital part of Kalecki's analysis, as has already been pointed out by Malcolm Sawyer.[2] It also deprives economists of important insights into monetary circulation and corporate finance that are absent in the work of the better-known English monetary economist, and that shed new light on the monetary and financial problems that we find in the twenty-first century.

The neglect of Kalecki's monetary analysis is in large measure the fault of its author. Although he was consistent in his monetary theory, he was so inconsistent in explaining it as to frustrate any reader wishing to grasp the essentials of that theory. I have tried to resolve this inconsistency by presenting his published remarks on money and finance in the first four chapters of this book, as they were expounded chronologically. A middle section then explains how Kalecki's monetary ideas, are distinguished, in particular from the 'classical' view that links interest to profits, a view that today spans virtually all schools of thought from the New Neo-Classical Synthesis to Marxists (although Marx himself was sceptical of this 'classical' view). This section also expounds some of the implications of Kalecki's views for contemporary money and finance. A final section concludes with some Kaleckian reflections on central banking and monetary policy.

But that neglect cannot be dissociated from the way in which macroeconomics itself has evolved. From the modelling of the Neo-Classical synthesis, providing a macroeconomics driven by aggregate variables, through monetarism and New Classical macroeconomics, the capitalist firm has been consistently eliminated in pursuit of 'micro-foundations' consisting of households acting as producers. This may be appropriate for what Marx called 'petty commodity production', with households having an option to exchange labour in addition to their own products for what they wish to consume, but not for a twentieth-century, let alone a twenty-first century, economy in which production is dominated by corporations. The difference is fundamental because households have income and expenditure, but not corporate finance. Corporate finance resides in corporations, and is the foundation of Kalecki's monetary analysis and, arguably, his macroeconomics.

The premise of this book is that the monetary analysis of Kalecki cannot just be recovered from his limited writing on the subject, such as the account given by Sawyer.[3] That analysis needs to be reconstructed from all parts of his work, because of the clear focus in his work on aggregate demand and the

[2] Sawyer, 'Kalecki on Money and Finance', 2001.
[3] Sawyer, 'Kalecki on Money and Finance', 2001.

business cycle as the 'central problem' of the capitalist economy.[4] At some point, around 1938–1939, Kalecki had come to the conclusion that monetary factors are 'not of fundamental importance for the mechanism of the business cycle'[5] and this seems to have justified for him continuing his neglect of systematic writing on money and monetary policy. But this does not mean that he neglected corporate finance as a factor in economic decision-making and macroeconomic dynamics, and there is a remarkable consistency, explored in Chapter 6, in what he did write. In this book, therefore, in addition to Kalecki's own explicit insights on money, I have reconstructed some of his ideas on the monetary circulation to which I have added some of my own observations on finance and credit to give a more systematic account of money and corporate finance in the present day. At this stage, after many years of research on Kalecki and, in parallel with this, on financial economics, it is very difficult for me to distinguish where Kalecki's ideas finish, and where my own ones emerge. The purist seeker after Kalecki's insights is recommended to read Malcolm Sawyer's excellent digest of Kalecki's monetary economics or, ideally and without Post-Keynesian bias, Kalecki's own writings. Nevertheless, this book remains a financial and monetary interpretation of Kalecki, rather than a financial or monetary departure from Kalecki.

Method of Analysis

There is a very particular reason for presenting to the reader a mixture of my own and Kalecki's ideas. In the wake of the financial crises of our time, the neglect of corporate finance by virtually all schools of thought in economics today, including Keynesian and Post-Keynesian economics, has become most glaringly obvious. Even the sub-discipline of finance in economics, goes little beyond the study of financial instruments, portfolio choice, and market valuation.[6] This book may therefore have some use in recovering Kalecki's monetary ideas for our time, and may even convince some of my fellow-economists of the value in those ideas. But its main value is, I believe, in presenting in a systematic way the key concepts and relations of money, credit, and finance that are necessary to understand finance and its crises today.

[4] Kalecki, 'Theories of Growth in Different Social Systems', 1970.
[5] Kalecki, 'The Long-Term Rate of Interest', 1939, p. 114.
[6] Shabani and Toporowski, 'A Nobel Prize for the Empirical Analysis of Assets Prices', 2015.

My extended immersion in the work of Kalecki accounts for the methodology that I use in these chapters (most notably in Chapters 7 and 8), namely that of successive approximations starting from a base model of a 'pure' capitalist economy. This is not only in line with the way in which Kalecki himself presented his work. Its purpose is not so much to uncover the assumptions that will make a particular conclusion consistent with premises or evidence[7] as to identify a simple, tractable, 'basic' system of structural relations that will give conclusions which may be modified as successive approximations to 'reality' are made. This makes for a more systematic investigation of monetary relations than the sympathetic introspection with which New Classical, New Keynesian and behavioural theories model optimizing (or sub-optimizing) behaviour. Such optimization may, at best, capture one moment in monetary circulation, but not its aggregate significance or outcomes. By comparison the asymmetries and market rigidities that characterize New Keynesian models may be seen as incidental rather than systematic.

In general the methodology used here precludes empirical or statistical verification because, until the final approximation, we are dealing with different 'levels of abstraction', or analytically imagined structures, in this case structures of payments and monetary transfers or monetary circulation. Such structures would not show up as statistical regularities that are outcomes of all the monetary transactions, and not just those associated with the basic model or any particular approximation. At the same time, the method advanced here provides a more rigorous testing of structural relations through successive approximations than mathematical models nested in congenial assumptions that use mathematics to secure their logic, while leaving their assumptions wide open for the entry and proliferation of error. Such formalism reduces monetary economics to a diet of conjecture and statistics that is fairly meaningless without the conjecture, but does little to prove or even test the underlying conjecture.

Wicksell observed something like this in the Preface to his classic work on monetary theory:

> I have on this occasion made next to no use of the mathematical method. This does not mean that I have changed my mind in regard to its validity and applicability, but simply that my subject does not appear to me to be ripe for methods of precision. In most other fields of political economy there is unanimity concerning at least the *direction* in which one cause or another

[7] cf. Leontief, 'Implicit Theorizing', 1937.

> reacts on economic processes; the next step must then lie in an attempt to introduce more precise quantitative relations. But in the subject to which this book is devoted the dispute still rages about *plus* as opposed to *minus*. As regards the influence on prices of easier credit, all three possible opinions are to be found among the most eminent writers.[8]

If there is a criticism that Kalecki may have accepted of his work it is perhaps that he may have been too confident about the explanatory power of his mathematical models. It was not their mathematical formulation that decided the fate of his theories, but the ideas contained in them. This book is offered to the reader with a view to exposing the monetary ideas hidden behind the modelling, rather than adding more equations to the model.

It follows from this that there is only a limited claim for the 'realism' of the basic assumptions in this analysis. In any case, the criticism, widespread among critics of the mainstream in economic theory, that such theory lacks 'realism' is overdone. What matters is not the realism of any starting assumptions, but whether those assumptions can survive successive approximation to reality. In other words, whether the fundamental relationships postulated in the basic model remain basic at the point when the model has become complicated to mirror reality. The notion at the heart of contemporary 'micro-founded' macroeconomics that households determine production and investment is unreal, but should have been disposed of as soon as the firm is introduced into the analysis.[9] Kalecki's capitalist firms determining the circulation of money in the economy through their production, investment, and financing decisions remains, as these chapters argue, at the heart of any modern economy. Such too, I believe, is the purpose of Keynes's assumption in his *General Theory* of a closed economy with no government and no foreign trade.

The clear focus in the chapters in this book is on the succession of money payments in an economy. This is largely ignored in the literature of monetary economics, where monetarists have been concerned with money stocks, and are content to assume away as constant the circulation of those stocks. Since the 1990s this concern has been replaced by a preoccupation with the rate of interest, rather than any underlying monetary circulation. In macroeconomics, New Classical economics, despite its initial monetarist pretensions, has

[8] Wicksell, *Interest and Prices*, 1936, p. xxx.

[9] This argument is further expanded in Toporowski, 'Microfoundations, Minsky and Classical Political Economy', 2016a.

removed money still further from consideration, by insisting on a distinction between 'real' and 'monetary' analysis, in which money incomes are removed and the analysis orientated towards efficient barter. Credit is reduced to money, and money is reduced to savings that may be any surplus commodities withheld from exchange.

Outside the academic journals that dominate monetary economics two schools of thought have emerged each claiming to secure a firmer grasp of monetary circulation in our economies. One of them has sought to focus money and credit around a principle of stock-flow consistency. The principle of course is correct for the purposes of accounting of stocks and flows. Its limitation for the analysis of monetary circulation is that the principle is usually presented as a system for the whole economy that becomes too complex to be entirely tractable as soon as one tries to break down the 'transactions' of the private sector as a whole into the actual transactions of differentiated individual households and firms within that sector. With Jo Michell I examine this limitation in a separate paper.[10] However, it should be said from the outset that the principle of stock-flow consistency is sound, and is adhered to in the chapters that follow.

The other school of thought is the French–Italian–Canadian group of economists who have sought to reconcile the monetary theories of Marx with Keynes by examining stylized 'circuits of money'. Their analysis, as represented by the work of Augusto Graziani, is discussed in Chapter 8 of this book.

The Structure of the Argument

This book is a set of essays made up of separate papers. They may be read individually, or taken together. The reader seeking a more summary view may read just the first part of the book, or, at its most brief, Chapter 6 in this book. Nevertheless, taken together these chapters form a logical structure. Kalecki's remark in his foreword to his *Essays in the Theory of Economic Fluctuations* applies very much to this volume:

> These essays, though formally independent, nevertheless constitute a whole. Each of them treats a problem which is interesting in itself, but at the same time it prepares the ground for the succeeding essays... (1939a, p. 7).

[10] Michell and Toporowski, 'The Stock-flow Consistent Approach with Active Financial Markets', 2012.

The logical structure goes from explaining and extending Kalecki's 'application' of his business cycle model to 'The Money Market', published for the first time in English in the Oxford University Press edition of the *Collected Works*. From this Kalecki's ideas developed to his consideration of international payments and debt, and the financing problems of developing countries. The section on Kalecki's fragments on money and finance concludes with a recent discovery that points to a striking departure from the classical view that payments on debt and interest have to come out of current income or profits. The second part of this book then starts with a summary of the fundamental principles of Kalecki's monetary thinking. This leads on to chapters comparing and contrasting his view with the Ricardian or classical theory of money and interest that is the foundation of current views on money and interest in most mainstream and heterodox economics (Chapter 7) and the circuitist theory of Augusto Graziani, whose monetary theory is close to that of Kalecki (Chapter 8). Chapter 9 considers the effect of fiscal policy on monetary circulation.

The final set of chapters explain central banking operations and conclude with a chapter arguing that monetary policy may affect the way in which firms finance their business expenditure, but not the level of that expenditure itself, which is what determines the business cycle. Hence, when central banks are set to manage (target) the business cycle (inflation or output), their monetary policy becomes endogenous to the business cycle. This last point then ties up with the exposition in Chapters 1 and 2, arguing that the rate of interest has no effect on the business cycle, which is determined by firms' investment.

Kalecki's monetary theory is a challenge to the Wicksellian orthodoxy that has dominated monetary theory for the last century and a half, with the brief interlude when it succumbed to the specious banality of monetarism. Kalecki's challenge is fundamental, delving deep into the circulation of money in capitalism.

PART I

KALECKI'S FRAGMENTS ON MONEY AND INTEREST

Kalecki's writings on monetary theory were rarely presented in a systematic form and, if presented systematically, it was to conclude that monetary factors did not have much influence on the business cycle, the concealed mechanism by which markets move between boom and recession. That business cycle determines prosperity or poverty, employment or idleness. Accordingly, in Kalecki's view, that cycle is the proper economic domain of politics and social reform, and he did not bother with politically redundant reflections on money and interest. However, this did not mean that his views on money were incidental, inconsistent and lacking in original insight. In fact, taken together, Kalecki's ideas reveal a profound view of money, credit, and finance.

These chapters put together the fragments of Kalecki's writings on money and credit, more or less in chronological order. Chapter 1 looks at his writings before the Second World War, when Kalecki's monetary thinking was organized around how investment was financed. Chapter 2 considers Kalecki's wartime writings, when he articulated his disagreement with the Wicksellian theory that the business cycle can be regulated by the rate of interest. Chapter 3 surveys that part of his wartime writings that dealt with interest and debt. This is followed by Kalecki's consideration of the debt and international monetary implications of post-war full employment, in Chapter 4. This part of the book finishes on a lighter note, but with serious implications, with a fable on the debt management that is an important aspect of money in a credit economy.

1

Kalecki's Monetary Theory before the Second World War

The Financing of Investment

This chapter examines Kalecki's pre-war monetary analysis, where he put forward for the first time his idea that, from the point of view of the economy as a whole, investment finances itself, because investment raises the circulation of money in the economy. However, investment is limited by the liquidity that enterprises possess.

1.1 Earliest References

Kalecki's first exposition of his monetary ideas came in his *Próba teorii koniunktury* (widely translated as 'Essay on the business cycle theory') published in Polish in 1933. Its key theoretical modelling of the business cycle appeared shortly afterwards in German, French, and English. Kalecki's *Essay* contains the elements of his analysis familiar to those who have read his work: Profits are equal to capitalists' consumption and their gross expenditure on capital equipment, that is the production of investment goods. Investment is given as a function of the expected profitability of investment, which in turn is determined by the actual gross profitability of existing capital, and the rate of interest. However, once investment exceeds the amount required as replacement of worn-out capital equipment, additions to the capital stock, or net investment, eventually reduce the gross profitability of existing capital. This then brings down the amount of investment, and the economy moves into a downturn. This is modelled using a difference equation so that, with stable lags, the system produces a regular cycle around a constant (flat) trend.

A key relation in Kalecki's system is the one between capitalists' expenditure on consumption and investment and the profits that they earn. Here, with a simplifying assumption that workers do not save, Kalecki put forward the essential idea that became his theory of profits:

Interest and Capital: The Monetary Economics of Michał Kalecki. Jan Toporowski, Oxford University Press.
© Jan Toporowski 2022. DOI: 10.1093/oso/9780198816232.003.0002

> The conclusion that the increase in capitalist consumption in turn increases their profits contradicts the common conviction that the more is consumed the less is saved. This approach, which is correct with regard to a single capitalist, does not apply to the capitalist class as a whole. If some capitalists spend money, either on investment or on consumer goods, their money passes to other capitalists in the form of profits. Investment or consumption of some capitalists creates profits for other. Capitalists as a class gain exactly as much as they invest or consume, and if – in a closed system – they ceased to construct and consume they could not make any money at all.[1]

He went on:

> The question may still arise of where capitalists find the means to increase the production of their investment goods, or their personal consumption. If we abstract from the 'technical' elements of the money market, we may say that capitalists as a whole do not need money in order to achieve this since, as shown above, the expenditure of some capitalists is converted into profits for others; the outlay on construction of a fixed asset is by no means frozen, as some people think, and released only as the capital invested is gradually written off – but it is already returned in the course of construction in the form of profits accruing to the firms whose sales (either of investment or consumer goods) are directly or indirectly connected with this construction.

A financial implication of this is that '...If during a particular period more money is spent, e.g., out of bank deposits, then *pro tanto* more money flows back into the banks in the form of realised profits, so that the sum of deposits remains unchanged.' However, Kalecki argued that some 'credit inflation' (additional borrowing) would be necessary for two reasons: First of all because the lag in delivery of investment goods would require additional working capital; and, secondly, to finance any increases in investment and consumption.[2]

With this observation, Kalecki marked out the fundamental distinction between his monetary economics and that of other theorists who have formed monetary theory in his time and well into the twenty-first century. He was later to express this distinction as follows:

[1] Kalecki, 'Essay on the Business Cycle Theory', 1933, p. 80. The page number refers to the complete version of this essay published in the English edition of Kalecki's *Collected Works*.

[2] Kalecki, 'Essay on the Business Cycle Theory', 1933, pp. 80–1.

> Many economists assume, at least in their abstract theories, a state of business democracy where anybody endowed with entrepreneurial ability can obtain capital for starting a business venture. This picture of the activities of the 'pure' entrepreneur is, to put it mildly, unrealistic. The most important prerequisite for becoming an entrepreneur is the *ownership* of capital.[3]

Capital, it should be noted here, refers to the monetary resources spent in the course of production and investment, monetary resources that then return as profits income to capitalists in the market exchanges that constitute the processes of production and investment. Kalecki went on to specify the significance that this distinction, between his monetary theory and that of 'abstract theories', had for his argument: 'The above considerations are of great importance for the theory of the determination of investment.'[4] This significance is discussed below. But his argument at that point was laying down the elements of his theory of business cycles in which, as is well known, investment is the key driving force. For this reason, perhaps, he overlooked the significance of his distinction for monetary theory. That significance may be summarized here as follows. In 'a state of business democracy where anybody endowed with entrepreneurial ability can obtain capital for starting a business venture' the terms on which that capital is made available by the credit system to entrepreneurs, along with the return on capital employed in business, wholly determines the scale and direction of business activity. In turn, those terms are determined by the credit policy of commercial banks, and the monetary policy of the central bank, regulating the liquidity of commercial banks, and setting the minimum rate of interest for short-term loans. As in the monetary theory that commonly accompanies 'abstract theories' postulating 'a state of business democracy', the circulation of money in this democracy is decided by credit policy and monetary policy; or else, in the 'abstract' theory of corporate finance, by the choice of the entrepreneur from among the different forms of financing available, a choice that, according to the fundamental Modigliani–Miller theorem in this theory, does not make any difference to the value of the firm.

Therefore the starting point of Kalecki's monetary theory is not the abstract properties or functions of money, or the suppliers of that money, whether bankers or the state, but the possession of money by capitalists or firms. This gives firms possessing monetary reserves, in modern times in the form of

[3] Kalecki, *Theory of Economic Dynamics*, 1954a, pp. 94–5.
[4] Kalecki, *Theory of Economic Dynamics*, 1954a, p. 95.

bank deposits, a degree of discretion in their expenditure and financing operations independent of the credit policy of banks and the monetary policy of the government and of the current income of those firms. The money that circulates in the economy, outside the government sector, is not bankers' money or credit, but the money or credit of the firms that put it into circulation through the process of production and investment, using banks as a mere institutional repository for the settlement of the accompanying payments and financing. In this respect, as will be argued in the next section of this book, the financial system of a capitalist economy is a comprehensive credit co-operative of capitalists, for those capitalists with monetary reserves.[5] In other words, the antecedents of modern business banking should be sought in the Bank of Amsterdam or the 'country banks' of the eighteenth and early nineteenth century, run by merchant capitalists with retail business that afforded liquidity to manage the credit operations of other capitalists, rather than in the banks set up to manage the sovereign finances of absolutist monarchs that are the origin of today's central banks.

The ability of firms with monetary reserves to spend it independently of current income gives rise to economic instability, the business cycle that was Kalecki's life-long research project. The expenditure item causing this instability is business investment: consumption being a matter of necessity, habit, and convention, is much more stable; industrial investment, however, takes time, and therefore necessarily lags behind investment decisions, or orders. This second distinction between current investment and investment decisions is one of the fundamental differences between Kalecki's macroeconomics and that of Keynes and his followers. By assuming that investment orders are delivered in the same period, Keynes and his followers missed a lag that is a central element in the business cycle. In his 1933 *Essay*, Kalecki put forward a simple investment function in which investment orders are an increasing function of gross accumulation (total investment deliveries in that period) and a decreasing function of the stock of capital equipment. Having explained the essential relationships in the analysis, Kalecki presented a second section, which he called 'Mathematical Development'. This is built around his investment function, from which he derived the conditions for regular 8–10 year

[5] The fundamental financing problem of small and medium-sized enterprises, the famous 'financing gap', stems not so much from an institutional lacuna that was somehow overlooked when modern banking institutions were being set up as from the roots of those institutions in capitalist banking. See Steindl, 'Capitalist Enterprise and Risk', 1945, which Kalecki cited with approval in his 1954 book *Theory of Economic Dynamics*.

cycles around a trend, using an equation for harmonic vibrations which can have a constant, decreasing, or increasing amplitude.

1.2 The 1933 Analysis of the Money Market

The Mathematical Development is then followed by a section entitled 'Applications'. The first of these was a section on 'The Money Market', which, outside Poland, only appeared in the 1935 French edition of the *Essay* in *Revue d'économie politique* (the French translation was done by his colleague, the multilingual Blanka Winawer at the Institute of Research in Business Cycles and Prices in Warsaw where they both worked in the 1930s). In this section, Kalecki showed how investment essentially financed itself by demonstrating that rising investment was possible with a constant overall total balance sheet of the banking system. In part investment is financed by having businessmen transfer what Kalecki called 'unattached deposits', that is bank deposits that are not designated for any particular planned expenditure, into 'investment reserve funds' or payment accounts. In the course of investment, the reserve funds are transferred to other capitalists who pay the costs of producing investment goods out of the reserve funds that they receive:

> It follows that, during the rising half of the cycle, the accounts of investment reserves and money in circulation increase at the expense of 'unattached' deposits. In the second half of the cycle, opposite transfers take place between accounts of the consolidated balance sheet. The creation of investment reserves and money in circulation takes place here – without an increase in bank credits, just by means of a change in the composition of bank liabilities: credit inflation consists in the fact that unattached deposits are transformed into investment reserves or money in circulation ...[6]

In a more sophisticated financial system, operating with bills, bonds, and stocks, Kalecki argued that the conversion of unattached deposits into investment reserves takes place through the issue, by companies intending to invest, of

[6] Kalecki, 'Essay on the Business Cycle Theory', 1933, p. 95. According to Tadeusz Kowalik, Kalecki got the idea that investments finance themselves from one of the co-editors of *Przegląd Gospodarczy*, T. Sławiński. Sławiński was a proponent of conservative monetary and financial practices, such as the gold standard and balanced government budgets. But he also argued that changes in the velocity of circulation of banknotes tended to alleviate shortages of credit (Osiatyński 1990, p. 473). However, the general idea goes back before the Polish discussions, through German monetary theory to Wicksell.

stocks and bonds which are sold to holders of unattached deposits. Here the rate of interest becomes a factor. But it is not the absolute, real, or nominal, rate of interest that matters, but the margin between the yield on stocks and bonds, and the rate of interest on bank deposits. That margin must be allowed to rise in order to persuade holders of unattached deposits to invest in bonds and stocks. At the same time, the rate on deposits will rise as banks experience the transfer of investment reserve funds between individual accounts and into money in circulation, and try to attract liquidity. Kalecki's conclusion from this was striking: the rate of interest effective for business and investment purposes is endogenous to the business cycle or, as he put it:

> 'Thus changes in the rate of interest are determined by the mechanism of the business cycle rather than determining it.'[7] (Kalecki 1933, p. 97).

The question that remained was how far the rate of interest could be relied upon to influence investment, the active factor in determining the business cycle.

1.3 Business Finance and Investment

In 1936, Kalecki arrived in London on his Rockefeller Fellowship where he started attending research seminars at the Department of Economics of the London School of Economics. When not attending those seminars, he was drafting his own papers. His first English paper appeared in the Department's journal *Economica*. It was Kalecki's alternative explanation of Keynes's 'liquidity trap', or the failure of business to respond to a loosening of monetary conditions by borrowing more for investment. Monetary policy had been loosened in Great Britain with the departure from the Gold Standard in 1931, allowing Bank Rate to be reduced from 3.9 per cent in 1931 to 2 per cent in 1933 (the equivalent rate in Poland had been reduced from 8.6 per cent in 1929 to 5 per cent by 1934). However, this had given little stimulus to business investment. In his *General Theory* Keynes had attributed this apparent unwillingness to borrow for new investment to increased 'liquidity preference' due to more pessimistic expectations among businessmen. Kalecki suggested that the problem was rooted in the structure of corporate finance.

At the heart of Kalecki's explanation was an idea that had been put forward by his friend at the Institute, Marek Breit. In a paper which Breit had

[7] Kalecki, 'Essay on the Business Cycle Theory', p. 97.

published in German in *Zeitschrift für Nationalökonomie*, with a shorter version appearing Polish, he had argued that banks increase the interest that they charge on loans in proportion to the ratio of debt to the internal funds (own funds or liquid assets) of a company. Thus, even low short-term money market interest rates may fail to stimulate investment, if the 'risk margin' charged to corporate borrowers has increased, due to the large amount of borrowing, in relation to the internal funds of a company. By draining those funds, excessive borrowing may effectively also drain the equity out of the firm. In this way, credit easing, or lower interest rates, may fail to evoke a boom in borrowing.[8]

Kalecki took up and extended the essential concept of financial risk that Breit had put forward. In Kalecki's version the analysis became a theory of investment, and a reason why increasing the supply of credit in financial markets would not increase investment, as suggested by the conventional theory, according to which the rate of interest brings the demand for and supply of credit into equilibrium.[9] Kalecki suggested that a constant prospective return on investment is more realistic than the decreasing returns advanced in their investment theory by most economists (decreasing returns being really only characteristic of agricultural or minerals production). Given such expectations of a constant return, determined by the current return on past investment, and the current rate of interest with increasing risk margins, the amount of investment that a firm can undertake is limited by the amount of its savings. Borrowing in excess of the firm's own liquid assets (we might today call it borrowing that is not 'hedged' by liquid assets) incurs a higher interest margin. A similar risk constraint would apply to funds raised from the stock market, through a rising cost of funds on bond issues. In the case of shares, existing shareholders would resist the 'watering-down' of their stock by additional stock issues, and firms would be faced with rising costs of selling more than an 'optimum size of issue'.

Kalecki's paper evoked a response from N. S. Buchanan and R. D. Calkins, who argued that Kalecki's analysis would apply only to a firm owned by a single proprietor, operating with unlimited liability. This would leave out joint-stock companies, the most important business organizations in modern capitalism. The analysis could not therefore be generalized to provide an

[8] Breit, 'Ein Beitrag zur Theorie des Geld- und Kapitalmarktes', 1935b and 'Problemy rynku pieniężnego i kapitałowego na tle depresji', 1935a.

[9] See Chilosi, 'Breit Kalecki and Hicks on the Term Structure of Interest Rates', 1982; Mott, 'Kalecki's Principle of Increasing Risk', 1985–1986; and Mott, 'Kalecki's Principle of Increasing Risk', 1982. Mott's reflections on Kalecki's approach to risk are brought together in his book *Kalecki's Principle of Increasing Risk and Keynesian Economics*, 2010.

'internal financing' constraint for the economy as a whole.[10] In his reply, Kalecki argued in general terms that 'the expansion of the firm depends on its accumulation of capital out of current profits' and discussed the limitations of capital market finance.[11] Bond issues reduce the return on share capital if the investment is unsuccessful, while share issues reduce the control of the controlling shareholders. The latter may be partially overcome by a holding company structure (floating off 49 per cent of a subsidiary). But the problem remains that, if the venture is unsuccessful, earnings per share will be reduced. Finally Kalecki suggested that portfolio diversification by rentiers will limit the amount of new shares in a company to which financial investors will be willing to subscribe. He pointed out that all of these difficulties may be overcome through the accumulation of internal savings from profits, i.e., entrepreneurial capital. This provides a cushion of reserves to reduce the financial risk of capital subscribers and will even 'widen the capital market for the shares of that company since, in general, the larger a company is the more important will its role in the share market be'.[12]

Kalecki had not only provided a more general analysis of financial risk and credit market impotence. He had, as Lange was later to point out, advanced a theory of the size of the firm that depended on financial factors: '...the size of the firm is thus limited by the capital owned by the entrepreneur'.[13] In contrast, the traditional Marshallian theory of the firm that prevailed in Britain at the time and has now taken over as *the* theory of the firm, argued that the size of a firm is determined by the profit-maximizing *scale* of production, i.e., the total industrial capacity that gives the lowest cost per unit of output. The Marshallian theory contains an element for the cost of capital, but does not really consider corporate finance. Moreover, strictly speaking, it is a theory of the *scale* of production in one plant or factory, rather than a theory of the firm as a corporate organization.[14] In America the common view, following Frank Knight, was that 'entrepreneurship' or enterprise was the 'scarce' factor that caused long-run average costs to rise.

Kalecki's pre-war writings on money and finance record ideas that did not really change as he developed and extended his monetary theory. Money and finance are perquisites of capitalists. Indeed, capitalists are defined by their ownership of money: workers may receive money for their labour, but return

[10] Buchanan and Calkins, 'A Comment on Mr. Kalecki's "Principle of Increasing Risk"', 1938.
[11] Kalecki, 'A Comment on the "Principle of Increasing Risk": A Reply', 1938a.
[12] Kalecki, 'A Comment on the "Principle of Increasing Risk": A Reply', 1938a.
[13] Lange, 'Review of M. Kalecki *Essays in the Theory of Economic Fluctuations*', 1941.
[14] Steindl, *Random Processes and the Growth of Firms*, 1965.

it to capitalists as they purchase their articles of consumption. The money of capitalists is thrown by them into circulation in the processes of production, investment, and exchange, and then accumulated in their bank deposits as profits, or firms' savings. That ownership of money is the key to the access of capitalists to credit, and the scale of their own financial resources limits the cost and the amount of debt which capitalists may take without risk onto their balance sheets. Interest rates do not determine the business cycle, but are endogenous to that cycle. Implicitly, the size of firms is not determined by the scale of production, but by the scale of their financial resources. The credit system therefore reinforces a business hierarchy, from large corporations that can access credit most easily, to small and medium-sized enterprises that have the greatest difficulty in accessing credit, because they have the least money capital to put up as security.

2

The Wartime Fragments I

Breaking with Wicksellian Theory

Kalecki had arrived in London in 1936 on a Fellowship from the Rockefeller Foundation that was to assist him in further studies on the business cycle. The Fellowship envisaged Kalecki meeting Keynes and discussing those studies with him. Joan Robinson was to put out the story that Kalecki was shaken by Keynes's publication of his *General Theory* since this was the book that Kalecki intended to write.[1] Kalecki's subsequent review, in Polish, of Keynes's book revealed the fundamental areas of agreement, in their common macroeconomic analysis. But his review signally omitted to mention what Keynes considered was the most original feature of that book, namely its monetary analysis.[2]

On conclusion of his Fellowship, Keynes had found Kalecki employment in Cambridge on a project examining various aspects of the business cycle. There were disagreements with Keynes's colleagues who were supposed to be supervising Kalecki's work.[3] At the end of 1939, he moved to Oxford. It was there that Kalecki finally took up the challenge of Keynes's monetary theory. Away from Cambridge, Kalecki was able to turn to a closer examination of credit and finance and to incorporating money and monetary policy in his overall analysis of capitalism. Circumstances were particularly favourable for such an examination. Keynes's monetary doctrines, in particular his insistence on the long-term rate of interest, determined in the bond markets, rather than the short-term rate in the money markets as a key influence on business investment, remained controversial. Ralph Hawtrey, who emphasized the importance of the short-term rate, had challenged Keynes's stress on the long-term rate in his (Hawtrey's) Marshall Lectures in 1937 on the grounds of the greater stability of that long-term rate.[4] J. R. Hicks, Roy Harrod, George

1 Robinson, 'Michał Kalecki, a Neglected Prophet', 1976.
2 Kalecki, 'Some Remarks on Keynes's Theory', 1936.
3 See Toporowski, *Michał Kalecki: An Intellectual Biography Volume 1*, 2013, chapters 13 and 14.
4 Hawtrey, *A Century of Bank Rate*, 1938. chapter VI.

Interest and Capital: The Monetary Economics of Michał Kalecki. Jan Toporowski, Oxford University Press.
© Jan Toporowski 2022. DOI: 10.1093/oso/9780198816232.003.0003

Shackle, Nicholas Kaldor, and others were all involved in investigations of the yield curve, linking short-term and long-term rates of interest.

Oxford too was open to new ideas. Hubert Henderson had organized the Oxford Economists' Research Group there in the 1930s, to investigate the economics of industry. The studies that were published as a result of these investigations are mostly known for the light they cast on industrial pricing and costs. It turned out that the leaders of industry had little idea of the calculations attributed to them by the standard economic theory; they did not even know what their marginal costs were, a concept of totemic significance in modern economics.[5] However, among those studies was one by James Meade and Philip Andrews, introduced by Henderson himself, reporting that the leaders of business ignored the rate of interest when deciding on fixed capital investment. All sorts of other factors were considered, the state of demand, pay-back periods, and so on but not the rate of interest.[6] Since investment was supposed to be the main factor in the business cycle, this lack of influence, direct or indirect, of the rate of interest on investment raised fundamental questions about the effectiveness of monetary policy.

The observations of Meade, Andrews, and Henderson were very much in tune with Kalecki's own observations of business procedures. Already in 1932 he had written:

> The question arises here whether...– the creation of credits by the central bank or a private bank – can be more than a passive instrument in the hands of the entrepreneur, and can become an active factor encouraging him to make use of its services. The answer to this question is affirmative, though with some serious reservations...banks can increase the demand for credit by lowering the rate of interest. Its reduction encourages investments, since it increases the profitability of future enterprises by a reduction in charges for interest payments. The rise in investment activity is financed from bank credits, and by lowering the rate of interest banks can thereby grant more credits than before. Indeed, this is the typical way in which the banking system intervenes to improve business conditions. However, to a large extent this influence is illusory. The rate of interest is not a decisive factor in undertaking investments. More important is the expected gross profitability of the enterprise, estimated on the basis of the profitability of existing enterprises.

[5] Lee, *Post-Keynesian Price Theory*, 1998, chapters 4 and 5.

[6] Meade and Andrews, 'Summary of Replies to Questions on Effects of Rate of Interest', 1938. See also Andrews, 'A Further Inquiry into the Effects of the Rate of Interest', 1940. As Andrews pointed out, this evidence confirmed the results of studies in the United States.

Kalecki went on:

> In a period of crisis, when this profitability falls considerably below its average level, with very slack employment of existing plant, a reduction of the rate of interest reinforces only weakly any inclination to invest and, in any case, takes a long time to produce perceptible effects. This method of intervention is deceptive because it acts by trying to influence the willingness of the entrepreneur to undertake investments. The reliable methods are those that can afford certainty that the scale of investment will in fact be enlarged. We have in mind investments undertaken by the government and aimed at mitigating the crisis or accelerating the business upswing.[7]

2.1 Monetary Circulation and the Money Market

On his arrival in Oxford, Kalecki got down to explaining to the readers of the Institute's *Bulletin* how the financial markets actually worked. In particular he wanted to dismiss the common view that government expenditure that was not covered by tax revenue had to be covered by 'credit creation' by banks. Behind this common view was a notion that deposits create loans. Among those who knew about banking operations, the idea that it is in fact the other way around, that loans create deposits, had already been put about by Hartley Withers, the editor of the *Economist*, even before the First World War. Among academic economists, the idea had been put forward by Dennis Robertson in a much-cited work of 1925, *Banking Policy and the Price Level.* However, among the wider community of economists, it was still widely thought by prominent economists like Hayek and even Keynes (up to the 1930s) that interest and banking was about making saving equal to investment and providing 'credit creation' in the form of loans to make up any shortfall of savings.[8]

For Kalecki, as for the Keynes of the *General Theory*, saving always equals actual investment plus the fiscal deficit, plus the trade surplus, because the trade surplus, fiscal deficit and investment were the means by which savings, in the form of unspent money surpluses, were deposited with firms and households. What distinguished Kalecki's approach from that of Keynes,

[7] Kalecki, 'The Business Cycle and Inflation', 1932/1990.

[8] Withers in fact had himself, during the First World War, advanced the view that fiscal expenditure was about mobilizing the circulation of money in *Our Money and the State* (1917), chapter II.

Robertson, and Hawtrey, was Kalecki's exposition of the macroeconomic circulation of money from government expenditure through to the recovery of that money as profits in the accounts of firms and capitalists. Supposing that government expenditure is financed by issuing short-term Treasury bills, the funds raised are then 'returned to the market' as the government spends the money which finds its way into other current or transactions accounts. Far from depleting the liquidity or reserves (including claims on the government) of banks, the borrowing adds liquidity to banks' balance sheets. If output and expenditure do not rise, then the surplus money in current accounts will be transferred by its owners to investment accounts, to be available to buy bonds, should the government decide to refinance its issue of Treasury bills with longer-term obligations.

Thus, profits are a way in which the routine activity of exchange in markets concentrates credit balances in the accounts of capitalists, as production and investment is the way in which that credit is distributed around the economy. The two processes, of production and monetary circulation, take place at the same time and not separately as commonly laid out in classical and Neo-Classical economic theory that analyses value and distribution (microeconomics) as a distinct sphere of enquiry from monetary theory or macroeconomics.

Kalecki proceeded to examine the financial operations of the government, in the first year of the war (from 1 September 1939, to the end of August 1940), its 'floating debt', so-called because it involved issues of bills and loans that were short- or medium-term, and would therefore require refinancing.[9] He was able to show that a large part of this debt was financed not by borrowing from banks or the 'public departments' like the Exchange Equalization Fund. Although there was an increase in bank current account deposits, netting out advances to the private sector and its loan repayments, this was largely unrelated to government borrowing.[10] In other words, the finance for the war effort was largely provided by the investment accounts in which the profits of the private sector from government expenditure were accumulating. Through government expenditure each successive budget deficit was providing the balances in investment accounts to finance that deficit.

[9] The floating debt nevertheless placed considerable demands on the money market on the days (usually Fridays) when bills had to be rolled over, obliging the Bank of England to provide reserves on those days in order to keep Bank Rate at the official level. See Sayers, *Central Banking after Bagehot*, 1957, pp. 67–8. Allen, *The Bank of England and the Government* Debt, 2019, chapter 6, provides a good summary of the financing of government borrowing at this time.

[10] Kalecki, 'The "Mysteries" of the Money Market', 1940a.

There was then the related question of the circulation of notes and coins. He was able to show more or less conclusively that such circulation was chiefly determined by the total wage bill in the economy.[11] This is not really surprising and merely reflected the institutional fact that workers did not have bank accounts. Cash circulation was very much a dependent variable, and in a later note Kalecki argued that inflation is driven by demand rather than by any monetary factors. An inflationary spiral occurs when real wages cannot catch up with the rise in prices. However, the cause of this is the rise in expenditure in excess of the supply of consumption goods, due to the rise in employment.[12] An increase in banknotes in circulation in 1941 may have been due to the rise in black market activity.[13]

At the beginning of his note on the money market, Kalecki made an observation on the rate of interest that was to be the start of a broader analysis of interest as a factor in economic activity. He noted that changes in current accounts 'are chiefly determined by... [changes] in the volume of transactions. A certain influence may also be exerted by the short-term rate of interest; for if it is low one will on the whole afford the convenience of having ready cash and not bother convert it into an earning asset. But if both the volume of transactions and the rate of interest are stable there is no reason to use the funds returned by government expenditure to increase current accounts'.[14] In a study of bank deposits shortly after this, Kalecki noted a much higher rate of increase of current (transactions) deposits as opposed to investment. However, much of this reflected changes in the wartime foreign exchange controls. In fact, he thought, 'there is no reason to expect a similar pace in the movement of current and deposit [investment] accounts, for... with a given short-term rate of interest current accounts increase more or less proportionately with the volume of transactions while the rise in deposit accounts depends on the rate of accumulation of liquid reserves and the attractiveness of deposit accounts as compared with other relevant accounts'.[15]

The question of the scope and significance of the rate of interest was one that Kalecki worked on through 1941 to verify his thesis that changes in the short-term rate of interest principally affected the velocity of circulation of

[11] Kalecki, 'Wage Bill and Cash Circulation', 1940b and 'Wage Bill and Cash Circulation: A Supplement', 1940c.
[12] Kalecki, 'What Is Inflation?', 1941a.
[13] Kalecki, 'Employment, Wage Bill and Cash Circulation', 1942a.
[14] Kalecki, 'The "Mysteries" of the Money Market', 1940a.
[15] Kalecki, 'The War-time Trend of Deposits', 1943a.

current accounts in banks. The result was his paper 'The Short-term Rate of Interest and Velocity of Cash Circulation'. Using data from clearings of the London Clearing Banks since 1930, he argued that the overall turnover in bank deposits consisted of two types of clearings: financial clearings and non-financial ones. The turnover in financial transactions was much higher than turnover in non-financial payments. However, if the data are adjusted reducing the weight of the financial transactions, in relation to current accounts, to the level that non-financial transactions have in relation to current accounts, then there was indeed a positive relationship between the turnover of current deposits in banks, and the short-term rate of interest. The higher financial turnover, he thought, was because of complex shifts in liquid asset portfolios between bank investment deposits and bills. For example, an increase in bank buying of bills would reduce their discount rate, and make them less attractive for banks customers than the investment accounts.[16]

2.2 The Critique of Wicksellianism

The common view among economists in 1930s had been (as it is today) that the rate of interest and bank credit creation are key determinants of the business cycle. Economists were inspired by Keynes's work in the *Treatise on Money* emphasizing the effect of the long-term rate of interest on investment; Hayek's book *Monetary Theory and the Trade Cycle*, which brought to the English-speaking world German ideas on the monetary business cycle; and, finally, Richard Kahn's translation of the book from which much of those German ideas were derived, Wicksell's *Interest and Prices*.[17] For example, Wicksell argued that the business cycle occurs because of differences between the money rate of interest and the 'natural' rate of interest, being the marginal productivity of capital, or the return on real investment. The rate of interest had this function because it determines the cost of finance, or is the opportunity cost of any real investment. During the boom the 'natural' rate of interest exceeded the 'money' rate of interest. The boom would continue until the money rate of interest rose, and the natural rate of interest fell, so that they became equal. In this way investment and inflation bring the money rate of interest into equality with the natural rate of interest. A money rate of interest

[16] Kalecki, 'The Short-Term Rate of Interest and Velocity of Cash Circulation', 1941b.

[17] Keynes, *Treatise on Money*, 1930/1971; Hayek, *Monetary Theory and the Trade Cycle*, 1933; and Wicksell, *Interest and Prices*, 1936.

above the natural rate causes deflationary processes to bring that money rate back to equality with the natural rate.

In his pre-war work, Kalecki acknowledged the influence of this view, even if only as conventional wisdom. But in 1941 he finally broke with the idea that interest plays this role. His earlier models had incorporated the rate of interest as an influence on the level of investment, the real factor, the fluctuations of which decided whether the economy was booming or in recession. His studies of money and finance in 1941 showed him that the rate of interest was largely of financial significance, and that any effect on investment was so hedged with complex financing arrangements as to be virtually insignificant. The common flaw in the business cycle theories of Wicksell, as well as those of Hayek and Keynes (in his *General Theory*), was that they had no theory of profits as monetary circulation, so they had no explanation of how investment generated returns. However, to complete his theory of interest, Kalecki had to deal with the complex, Keynesian theory that emphasized the long-term rate of interest, rather than the short-term money market rate of interest, as an influence on the level of business investment. Two years later he presented the fruits of his researches in a slim volume, *Studies in Economic Dynamics*. At first glance this appears as a revised version of his 1939 volume *Essays in the Theory of Economic Fluctuations*. There are indeed overlaps in the topics discussed, in the analysis of profits, costs, and distribution. However, the new analysis is on the theory of interest. The key additional material is an essay on the short-term and the long-term rate of interest, and an extended discussion of the long-term rate in the essay on the theory of profit.

In his discussion of the short-term rate of interest, Kalecki noted 'changes in the short-term rate have a rather small immediate effect upon the long-term rate; and it is chiefly the latter that is relevant for investment activity. Thus, only after the new level of the short-term rate of interest has been maintained for a rather prolonged time will it affect appreciably the rate of investment'.[18] He added a criticism of the quantity theory of money, according to which a rise in the quantity of money is supposed to increase the amount of transactions, eventually raising the price level: '...the *immediate* influence of the increase in the supply of cash will be not to raise the money

[18] Kalecki, *Studies in Economic Dynamics*, 1943/1991, p. 142. Kalecki's view of a slow impact of changes in the short-term rate, contrasts with the common view of central bankers and monetary theorists today whose Dynamic Stochastic General Equilibrium models lead them to suppose that even slight changes in interest rates are monetary 'shocks'.

volume of transactions but to reduce the velocity of circulation and the short-term rate of interest'.[19]

At the time of his statistical study of the short-term rate of interest, in 1940, Kalecki had integrated his view of the money market with an analysis of the long-term rate of interest. Like Hawtrey, Shackle, Hicks, and others, he measured the long-term rate of interest by the yield on Consols (the perpetual government stocks). Kalecki pointed out that it was not necessary to sell the stocks in order to raise cash: the relative stability of the price of Consols meant that banks were willing to advance loans on the security of Consols up to quite a high percentage of their value.[20] He concluded that the long-term rate of interest reflected the expected discount rate over the next few years. However, unlike Hicks' 'pure expectations' theory of the long-term rate, according to which the long-term rate would settle at the *average* of the expected short-term rate, plus some 'risk factor' specific to the borrower,[21] Kalecki thought that the estimated average of future short-term interest rates would only partially reflect any current changes in actual interest rates, and that the long-term rate changes less than the average short-term rate expected over the next few years. In other words, the long-term rate was more stable than the average expected short-term rate.[22] This was confirmed by data on the yields on Consols, and his estimates of the average discount rate from 1849 to 1938. It is worth pointing out here that Kalecki used the *actual* average of the discount rate as the *expected* average. However, his estimated equation predicted the yields on Consols in 1940 and 1941 with remarkable accuracy. He concluded that in any case, the government can control the long-term rate of interest on its borrowing by financial operations along the yield curve: issuing bills and using the proceeds from them to buy in long-term bonds, until its preferred long-term rate of interest is obtained.[23]

The following chapter of his *Studies in Economic Dynamics* is entitled 'A Theory of Profits' and largely consists of the paper of the same name which had appeared in the *Economic Journal* (see Chapter 5 in this volume). However, its conclusion, examining the relationship between the rate of profit and the rate of interest was now changed, not just in its substance, but also in its conclusion. That conclusion was not just confined to Kalecki's usual inner

[19] Kalecki, *Studies in Economic Dynamics*, 1943/1991, p. 142.

[20] Kalecki acknowledged the source of this information as P. W. S. Andrews, 'A Further Enquiry...', 1940, pp. 37–8.

[21] Hicks, *Value and Capital*, 1939, pp. 144–52.

[22] Kalecki, *Studies in Economic Dynamics*, 1943b, pp. 39–40.

[23] Kalecki, *Studies in Economic Dynamics*, 1943b, pp. 45–6.

world of reflection on the theory of the business cycle. It represented a fundamental critique of the Wicksellian theory and its modified version in the interest rate theory of Keynes.

As previously mentioned, the Wicksellian theory regarded the business cycle as being driven by differences between the rate of interest in the money markets and the marginal productivity of capital, or the natural rate of interest. Without a theory of profits, Wicksell and his followers were reduced to a circular argument in which a boom was evidence that the natural rate of interest must be higher than the money rate of interest, and the recession meant that the natural rate was lower, but the cause of it all, the natural rate in relation to the money rate, could not be observed.[24] Kalecki's 'A Theory of Profits', published in the *Economic Journal* in 1942, explained how the money flows that constitute profits arose from capitalists' expenditure on investment and their own consumption. From this he had derived an average rate profit on capital. Kalecki had concluded with a small section outlining the possibility that the rate of profit may fall to the level of the long-term rate of interest.

In the version of this paper that came out in *Studies in Economic Dynamics* Kalecki addressed in detail the issues raised by Keynes's monetary analysis, as expressed in Joan Robinson's paper 'The Long-Period Theory of Employment'. In her paper, the long-period is defined as the equilibrium point where the (decreasing) marginal efficiency of capital is equal to the rate of interest.[25] The marginal efficiency of capital was Keynes's term for the expected return from business investment, from which was deducted the long-term rate of interest, representing the cost of financing that investment. In Keynes, in the short term, that expected return from investment was subject to uncertainty and volatile expectations.[26] In the long-run, Joan Robinson argued, uncertainty and expectations fell out of the analysis, and the rate of interest converged on the marginal efficiency of capital. She argued that unemployment may still remain intractable in this long-term equilibrium, since she dismissed the effectiveness of the 'Keynes effect', the possibility that unemployment would cause wages and prices to fall, causing interest rates to fall until investment restarted. The only way of obtaining full employment would be by successive reductions in interest rates: each reduction would stimulate investment, until

[24] Such is scientific progress in economics, that much the same is true of monetary theory in the twenty-first century. Recent attempts to estimate the 'natural' or 'real equilibrium' rate of interest do so on the basis of a money rate of interest, rather than on the basis of any actual productivity of capital, e.g., Williams, 'Monetary Policy in a Low R-Star World', 2016.

[25] Robinson, 'The Long-Period Theory of Employment', 1936.

[26] Keynes *General Theory*, chapter 11.

the capital stock stabilized, so that in order to maintain a given level of investment, successive cuts in interest rates were necessary.[27]

In his revised version of 'A Theory of Profits' Kalecki added a new conclusion which he entitled 'The Rate of Profit and the Rate of Interest in the Long Period'. In this Kalecki's examined exactly the same question as that Joan Robinson had looked at six years earlier: the relationship of the rate of profit to the long-term rate of interest to determine whether it was possible for the economy to sustain over a long period a level of activity in which the long-term rate of interest is in excess of the rate of profit. As previously he defined the long-term rate as the average expected short-term rate, with a risk premium and net of tax.

Kalecki's conclusion in the earlier version of the paper was that capitalists' consumption, being more stable than fixed investment, would, if high enough, tend to keep the rate of profit above the rate of interest. But were that profit rate to be very low, there was always the possibility that the short-term rate of interest would be reduced to below the long-term rate, thereby reducing that long-term rate. If that was insufficient to prevent 'dissaving' by capitalists (their running down of their existing productive capital stock) then the possibility that a long-period economic 'deadlock' may arise.[28] In his revised conclusion, Kalecki pointed out that in a state where investment is reduced to a minimum, the average rate of profit would remain stable and may even equal the long-term rate of interest because of the stable part of capitalists' consumption, and the minimal level of fixed investment required for depreciation. In that situation, the short-term rate of interest may end up below the average rate of profit. But the long-term rate of interest will not fall below the floor given by risk involved in fluctuations in bond prices. In long periods, therefore, the relationship between the rate of profit and the rate of interest 'depends to a great extent on...the ratio of the average of the stable part of capitalists' consumption over the period...to the volume of capital...at the beginning of the period'. The long-term rate of interest sets a critical level for this ratio. If the ratio exceeds this critical level, then over successive long periods, the rate of profit will exceed the long-term rate of interest. If the ratio falls below the critical level, then the rate of profit may equal the long-term rate of interest, or fall below it.[29]

[27] Robinson, 'The Long-Period Theory of Employment', 1936. See also Harcourt and Kerr, *Joan Robinson*, 2009, pp. 25–6.
[28] Kalecki, 'A Theory of Profits', 1942b.
[29] Kalecki, *Studies in Economic Dynamics*, 1943b, p. 58.

It was, however, in his following chapter on the business cycle that Kalecki considered what effect the long-term rate of interest has on the all-important investment. Not much, he concluded 'because of the stability of the long-term rate of interest as compared with the rate of profit it seems to be not very important'.[30]

The addition of the new section on the long-term rate of interest in the second version of the theory of profits makes it possible to date quite precisely when Kalecki finally abandoned the Wicksellian theory that the business cycle is driven by the difference between the rate of profit and the rate of interest, namely in 1940 and 1941, as he realized that the greater stability of the long-term rate of interest made it more of a constant factor in investment decisions and capitalists' consumption. He revised his paper 'A Theory of Profits', from the version in the *Economic Journal* for his *Studies in Economic Dynamics* to show that interest is not a stream of dead money draining income from the economy, but is a distributional variable transferring income or credit resources to rentiers whose consumption off-sets the drain from the incomes of net debtors.

Kalecki's theory of profits provides the crucial factor left undefined in the theories of Wicksell and Keynes. Both Wicksell and Keynes placed the rate of interest in a key position in determining the level of investment, and then proceeded to explain why this determination may prove to be ineffective: in Wicksell's case the falling natural rate of interest, in Keynes's case 'animal spirits' and uncertainty. With his theory of profits, Kalecki defined actual profits as the main factor determining investment and the business cycle, and found that the rate of interest had only a weak and decreasing influence on investment. But his theory of profits, accumulated as bank deposits, also explained how investment was, in fact, 'self-financing'.

In Kalecki's view, the rate of interest was a purely monetary and financial variable. The rate of interest does not reconcile investment and saving, but the *margin* on the short-term rate of interest creates the financing structures to reconcile the financing and liquidity (i.e., refinancing) needs of business with the liquidity provided by banks of issue (or central banks), or those intermediaries willing to advance bank deposits against illiquid assets. In this respect Kalecki was in agreement with Keynes. Where Kalecki differed from Keynes was in seeing the distribution of profit around the economy as the mechanism by which money spent on investment or capitalists' consumption returns to be saved by those capitalists: a more elegant reflux than Keynes's

[30] Kalecki, *Studies in Economic Dynamics*, 1943b, p. 64.

elaborate 'revolving fund' of credit for financing investment.[31] For Keynesians, those margins represent various shades of uncertainty as financing maturities lengthen.[32] For Kalecki they were the margins that were required to induce a particular amount and maturity of financing. This was the position that Joan Robinson eventually reached.[33] However, there was one distinctive detail in Kalecki's analysis that remained very much his own. This was the link between the rate of interest and the liquidity of a firm's assets, the relationship that Kalecki called the Principle of Increasing Risk.[34] That relationship is between the *margin* over the short term rate of interest and general financing need at any one time. That financing need may be for the purposes of investment, but may simply be in order to refinance existing obligations. In this way, Kalecki broke the Keynesian link between the rate of interest and a 'natural' state of uncertainty, reaffirmed Keynes's original insight into liquidity, and extended it to business financing.[35]

2.3 A Provisional Conclusion

On his arrival in Oxford Kalecki developed the monetary analysis that had played perhaps too minor a part in his earlier studies on the business cycle. At the centre of that monetary analysis was not an explanation of the universal properties of money, or its essence, but the circulation of money through the expenditure of households, capitalists, and firms, and the government. The circulation of notes and coins was not, in his view an enigma, and was explained by household consumption. The other type of money was bank deposits, the transfers of which between transactions accounts and investment accounts provided the link with finance. Kalecki's theory of profits showed the macroeconomic flows by which profits are accumulated as deposits in the bank accounts of capitalists and firms. The chief source of those profits was firms' fixed capital investment and capitalists' consumption. The accumulated profits provided the financing of investment, and the means of servicing debt-financed investment. Where those profits were due to government expenditure financed with debt, the accumulated deposits constitute the liquid funds available to finance government debt. The short-term rate of

[31] See Keynes, 'Alternative Theories of the Rate of Interest' and his subsequent discussion with Ohlin, Hawtrey, and Robertson in Keynes, *The Collected Writings*, 1973, pp. 201–34.

[32] See, for example, MacLachlan, *Keynes's General Theory of Interest: A Reconsideration*, 1993.

[33] Robinson 'The Rate of Interest', 1951.

[34] Kalecki, 'The Principle of Increasing Risk', 1937.

[35] See Mott, *Kalecki's Principle of Increasing Risk and Keynesian Economics*, 2010.

interest was a factor only in the turnover of bank deposits, while the long-term rate of interest, the indicator of the financing costs of fixed capital, would tend on the whole to remain below the rate of profit, unless disinvestment set in and capitalists' became uncharacteristically frugal in their consumption.

After *Studies in Economic Dynamics* Kalecki never came back to his reflections on the role of the rate of interest in the long term evolution of capitalism. In the next synthesis of his theory, *Theory of Economic Dynamics*, published in 1954, the scope of his analysis was compressed to distribution and the business cycle. His monetary analysis was reduced to his empirical observations about the short-term rate of interest influencing the velocity of circulation of money and the greater stability of the long-term rate of interest indicating, in his view, the irrelevance of monetary factors in economic dynamics.[36] In 1932 he had asked the question '...how can capitalists invest more than remains from their current profits after spending part of them on personal consumption?' and had answered 'This is made possible by the banking system in various forms of credit inflation. Hence...without credit inflation there would be no fluctuations in investment activity and consequently there would be no major business fluctuations. *Business fluctuations are strictly connected with credit inflation*.'[37] This might be understood as highlighting the credit policy of banks in the determination of business investment, and business conditions generally. However, ten years later, Kalecki had more clearly shown that credit was much more accommodating than might appear from consideration of credit policy, because capitalists hold financial assets and this allows them to determine for themselves the velocity of circulation of credit to afford the means of financing investment.

There remains the puzzle as to why Kalecki put forward his criticism of the Joan Robinson's Wicksellian interpretation of Keynes's theory 'in the long term' in an analysis that he subsequently dropped. One possible explanation is that there is in fact an inconsistency between a theory of investment based on an aggregate *average* rate of profit in relation to the long-term rate of interest, suggested by Kalecki's 'The Rate of Profit and the Rate of Interest in the Long Period', and Kalecki's theory of the firm, in which firms have

[36] Kalecki, *Theory of Economic Dynamics*, 1954a, chapters 6 and 7.

[37] Kalecki ,'The Business Cycle and Inflation', 1932/1990, p. 148. See also Sawyer, 'Kalecki on Money and Finance', 2001. The link between macroeconomic flows and credit circulation is also noted by Gary Dymski: '...Kalecki's framework cannot be encompassed in a real analysis; his building blocks can be *consistently* only in a monetary analysis.' See Dymski, 'Kalecki's Monetary Economics', 1996, p. 122.

differentiated rates of profit according to their 'degree of monopoly'.[38] Or perhaps Kalecki's argument here is just incomplete. Once allowance is made for differentiated rates of profit among firms, then we have a *spread* of rates of profit and a *spread* of rates of interest, including long term rates of interest, making averages less likely to be observed in practice, and less of an influence on actual economic decision-making. As Joan Robinson observed: 'Keynes's theory treated the rate of interest as determined by the demand and supply of money. This was a useful simplification in the pioneering days of the theory, but it was always obvious that there is no such thing as *the* rate of interest and that the demand and supply of every type of asset has just as much right to be considered as the demand and supply of money.'[39] And Kalecki's 'Principle of Increasing Risk', relating the interest that banks charge on business loans the ratio of existing borrowing to liquid assets held by a given borrower, undoubtedly implies a range of interest rates for any given loan maturity.[40]

The effect of such a differentiation may be illustrated in a consideration of a system in which firms are either monopolies, enjoying a positive rate of profit due to their market power, and small and medium-sized enterprises whose rate of profit is zero or negative. (Firms continue in business when they are making a loss usually because there is unemployment, or under-employment, and running a loss-making small business is a more dignified alternative to unemployed idleness, especially if the loss can be covered from the earnings a household member who may enjoy employment.) In such a situation, the smaller firms borrow to cover the excess of their expenditure over revenue (in the cases where rates of profit are negative); or to pay interest on previous borrowing. By a macroeconomic process of production and exchange, the deposit counterpart of their borrowing to cover their excess expenditure passes into the possession of the monopolies. By circulating through the financial balance sheets, the deposit counterpart of the borrowing by the smaller firms

[38] Kalecki made this explicit in a section on 'Price fixing by a firm' that he added to the chapter on 'Costs and Prices' in *Studies in Economic Dynamics*, when he revised that chapter for his *Theory of Economic Dynamics* in the early 1950s. See *Theory of Economic Dynamics*, 1954, pp. 12–14. Cf. '...there is no such thing as a "natural" rate of interest...there is...no general law to determine the limits of the average interest, or average rate of interest, as distinct from the continually fluctuating market rate of interest...the general rate of profit appears as an empirical, given reality in the average rate of interest, although the latter is not a pure or reliable expression of the former...On the other hand, the general rate of profit is never anything more than a tendency, a movement to equalise specific rates of profit' (Marx, *Capital Volume III*, 1974, pp. 364, 366). Marx's scepticism about the incarnation of averages is applicable to Kalecki's argument here. See his (implicitly) dismissive comment on Adolphe Quetelet's notion of 'average man' in *Capital Volume I* (Everyman edition) p. 337.

[39] Robinson, 'The Rate of Interest', 1952, p. 5.

[40] Kalecki, 'Principle of Increasing Risk', 1937.

to pay interest passes into the possession of monopolies as interest on their deposits.

In this way, the credit cycle depends on the banks' willingness to lend to the smaller, least credit-worthy, firms. The recurrent call to lend to the small and medium-sized enterprises that are supposed to embody the spirit of entrepreneurial capitalism, is less a declaration of confidence in their enterprise than a symptom of the state of credit in a situation of under-employment, as monopolies accumulate bank deposits and the integrity of bank balance sheets can only be retained through the extension of lending to the least credit-worthy businesses as the only willing borrowers.

3
The Wartime Fragments II
Interest and Debt

3.1 Money and Debt

Two further excursions into monetary and financial theory concluded Kalecki's studies of interest and finance during his stay in Oxford. In April 1943, he published in the Institute *Bulletin* his critical deconstruction of 'The Burden of National Debt'. In his earlier note on 'The "Mysteries" of the Money Market' he had already shown that there was no immediate problem in financing current borrowing, because the government expenditure financed by borrowing accrued in bank deposits available for the purchase of government bonds (see previous chapter). His new note was intended to show that, despite the huge increase in government borrowing, the 'burden' of financing the debt was unlikely to be greater than it was in 1938–1939. He pointed out that interest on the debt was subject to taxation, which reduced the net cost of the debt, and servicing of the debt should also be deflated for the rise in prices. With an estimate that nominal national income at the end of the war would be at least 30 per cent higher than it was in 1938–1939 due to price inflation, he calculated that, net of tax, the real interest cost of the National Debt, as it stood in 1942–1943, would after the war be approximately the same as it was in 1938.[1] However, he conceded that the Debt was likely to rise still further, and this made it necessary to consider how to deal with the cost of servicing such a debt.[2]

Kalecki proceeded to show how 'it is possible to devise special taxes for financing the interest on National Debt which will render its increase harmless, in the sense that it will have no repercussions on output and employment; that therefore it is not necessary to consider the reduction of the budget deficit as such an important problem of war finance; and that a regime under which

[1] Kalecki, 'The Burden of The National Debt', 1943a.

[2] In the event, by 1945 the national debt rose some 2.5 times in relation to its level in 1938, while prices rose 40 per cent.

Interest and Capital: The Monetary Economics of Michał Kalecki. Jan Toporowski, Oxford University Press.
© Jan Toporowski 2022. DOI: 10.1093/oso/9780198816232.003.0004

budget deficits would be used whenever necessary to maintain full employment does not involve insuperable difficulties'. He proposed that the interest on the National Debt should be financed by an annual tax on all privately owned capital (including holdings of government bonds). This would be 'neutral' in the sense of leaving capitalists as a whole with the same amount of money (bank deposits) that they started with: the tax paid by capitalists would be returned to them in the form of interest on their holdings of government bonds. The tax would also be 'neutral' in the sense of not affecting in any way incentives to invest and produce, since the profitability of these activities would not be affected by the tax.[3] As an alternative that would also not affect those incentives Kalecki suggested an income tax with exemptions for income that is invested in fixed capital. Either of these two methods would remove the financial burden of government debt. 'Consequently, to keep down the Budget deficit in war-time in order to reduce the increase in the National Debt ceases to be the primary objective of war finance. And, if to maintain full employment in peace-time requires budget deficits, there is no reason to be scared by the rising National Debt.'[4]

Kalecki reinforced his point that technically the National Debt should not be a problem, if financed within the economy, in his contribution to a set of studies of *The Economics of Full Employment* that were prepared and published by the Oxford Institute of Statistics. Kalecki's chapter was titled 'Three Ways to Full Employment'. The three ways were: deficit spending on public investment and social welfare, financed by borrowing; stimulating private investment; and redistributing income from those on higher incomes to households on lower incomes. He reiterated his previous arguments that a fiscal deficit always finances itself, in the sense that the spending ensures that funds accrue in bank accounts to finance the government borrowing. The rate of interest would not rise as long as the central bank expanded commercial banks reserves sufficiently to allow commercial banks to maintain their cash ratios. If the rate of interest on government bonds started to rise, then the government could always switch its saving to shorter-term bills. In this way, as with the wartime fiscal deficit, the government borrowing could continue

[3] See Kalecki, 'A Theory of Commodity, Income and Capital Taxation', 1937. See also Toporowski, *Michał Kalecki: An Intellectual Biography, Volume 1*, 2013, pp. 94–6. Keynes had advocated a capital levy of this kind to deal with the debt left over from the First World War, describing the tax as 'the fairest and most expedient method of adjusting the burden of taxation between past accumulations and the fruits of present efforts, whenever, in the general judgement of the country, the discouragement to the latter is excessive'. *Tract on Monetary Reform*, 1923, p. 70.

[4] Kalecki, 'The Burden of the National Debt', 1943a. This note is further discussed in Chapter 10 below.

without affecting the rate of interest. Wage pressure on prices of consumer goods could be regulated by a combination of price controls, subsidies, and income tax. Concerns about the 'burden' of the National Debt could be met by servicing it from the proceeds of a capital levy, or a tax on profits with the amounts of fixed capital investment deducted from the profits liable to tax. This last Kalecki called a modified income tax that would have a neutral effect on output and employment. Here Kalecki pointed out that domestically financed government debt is merely a redistribution from tax-payers to bond-holders: the National Debt is not 'a burden to society as a whole because in essence it constitutes an internal transfer'. Obviously when bond-holders are capitalist rentiers, and tax-payers are less wealthy, such a redistribution is regressive. But it is not difficult to see that his proposed capital levy is ingenious precisely because it adjusts the tax system to make it more progressive as tax-payments to bond-holders make the system more regressive.

Kalecki found the regulation of private investment to be the most problematic way of securing full employment. The optimal amount of such investment was the amount that would keep productive capacity growing with the level of consumption and total expenditure. However, investment is the least stable part of expenditure in an economy and did not respond reliably to any of the incentives to such undertakings. It was therefore unlikely to be regulated by the rate of interest, where the relevant long-term rate of interest is relatively stable, indicating only a very weak relationship between policy rates of interest, which are short-term, and the level of private investment, or by tax allowances. Either of these measures would require cumulative reductions to maintain their effect so that, in time, a government would be unable to reduce interest rates or taxes any further. Private investment adds to productive capacity and, if excess capacity emerges, because the rate of investment required to maintain full employment is less than that required to maintain full capacity utilization, then excess capacity will tend to depress investment. The third way of achieving full employment is by redistributing income to achieve higher consumption by taxing higher incomes and subsidizing, with welfare payments, those on lower incomes. The tax on higher incomes would have to be 'modified' by allowing deductions for business investment, so that the redistribution does not adversely affect private investment. The redistribution would result in a more equal distribution of income after tax. Such redistribution was likely to meet with much stronger opposition than the policy of deficit financing. It may therefore be necessary to reinforce redistribution with a deficit spending by the government. The combination of deficit financing and redistribution through taxes, subsidies, price controls, and welfare payments was, in Kalecki's view, the most reliable way of securing full employment. At the same time, it would be necessary to ensure that private investment provided sufficient capacity for demand, given full employment and labour productivity. Private investment could be encouraged by making fixed investment deductible against tax, or by replacing income tax by wealth taxes, which will have no effect on the profitability of investment. Such incentives to investment could be supplemented by public investment, for example, in slum clearance.[5]

Keynes, who had urged 'the socialisation of investment' as a solution to the problem of unemployment, was impressed. He wrote to Kalecki to thank him for the book. 'Your own contribution seems to me most striking and original, particularly pages 44–46 [where Kalecki advanced the idea of the National Debt as merely a redistributional mechanism and proposed a wealth tax, or a tax on profits from which investment could be deducted]; also most beautifully compressed. It is a great comfort to read something so short and so much to the point. I am very much taken with your modified income-tax [i.e., the tax on profits]. It will be alleged, I am afraid, that the difficulties of transition would be excessive, since it would mean that a new business might have next to no tax to pay for years, which would appear to give it a great competitive advantage. Nevertheless, there is, I think, a good answer to this, and such criticisms, which would be certain to arise, would be based on a fallacy.'[6]

After the war, Kalecki's comment on the management of the national debt was lost, consigned to the discussions of 'War Finance' that were deemed no longer relevant in peacetime. But, as he pointed out, the principles of debt management in wartime were just as relevant in peacetime.

3.2 Credit and Debt

Somewhat more widely cited than his observations on the management of the National Debt was an even shorter note by Kalecki in which he pointed to the dangers for credit and debt of reasoning in terms of 'real' price changes. Arthur Pigou had published a paper 'The Classical Stationary State' in the *Economic Journal* taking issue with the Keynesian theory of wages and its place in macroeconomic equilibrium.

[5] Kalecki, 'Three Ways to Full Employment', 1944/1990.

[6] Letter of J. M. Keynes to M. Kalecki dated 30 December 1944, in *The Collected Writings of John Maynard Keynes Volume XXVII*, 1980b, pp. 381–2.

Pigou was the Professor of Political Economy at the University of Cambridge and one of the leading 'classics' to whose enlightenment Keynes's *General Theory* was dedicated. Keynes and Kalecki had been arguing that, under perfect competition, a state of unemployment would cause wages to fall and that, faced with a shortfall in demand at current prices, prices would then fall. In real terms, therefore, there would be no change in output or employment.[7] Pigou conceded that in a competitive economy, this would indeed happen. However, he advanced what came to be known as the 'Real Balance Effect' to explain how, in spite of falling wages and prices, the economy may still converge on full employment. This was because a given stock of money would increase in value as prices fell. As the value of money balances increased, money demand for exchange transactions would decrease, and the rate of interest would fall. With the diminished incentive to save, and growing real wealth, owners of money balances would start to spend additional amounts of money. In this way, rising demand would evoke an increase in output and employment.[8]

Kalecki found Pigou's argument confused. He took particular issue with Pigou's assumption that the banking system could keep the nominal supply of money constant while wages and prices were falling. This was possible if the money supply was a commodity like gold, or government debt that is a private sector claims on the government. But for the most part bank deposits are backed by loans to the private sector. Falling prices would then raise the real value of debts leading to 'wholesale bankruptcies' preventing the achievement of a new equilibrium: 'if the workers persisted in their game of unrestricted competition, the government would put a stop to wage decreases under pressure from employers'.[9]

Kalecki's argument was similar to that of Irving Fisher's earlier 'Debt Deflation Theory of Great Depressions', in the sense that Fisher also recognized the dangers of assuming 'real' price adjustments in a monetary system in which credit is backed by debt, and such bank credit is fixed, as assumed by Pigou, in nominal terms.[10] It is, however, worth bearing in mind that for Fisher the business cycle was made up of such price adjustments setting off cumulative changes in the real value of debt and interest. Furthermore Fisher's famous 'equation of exchange', which underlies his analysis, is very different from the analysis of Kalecki. Fisher's equation has the money supply multiplied by its

[7] Kalecki, 'Some Remarks on Mr. Keynes's Theory', 1936.
[8] Pigou, 'The Classical Stationary State', 1943.
[9] Kalecki, 'Professor Pigou on "The Classical Stationary State": A Comment', 1944.
[10] Fisher, 'The Debt Deflation Theory of Great Depressions', 1933.

velocity of circulation equal to the price level multiplied by the volume of real transactions. That velocity of circulation is the number of times that a given stock of money is turned over in a given period and for Fisher was made up of two different velocities, one for cash (notes and coins) and the other one for bank deposits. The velocities are supposed to be fixed by habit and institutional factors, and therefore the velocities are fixed in relation to each other.[11] For Kalecki, the price level was determined by 'prime costs', or wages and the prices of raw materials. Total output or real transactions are determined by the level of investment, because that is the main factor in the flow of profits. In turn the amount of bank deposits is determined by the financing needs of any given amount of investment and the deficit financing of the government. The velocity of cash circulation is fixed by the wage bill for the economy as a whole or household consumption. But it is the velocity of circulation of bank deposits that, given a certain level and composition of financing, accommodates the stock of bank deposits to actual investment and government expenditure.[12]

Keynes was intrigued by Kalecki's observations. In preparing publication of Kalecki's comment on Pigou, Keynes wrote to Kalecki on 22 February, suggesting that, 'On Pigou's assumptions, the *real* rate of interest in Irving Fisher's sense would be constantly rising. This would have two effects. People would save more, and not less, as Pigou assumes…[and] If the real value of money is constantly increasing, there will be a strong pressure to repay debts. Thus, at the limit, it would become impossible for the banks to keep the stocks of money constant except so far as it was backed by gold…Pigou is assuming simultaneously two contradictory hypotheses…would even the creation of more national debt help, since this would increase personal incomes paripassu?'

Kalecki replied on 28 February 1944. 'Your point on the rising *real* rate of interest is valid only in the period of adjustment.' Once equilibrium was established wages and prices would stop falling. However, during the adjustment, the rising real interest rates would 'tend to reduce employment, but an even more important influence in this direction will be exerted by wholesale bankruptcy and resulting "crisis of confidence"' mentioned in Kalecki's comment. On the role of government debt, Kalecki observed 'If in the initial situation there exists a large National Debt this makes Pigou's adjustment easier because the increase in the real value of the National Debt does mean an increase in the real wealth of firms and persons. (If the

[11] Fisher, *The Purchasing Power of Money*, chapters 5 and 6; see also Laidler, *The Golden Age of the Quantity Theory*, 1991, pp. 68–74.

[12] Kalecki, appendix on 'The Money Market', in *An Essay on the Theory of Business Cycle*, 1933/1990.

interest on Debt is financed by taxation its existence does not affect the aggregate disposable income.)'[13]

Keynes replied on 8 March to agree that the real rate of interest would not continue rising indefinitely. But he thought that by the time it reached its equilibrium 'substantially all bank loans would have been paid off. Thus I do not see how the banking system is going to maintain the quantity of money constant unless it is prepared to issue national debt as a backing for it. Assuming that interest is paid on this out of taxation, it cannot affect the wealth of the community one way or another...Pigou is in reality depending entirely on the increase in the value of gold. The whole thing is really too fantastic for words and scarcely worth discussing.'[14]

3.3 Monetary Policy after the War

In March 1945 Kalecki resigned from the Oxford Institute of Statistics. Later in the year he moved to Montreal, to work at the International Labour Organisation. It was an opportunity to engage with economic discussions in Canada and the United States, where a strong tradition centred on the University of Chicago attributed the Great Depression to monetary factors, and New Deal policies of the Roosevelt administration. In contrast, in his pre-war and wartime work Kalecki had advanced the view that monetary policy, and monetary circulation, is endogenous to the business cycle and that monetary considerations need not deter the chief aim of political economy, namely full employment, achieved by means of fiscal policy.

[13] Letters of Keynes to Kalecki dated 22 February 1944, and Kalecki to Keynes dated 28 February 1944 in Osiatyński, *Collected Works of Michał Kalecki Volume 1*, 1990, pp. 567–8. This correspondence between Kalecki and Keynes was originally published by Don Patinkin in his *Anticipations of the General Theory?*, 1982, pp. 96–103. Patinkin, whose work is one of the summits of the neo-classical synthesis interpretation of Keynes's theory, was a proponent of the real balance effect. To Kalecki's observation that the interest on the National Debt does not affect aggregate income if that interest is paid out of taxation, Patinkin had added the following footnote: 'Note Kalecki's view (with which Keynes in the reply which follows concurs) that government debt serviced by taxation is not part of wealth.' Patinkin is confusing the net wealth of society as a whole, for which debts and credit claims sum to zero, with the net wealth of the private sector. The net wealth of the private sector includes the private sector's claims on the government. In any case, what he attributes to Kalecki and Keynes is *not* their view. Kalecki was referring to *interest* not wealth. As he expressly pointed out, interest on government debt paid from tax revenue is merely a redistribution of aggregate income, and therefore cannot add to that income. In his 'Mysteries of the Money Market' (see above), which Patinkin seems not to have read, Kalecki explained exactly how the National Debt adds to the stock of private wealth: The expenditure financed by debt creates the profits that lie in capitalists bank accounts, available to buy government bonds.

[14] Letters of Keynes to Kalecki dated 8 March 1944, in Osiatyński, *Collected Works of Michał Kalecki Volume I*, p. 568.

In Montreal, Kalecki was invited to participate in a symposium put together to discuss a paper on fiscal and monetary policy by Lloyd W. Mints. Mints taught Money and Banking at the University of Chicago, and the policy framework that he suggested reflected many of the ideas that are associated with the work of his colleagues Henry Simons and Milton Friedman.[15] The most obvious shared idea is the monetarist notion that the quantity of money determines the price level, so that once the money supply is fixed, competition can be relied upon to keep prices likewise stable. A second common Chicago theme was their desire to abolish the Federal Reserve System for providing reserves to US banks, and the transfer of this function to the US Treasury, where reserves would be supplied through the Treasury's open market operations. This would integrate fiscal with monetary policy. The desire to eliminate the Federal Reserve was reinforced by their conviction that the Federal Reserve had been too cautious in the 1930s and had allowed the money supply to fall, thereby causing prices to fall in the period from 1929 to 1933.[16] Mints's only substantial differences with his colleagues were that he wanted the money supplied through open market operations by a specialist Monetary Agency created by Congress. He did not mention the 100 per cent reserve policy, requiring banks to hold the equivalent of their payment or sight deposits in cash form, and urged the gradual elimination of the government debt in favour of monetizing fiscal deficits. Fiscal deficits, along with open market operations, would be the means for supplying money to the economy. Mints wanted this to be associated with a stable level of government expenditure, so that counter-cyclical fiscal policy would consist of lowering the tax rate to create a fiscal deficit if prices were falling, and raising taxes if prices were rising. He considered that a sales subsidy (a negative sales tax) would be a more efficient and flexible means of stimulating aggregate demand than public works.[17]

Needless to say, Kalecki was not convinced by the proposal. He analysed the three substantive elements of Mints's programme. Increasing aggregate demand by open market policy and raising tax exemption schedules was likely to have only a weak effect on actual demand. This is because the channel through which the money supply affects demand is the long-term rate of interest. It would require very considerable open market purchases of securities

[15] Mints, 'Monetary Policy', 1946; Simons, 'A Positive Program for Laissez-Faire', 1934; Friedman, 'A Monetary and Fiscal Framework for Economic Stability', 1948.

[16] This criticism of the 'Fed' was originally made by Irving Fisher, and recurs in Friedman and Schwartz, *A Monetary History of the United States 1867–1960*, 1963.

[17] Mints, 'Monetary Policy', 1946.

to lower the long-term rate of interest. While this lowering may eventually have some effect on investment, its impact on consumption, through the 'wealth effect' (increase in the value of financial wealth), would be weak because of the low proportion of additional wealth that rich people actually consume. In any case, stimulating private investment to fill the deflationary gap would create excess capacity, and would therefore be 'self-defeating'. Increasing consumption by raising tax exemption levels would have a weak effect, because it would increase the disposable incomes of the better off.

(It should be borne in mind that in 1946 most households in the United States and in Europe earned incomes below the threshold that would make them liable to income tax. Their disposable incomes would therefore not be affected by increases in that threshold.)

Kalecki agreed with the proposal to subsidize consumption, but suggested that it would be more effective if the subsidy were concentrated on items of mass consumption, rather than a general sales subsidy. Increases in wages in relation to prices would also have a beneficial effect in helping to eliminate the deflationary gap by redistributing income from profits that have a higher propensity to save.[18]

Kalecki disagreed too with Mints's argument that the government should eschew public works. As Alvin Hansen also pointed out, there was considerable scope for public investment in health services, education, housing and infrastructure. Indeed, public investment should be undertaken to offset fluctuations in private investment. Hansen and Kalecki agreed too that public investment puts less stress on the labour market than offsetting changes in private investment by changes in the volume of consumption, because labour can be more easily redeployed between public and private investment. Once the economy stabilized at full employment there would be less fluctuation in investment in any case.[19]

Then there was effect of monetizing the fiscal deficit on the cash position of the banks. 'Presumably the government would obtain the currency from the central bank by way of interest-free loans. A large part of the currency issued would find its way back into the private banks, but the banks would be under the obligation to "sterilize" the additional cash.'[20] Kalecki pointed out that

[18] Kalecki, 'A Comment on "Monetary Policy"', 1946/1990a.

[19] Kalecki, 'A Comment on "Monetary Policy"', 1946/1990a.

[20] Kalecki, 'A Comment on "Monetary Policy"', 1946/1990a. In the version of the paper published with the symposium, Mints recommended the elimination of central banking, so that the Monetary Agency of the Treasury would issue to its head office the money required to finance the fiscal deficit. Mints also specifically argued against the raising of the banks' cash ratio by the bank regulators, unless it was intended that the rise would be permanent.

with a large deflationary gap (excess of household saving over investment), and therefore a large long-term fiscal deficit, the cash ratio of banks would rise continuously. This would induce banks to raise charges on their demand deposits, and lower the rate of interest on time deposits. The interest that is 'saved' by the government, because its deficit is monetized and not financed by borrowing, would be paid for, at least in part, by the public, through being charged more for their sight deposits and getting less interest on their time deposits. Kalecki suggested that a better way of financing the fiscal deficit would be by issuing short-term bills. This he argued would bring down medium and long-term interest rates, as securities with these longer maturities become scarce, relative to short-term securities. The falling rate of interest should ensure that the rise in interest costs remains below the rate of growth of the economy. And if those costs should turn out to rise faster than national income, then the debt could still be managed by a modest annual wealth tax to pay at least part of the interest on government debt.

In his conclusion, Kalecki turned to the question of wages and price inflation. Because of imperfect competition, wage flexibility was unlikely to eliminate frictional unemployment, or at least large falls in wages may be required to eliminate unemployment, and even that may take some time. Rather than reducing wages for all workers in order to secure employment for the margin that is unemployed, it would be far more effective to offer retraining with a decent level of income support to the workers unemployed. Concerning the pressure of trades unions, using the situation of full employment to force up wages, and thereby causing prices to rise, Kalecki pointed out that this would not cause prices to rise unless the rise in wages exceeded the increase in labour productivity.[21]

[21] Kalecki, 'A Comment on "Monetary Policy"', 1946/1990a.

4

The Monetary Consequences of Financing Full Employment in an Open Economy

Kalecki's pre-war excursions into monetary theory, like Keynes's work on the same subject in his *General Theory*, were conducted under the assumption of a closed economy, in order to isolate the endogenous destabilizing features of capitalist production and investment. However, Keynes's geographical location in the capital city that was most vulnerable to movements of international reserves, and his work on international monetary policy, meant that few of his major writings, with the notable exceptions of his *Treatise on Probability* and his *General Theory*, reached the printer without some consideration of international monetary arrangements. Kalecki was very well aware of fragile and volatile nature of cross-border payments and exchanges in the inter-war period. But he did not enter into a systematic analysis of this aspect of monetary theory until his work brought him to comment upon the plans drawn up in the middle of the Second World War for a new post-war international monetary order. Then it was inevitable that he would remark upon the work of Keynes, as well as the arrangements that emerged from Bretton Woods.

4.1 Trade Disequilibrium and Full Employment

Kalecki had earlier expressed his critical view on the possibilities of full employment without international co-operation. In his articles for *Przegląd Socjalistyczny* in 1932, he had alluded to the difficulties posed by the foreign trade account in trying to achieve and maintain full employment. On a unilateral basis, if one government alone attempts to reflate its economy, it risks difficulties in balancing its foreign trade, as domestic demand rises faster than demand among its trading partners. These difficulties could be overcome on a multilateral basis if reflation is co-ordinated with other governments, in order

Interest and Capital: The Monetary Economics of Michał Kalecki. Jan Toporowski, Oxford University Press.
© Jan Toporowski 2022. DOI: 10.1093/oso/9780198816232.003.0005

to ensure that all imported more so that all exported more. But this would be prone to imperialist rivalry, undermining international co-operation.[1]

These articles were only known to a small Polish audience. But the arguments around them were common in the financial and economic diplomacy of the inter-war period, where they inhibited government action to alleviate the economic depression. The failure of the London Conference in 1933 had given way to tariffs, currency blocs, and bilateral payment agreements between governments. After the outbreak of war, financial and economic diplomacy gave way to autarky. At the start of the Second World War regulations were introduced in Britain to give the government control over foreign assets and payments. This in effect reduced international payments to bilateral clearing between the British government and the governments of its allies and neutral states, while freezing payments to 'hostile powers'. Already in 1941, partly in response to German plans for a payments union in Europe, economists employed in the War Cabinet were working on the question of how bilateral payments could be replaced after the war by multilateral payments, that is, payments directly between traders in different countries and in currencies that were directly convertible against each other. While there was general agreement that free trade was desirable, Keynes and his US equivalent, Harry Dexter White, wanted to establish a system of multilateral payments in which exchange rates were fixed but adjustable, although they were famously to differ on how this was to be achieved.

In April 1943, Keynes's proposals were published in London as a government White Paper, simultaneously with the publication in Washington of White's proposals.[2] The key difference between them was that Keynes wanted a Clearing Union with a currency, provisionally called 'bancor', issued by an International Clearing Bank, that would serve as the benchmark against which exchange rates would be fixed. Trade surpluses would be automatically deposited in an investment fund for on-lending to deficit countries, and interest payments, deducted from surpluses above a certain quota necessary for trade, were supposed to discourage excessive surpluses. Governments in deficit would have automatic borrowing rights, subject to similarly modest interest payments. The White proposal recommended an exchange rate stabilization fund, into which member countries would pay gold, foreign

[1] See Toporowski, 'Multilateralism and Military Keynesianism', 2016b.

[2] White Paper, *Proposals for an International Clearing Union*, London, 1943, and *Preliminary Draft Outline of a Proposal for an International Stabilisation Fund*, Washington, DC, 1943.

currency, and government bonds, in exchange for overdraft facilities with a right to automatic borrowing against a quota set by the deposits of the government in the fund. Above quota borrowing would require the agreement of a majority of depositors in the fund (weighted by their deposits).[3] In May 1943, the Government of the United States started meetings with representatives of Allies and governments associated with them, to discuss and agree financial and monetary arrangements for the post-war peace, with a clear view to avoiding the financial difficulties that had exacerbated economic instability in the 1920s and 1930s.[4]

The revival of economic diplomacy and his position in Oxford gave Kalecki a chance to address a much broader audience about the international financial conditions for, and consequences of, full employment. In the summer of 1943, a special supplement of the Oxford Institute's *Bulletin* was prepared by members of the Joint Committee of Nuffield College and the staff of the Institute of Statistics. The editor of the Supplement explained the rationale for it as follows:

> The subject matter of international trade and finance is of a highly technical nature and discussions of these problems tend, therefore, to be confined to 'experts', city circles and business men. It is, of course, appropriate that the efforts to come to a satisfactory plan should be left to the experts of the Allied Nations whenever technical details are concerned. It is important, however, that a wider circle than the mere experts should understand the general issues involved and help to shape the line along which agreement should be sought by the experts. For, although questions of social security and full employment would appear to affect the life of the average citizen more immediately and fundamentally, there can be no doubt that his welfare and standard of living will be greatly influenced by the sort of international order or disorder in the economic relations between States which will emerge after the war.[5]

Apart from the editorial, approximately two-thirds of the Supplement consisted of a long article by Ernst ('Fritz') Schumacher summarizing the key mechanisms of the Plans proposed by Keynes and White. As the author of an

[3] In effect, it was the US Treasury's proposals that won out at the United National Monetary and Financial Conference at Bretton Woods in July 1944.

[4] These talks, and Keynes's part in them, are detailed in chapters 9–11 of Skidelsky, *John Maynard Keynes Volume 3*, 2001 and Keynes, *Collected Writings Volume XXV*, 1980a.

[5] 'Lessons of the Past', *Bulletin of the Oxford Institute of Statistics*, 1943.

earlier paper on multilateral clearing, Schumacher was a highly appropriate person to summarize with authority Keynes's and White's proposals.[6] Given that one of the other two papers in the Supplement was co-authored with Kalecki, it could be said that the Supplement owed more to Schumacher than to the Institute that published that Supplement. Schumacher's summary endorsed the view in both plans that free trade alone could not secure full employment. Market forces alone would not make trade balances converge on equilibrium, and the absence of equilibrium would deflate demand in trade deficit countries, reinforcing a tendency towards deflation in the global economy as a whole. However, he considered that both plans were inadequate to provide the liquidity necessary to maintain multilateralism and this brought with it the danger that individual governments would revert to rationing foreign exchange or bilateralism, that is, settlements between central banks on a net basis. The net basis (transferring only the foreign currency or gold equivalent to the *balance* between imports and exports during the settlement period) would inevitably encourage the direction of exports towards countries from which excess imports were being purchased, or else limitations on those imports. In this way, bilateralism tends to undermine free trade.

According to Schumacher, although the Keynes Plan was superior in offering a higher level of international reserves to support free trade, it suffered from a lack of clarity about the concept of equilibrium. 'Under the British Plan "equilibrium" is defined as the absence of bancor credits and debits.' However, this supposes that the flow of bancor credits and debits is determined by trade flows. In fact, the balance of payments consists of three parts: the balance of trade and income payments (the current account); the balance of long-term capital flows, and the balance of short-term bank transactions. These last are the bancor credits and debits. The flaw in the Keynes Plan was its presumption that long-term capital flows are balanced or non-existent, so that the balance of trade and income payments is equal to the net flow of bancor credits and debits. But if there are long-term capital flows then their balance can seriously disrupt the flows of short-term bancor credits and debits.[7] Keynes did indeed advocate capital controls to eliminate such

[6] Schumacher, 'The New Currency Plans', 1943b. See also 'Multilateral Clearing', 1943a. Schumacher had been a German Rhodes Scholar at Oxford, but ended up as an agricultural labourer working on the farm of Robert Brand, the Managing Director of Lazard Brothers, who was, with Keynes, one of the British delegation to the Bretton Woods Conference. In 1941, Brand passed on to Keynes a memorandum written by his farm labourer entitled 'Some Aspects of Post-war Economic Planning'. See Keynes, *Collected Writings Volume XXV*, 1980a, p. 21.

[7] Schumacher, 'The New Currency Plans', 1943b.

disruption.[8] But then he could not also claim, as the White Paper stated, that foreign exchange transactions can be 'carried on as freely as in the best days of the gold standard', that is, as Schumacher noted, without even having to notify the monetary authorities of the transaction.

4.2 The Kalecki/Schumacher Plan

The third paper in the Supplement was jointly written by Schumacher and Kalecki. Like Schumacher's summary paper on the White and Keynes Plan, the paper co-authored with Kalecki found the Keynes Plan to be preferable to the White Plan. But the Keynes Plan would not be effective unless modified and extended. Kalecki and Schumacher started with a fundamental critique of the whole idea that the aim of international trade policy should be balanced trade:

> Both the British and the American Currency Plans are based upon the idea of 'equilibrium'...they aim at creating rules and machinery through which, after a start has been made (after the war), each country would be 'kept in balance' with the rest of the world. Neither of them succeeds in giving more than a purely formal definition of 'equilibrium', a definition which...is not necessarily relevant. It may be questioned whether the very concept of equilibrium is sufficiently precise and significant to be introduced at this level at all. There is no merit in a general policy aiming at *Current account equilibrium* for all countries, because different countries are at different stages of economic development, and a regular flow of investment from the more highly developed to the more backward regions of the world may redound to benefit of all. This is implicitly recognised in both schemes, since they are both to be supplemented by proposals for an International Investment Board.[9]

[8] Skidelsky, *John Maynard Keynes Volume 3*, 2001, p. 231.

[9] Kalecki and Schumacher, 'International Clearing and Long-Term Lending', 1943. Kalecki's associate from his pre-war days in Poland, Oskar Lange, was rather more sanguine about the Keynes Plan, and defended it in a lengthy letter to the *New York Times*, on 9 April 1943. Lange's only criticism was that the proposed method of determining the 'fundamental disequilibrium' of exchange rates by a majority vote of the Board of the International Monetary Fund offered too much scope for political manipulation. See Lange, Dzieła, 1985, pp. 198–200. The International Investment Board proposal was realized at Bretton Woods in the form of the International Bank for Reconstruction and Development, or the World Bank.

Kalecki and Schumacher did not think that charging governments for surpluses deposited in the international clearing bank would provide an adequate incentive to expand domestic demand in their countries. They concluded that the long-term goal of current account equilibrium should be abandoned, to allow governments to pursue whatever levels of aggregate demand they may wish to have. However, this, in the view of Kalecki and Schumacher, suffers from the disadvantage that governments may in those circumstances resort to over-valuing their currencies in the foreign exchange markets in order to hold down import costs. The authors argued that therefore currency support arrangements should be differentiated, according to whether a country has a trade deficit, because it is in the process of industrialization, or because there are other reasons for the deficit. They suggested an extension of the powers of the International Investment Board at the International Clearing Union. The proceeds of the trade surpluses of the surplus countries would be deposited with the Investment Board. The Board would direct the surpluses to industrializing countries that had used up a quarter of their quotas as loans. However, industrializing countries that went on to use up half of their quotas would be required to devalue their currency.

The direction of loans to developing countries was supposed to allow for the additional imports required for industrialization. A further twist to the scheme was recommended by Kalecki and Schumacher to reinforce equilibrating mechanisms in industrialized countries. The International Investment Board, they suggested, should be given the power to direct that loans to industrializing countries had to be spent in industrialized countries that were in trade deficit. In this way the weak equilibrating mechanism in the Keynes Plan, of charging interest to deficit *and* surplus countries, would be assisted by recycling the surpluses of industrialized countries through orders for industrial equipment for developing countries from industrialized countries in deficit. Kalecki and Schumacher defended this proposed breach in 'the free play of market forces' by pointing out that the White Plan had a similar suggestion to ration the exports of surplus countries. The difference between the two proposals was that the White Plan 'is neither expansionist nor multilateral' while the scheme proposed in Oxford provided liquidity to assist current account equilibrium in industrialized countries, while at the same time facilitating the 'unbalanced equilibrium' required in developing countries.[10]

Unlike the Keynes Plan, which sought to eliminate private capital flows, but then declared that this elimination was 'not essential' to the international

[10] Kalecki and Schumacher, 'International Clearing and Long-Term Lending', 1943.

clearing scheme,[11] the Kalecki/Schumacher scheme did not altogether ban private sector capital flows. Its authors argued that *net* foreign short-term lending in the private sector would need to be eliminated, presumably leaving scope for short-term lending balanced on the balance sheet of the central bank. But long-term private sector or intergovernmental lending would be allowed, providing that the lender country had exhausted half of its bancor quota. In this way, surplus governments would only be able to engage in international lending after they had committed half of their quota to trade. However, the function of the International Investment Board would be to support current account equilibrium in countries that needed for development purposes to run current account deficits and which did not wish to become indebted to other governments and private finance. To be able to do this efficiently, Kalecki and Schumacher argued that the International Investment Board and the International Clearing Union needed to be combined in one institution, rather than separating international investment from the clearing of trade payments. In effect, this would ensure that international investment targeted at deficit countries would rise with growing trade imbalances. In contrast, the Keynes Plan offered limited resources to international investment, and the White Plan even more modest finance.

Two other aspects of their proposal deserves note. This is the authors' dissent from the classical doctrine that the purpose of international monetary arrangements was to assure convergence on equilibrium in the current account of the balance of payments. Kalecki's and Schumacher's argument, that countries in the process of industrialization require financing to be able to run trade deficits, was to become a feature of the development economics that emerged after the war, as well as Kalecki's later approach to the economics of the developing countries.[12] The other aspect of their proposal that is perhaps even more radical, and links Kalecki's pre-war ideas on full employment with his later work on multilateralism, is the idea that trade imbalances were the inevitable outcome of attempts to reach full employment by aggregate demand management. The reason for this was that capital equipment for industrial production was not distributed among countries in such a way as to secure trade balance with full employment. The condition for full employment with trade balance was investment in productive capacity in the developing countries. The Neo-Classical view that prices, including exchange rates, could adjust the demand of the full-employed and their families to the

[11] White Paper, *Proposals for an International Clearing Union*, London, 1943, paras 32 and 33.
[12] See United Nations, 'Growth, Disequilibrium and Disparities', 1950.

resources available through balanced trade was placing demands on market mechanisms that those mechanisms could not deliver.[13]

The final paper in the supplement was by the Hungarian economist Thomas Balogh who was, at that time, a lecturer at Balliol College. Balogh had been one of the earliest critics of the Keynes Plan.[14] In his paper, entitled 'The Foreign Balance and full Employment', he examined some of the difficulties that may be envisaged in implementing the Schumacher/Kalecki Plan. His endorsement of that Plan clearly suggests that the Plan was a common view of the authors contributing to the Supplement. If so, then it is an extraordinary achievement by Kalecki and Schumacher, who had a mere three months to come up with a consensus on the complexities of the Keynes and White Plans that would satisfy them all.

Balogh reiterated their common view that market forces would tend to work in deflationary ways in the international economy. They would be overcome by the Schumacher/Kalecki scheme for generating and financing exports of capital equipment to the developing countries. One problem that he foresaw was that a requirement to use development loans to buy from mature economies in trade deficit may end up with the developing countries buying at a higher cost than they may be able to buy from surplus countries. Balogh's answer to this was to argue for subsidies to make the cost of industrial equipment exported by deficit countries equal to that of surplus countries. He dismissed the idea that currency devaluation could do the job better, since exchange rate devaluation was a *general* subsidy from the domestic market to export markets, while targeted subsidies were likely to be less costly. Among the counterarguments to this, the possibility of retaliation was less likely if all economies are enjoying high employment. The charge that subsidies might constitute 'dumping' could just as easily be levelled against currency devaluation, or policies of wage reductions. In any case, subsidies would be superior to bilateral clearing agreements, which often resulted in the exchange of goods for which there was not much of a market in either country. Finally, Balogh considered whether the scheme put forward by Kalecki and Schumacher would work equally well if adopted by a smaller group of countries instead of the whole world. In his view, such a partial scheme would work less well, because its member governments would need to take measures to counteract the effects of business cycles in countries outside the scheme and this may involve quotas for trade with countries outside the bloc. The effect of such a reduced area of the

[13] Cf. Samuelson, 'Theoretical Notes on Trade Problems', 1964.
[14] Skidelsky, *John Maynard Keynes Volume III*, 2001, pp. 334–5.

scheme would therefore depend on the degree of self-sufficiency of the bloc: in a large, self-sufficient bloc like the sterling area the loss of labour productivity due to the reduced, in relation to the world economy, scope for the international division of labour would likely be small.[15]

4.3 The International Monetary Fund Emerges

In April 1944, the British Government published a White Paper, presenting the outcome of the earlier negotiations between Keynes and White on the proposed International Monetary Fund (IMF). The Government still had strong reservations about the proposed fund. Chief among them was the reduction in the resources of the fund, in relation to the Plan put forward by Keynes on behalf of the Government, and the realization of the international investment facility as an International Bank for Reconstruction and Development, which was clearly not going to direct its resources to Great Britain, whose reconstruction and development needs were nugatory by comparison with the colonies, developing countries, and countries on the mainland of Europe. The British negotiators had therefore agreed to a reduction in the loan capacity of the Fund.[16] Schumacher and Balogh wrote an extended comment on the White Paper for the Oxford Institute's *Bulletin*. They objected to the inadequate resources of the IMF, and the requirements imposed on its members. Among those requirements were the obligations to maintain free trade in accordance with criteria laid down by the Fund, rather than their development needs, and to seek balanced trade which, in Schumacher and Balogh's view, could only be deflationary. They commended the Kalecki/Schumacher Plan as a more effective way of avoiding deflation and offering a more discriminating way of securing trade equilibrium.[17]

Balogh was active in London, writing to *The Times* and briefing parliamentarians on the schemes being prepared for the Bretton Woods conference. Pre-occupied with his preparations for the Bretton Woods Conference in July 1944, Keynes could not have been unaware of the criticisms emanating from Oxford of his plans and agreements for the new international economic order. Balogh's extensive chapter on international trade policy to the volume on

[15] Balogh, 'The Foreign Balance and Full Employment', 1943.
[16] White Paper, 'Joint Statement', 1944b; *Skidelsky, John Maynard Keynes Volume III*, 2001, pp. 338–40.
[17] Schumacher and Balogh, 'An International Monetary Fund', 1944.

The Economics of Full Employment, where he reiterated his criticisms of the Keynes Plan for its failure to take into account the impact of deflationary policies abroad, therefore came as no surprise to Keynes. In his letter of 30 December 1944 to Kalecki, complimenting him on *The Economics of Full Employment*, Keynes took issue with the section in the volume on International Aspects. '…the section on International Aspects…seems to me a frightful muddle, which leaves the reader more in a fog and stupider than when he began. It does not even make a beginning at the basic analysis needed to tackle this rather difficult and intractable problem.' He seems to have had some difficulties himself in identifying Balogh's muddle: 'I wish I had time to think it properly through myself. It is not so difficult that it is impossible to write sense about it.' Balogh had, in Keynes's view, misquoted his speech in the House of Lords. 'What is happening to Balogh? He has done some excellent stuff in the past, but much of what I have seen of late strikes me as extremely confused.'[18]

Joan Robinson was less deprecating. Her review of the book devotes almost as much space to the section in the book on International Aspects as it does to Kalecki's 'Three Ways to Full Employment.' She outlined the problem of the deflationary bias in international trade, as governments sought to bring their foreign trade balance into equilibrium, and the danger that this may lead to autarky. Her review concluded with a discussion of Balogh's suggestion that a smaller group of countries committed to full employment may form a bloc in which they would give each other preference for the purposes of their imports. 'This amounts to something like making the scarce-currency clause of the Bretton Woods proposals permanent. An adequate discussion of this scheme, which raises wide issues of international policy as well as detailed questions the technique for planning trade in a mainly private-enterprise system, requires a volume to itself.'[19]

Joan Robinson put her finger on the problem. There is little evidence that any of the policy-makers or negotiators with the United States Government were reading the analysis of international trade and finance that was coming out of Oxford. Keynes himself, as he indicated, was aware of Balogh's briefings

[18] Keynes letter to Kalecki, dated 30 December 1944, in *The Collected Writings of John Maynard Keynes Volume XXVII*, 1980b, pp. 381–2. With the negotiations for an American loan after the war, Keynes's opinion of Balogh soured still further, and he called him a 'Jewish Nazi' (Skidelsky *John Maynard Keynes Volume III*, p. 543.)

[19] Robinson, review of *The Economics of Full Employment* 1945. The 'scarce currency' clause was an arrangement introduced by the American government allowing governments to discriminate in foreign trade against countries with persistent trade surpluses. See Kahn, 'Historical Origins of the International Monetary Fund', 1976, pp. 16–19.

against the agreed scheme, but read only Balogh's account in the volume on *The Economics of Full Employment*. Kalecki and Schumacher's attempt to integrate the developing countries into a supportive global financial system had to wait for a further decade before poorer countries disadvantaged in international trade found their voice in the counsels of the United Nations.

4.4 After the War

After the war, working at the International Labour Organization, Kalecki returned to the question of full employment in an open economy. 'Multilateralism and Full Employment' starts by pointing out that the new International Monetary Fund, the International Bank for Reconstruction and Development and the US loan to the UK 'aim at establishing a workable system of multilateral international trade...the principle of multilateralism requires that each country should be guided in its purchases in other countries by the price and quality of goods without taking into consideration whether the supplying countries are or are not buyers of the produce of the country in question'.[20] The question that Kalecki addressed was whether countries seeking to maintain full employment would be able, under a multilateral system, to export sufficiently to pay for the amount of imports that they would have with full employment. If this cannot be achieved under multilateralism, then the governments of countries trying to maintain full employment may decide that they can 'achieve more security in [their] foreign trade by concluding a series of bilateral agreements with other countries' directing import and export trade to those countries. Alternatively, a group of such countries may enter into a regional bloc, in which multilateralism operates for trade within the bloc, and proceeds of exports outside the bloc are pooled and rationed among the members of the bloc.[21]

In general Kalecki felt that world multilateralism was more efficient than bilateralism or regional blocs, and it would not 'raise the political issues which may be involved in the formation of regional blocks. It is therefore superior to other systems provided it is workable, i.e., provided that it is operated under conditions of such a kind that no difficulties in balancing imports of goods and services with exports arise for full-employment countries.' Kalecki therefore proposed to analyse the conditions under which full employment could

[20] Kalecki, 'Multilateralism and Full Employment', 1946/1990b.
[21] Kalecki, 'Multilateralism and Full Employment', 1946/1990b.

be achieved and maintained in a multilateral system of international trade. Kalecki's paper not only laid down the conditions for full employment under what is commonly regarded as 'free trade'. He also showed that this requires quite restrictive conditions of international credit and debt.

The key problem arises because in a situation of full employment in all countries, some would have trade surpluses, and some would have trade deficits. The surplus countries would continuously accumulate gold and foreign currency reserves. The deficit countries would be faced with a continuously deteriorating foreign exchange position. A condition for multilateralism to work well would be if governments in all surplus countries managed domestic demand in such a way as to eliminate all trade surpluses. In other words, full employment is not based on a trade surplus.

However, this situation would work only if all countries maintained full employment. If employment fluctuates in some countries, then this will cause problems in balancing foreign trade: countries where employment falls short of full employment will in effect be reducing the exports of other countries, and this will transmit economic contraction to other countries. Import duties would mean the failure of multilateralism, and devaluation may increase the value of exports in domestic currency, but would be unlikely to generate additional foreign exchange. Exercising the 'scarce currency' clause of the International Monetary Fund Agreement, allowing discrimination against the exports of countries running persistent trade surpluses, would in effect mean a suspension of full multilateralism, and a move towards a regional bloc of the countries whose currencies are not 'scarce' (because they are in trade deficit).[22]

The situation was modified if countries with less than full employment gave long-term loans in their currency to full employment countries. The condition for stable full employment then becomes one where 'all countries maintain full employment based on domestic expenditure and on foreign net expenditure financed by long-term loans. Thus, each country must maintain such a domestic expenditure that this expenditure plus export surplus financed by foreign lending (or minus export deficit financed by foreign borrowing) is adequate to assure full employment.' However, the difficulty with this solution is that the terms on which long-term international lending is offered may arouse a reluctance on the part of the lenders and borrowers to expand international lending up to the scale necessary to overcome the difficulties with multilateralism.

[22] Kalecki, 'Multilateralism and Full Employment', 1946/1990b.

> The higher, on average, and the more stable the employment in not fully employed countries and the greater their propensity to import...the greater the chance that the achievable level of international long-term lending will be adequate for the solution of the problem.
>
> It follows...that there are two alternative conditions which ensure the smooth functioning of the multilateral system of international trade: (i) that each country should maintain full employment based on domestic expenditure, and on net foreign expenditure financed by international long-term lending; (ii) that the level of current long-term lending from not fully employed countries should be sufficiently high...... An ideal basis of multilateralism, however, will be the maintenance throughout the world of a volume of domestic expenditure which, in combination with foreign net investment financed by long-term loans, is adequate for securing full employment.

Failing this, Kalecki believed, countries would have difficulties in balancing their inflows and outflows of foreign exchange. This will commonly happen if employment fluctuates in the major industrial countries. If long-term international lending does not expand to overcome these difficulties, then multilateralism will break down and be replaced by a different system of international trade.[23]

The post-war international monetary order rapidly moved to an international dollar area, in which prospects for full employment were blighted by their incompatibility with foreign current account balance.[24] With the breakdown of fixed exchange rates, from the 1970s onwards, floating exchange rates were sold on a prospectus, to which Keynes had richly contributed, that devaluation offered free competitive advantage. It was the Oxford economists, Schumacher, Balogh, and Kalecki who pointed out that, for an open economy, the cost of the export advantage bestowed by devaluation is imported inflation and the consequent reduction of the domestic market. The answer was the management of trade and international debt. The American economist Hyman Minsky, in what was for him a rare intervention on how the problems of multilateralism with inadequate reserves had turned the international monetary system into what was in effect a US dollar currency area, was later to echo (unconsciously) Kalecki's conclusion:

[23] Kalecki, 'Multilateralism and Full Employment', 1946/1990b. See also López and Assous, *Michał Kalecki*, 2010, chapter 7.

[24] See Thirlwall, *Balance of Payments Theory and Export-Led Growth*, 1980, chapter 11.

There is a vast network of dollar-denominated debt which leads to large cash flows to United States entities and to the non-U.S. banks and nationals that own dollar-denominated assets…For its currency and financial centre to function as the world's currency and financial center two criteria need to be satisfied; the rest of the world can acquire sufficient amounts of its currency so that payment commitments can be fulfilled, and the central bank and national economic policy of the key currency country can make its currency scarce without extracting too high a price [in exchange rate and rate of interest – JT] from either the home or foreign countries… There is no solution [to the international debt problem – JT] without a large United States trade deficit…

… One key requirement is for the United States to achieve and maintain a closer approximation to full employment without restricting imports. But the United States cannot now do it alone. The other rich countries – Japan and Western Europe in particular – need to help by maintaining their own prosperity. Since 1980s the United States, Japan and the affluent countries of Europe have not done their part. Without international understanding and cooperation a 'cross of debt' will replace Bryan's 'cross of gold'.[25]

[25] Minsky, 'Conflict and Interdependence in a Multipolar World', 1986. There is no evidence to suggest that Minsky knew the Kalecki, Schumacher, and Balogh critique of the Bretton Woods agreement. In his research on the operation of the US dollar as a world currency, Minsky might have come across the work of the Harvard economist John H. Williams who worked for the Federal Reserve and who, in advance of Bretton Woods, was advocating the coalescence of currencies around the 'key currencies' of sterling and the US dollar. See Williams, 'Problems of Post-War International Monetary Stabilization', 1943. Minsky's 'cross of gold' reference was the rallying-cry of the 1890s populists against the gold standard given by the Democratic candidate for the President, William Jennings Bryan who famously denounced corporate international finance with the words '…we shall their demands for the gold standard by saying to them, you shall not press down upon the brow of labor this crown of thorns. You shall not crucify mankind upon a cross of gold.'

5
A Fable on Debt and Debt Management

A key feature of Kalecki's monetary economics is the financial circulation of money, that is the circulation of money that settles payment obligations under debt contracts. Kalecki explained debt resolution by means of a fable about monetary circulation between mutually indebted individuals. This is reconstructed below and the processes of debt payment in that fable are generalized to show how interest and debt payments depend on the financial circulation of money, rather than profits or income derived from the non-financial economy. Financial circulation makes debt payments dependent upon the liquidity in the financial system and marks a break with the classical theory of interest in which interest is tied to the rate of profit. Bank lending, securitization, and central bank buying of financial assets all have their part to play in maintaining debt payments to avoid default and financial crisis.

In 2015 I published a reconstruction of a Kalecki fable on credit and debt.[1] At the time I thought that it provided an intriguing insight into the working of the monetary transmission mechanism in the financial system. Although my discussion of that working remains, I think, fundamentally correct, I have since been able to think through more carefully the implications of Kalecki's fable for debt and debt management. These are essentially new implications and have radical consequences for policies of debt management. I therefore present those implications and consequences in this chapter, along with the version of the fable that I published in 2015.

Kalecki would occasionally tell stories illustrating the paradoxical, even irrational, aspects of capitalism, usually to show how inefficient the market system may be, no matter how rational may be the calculations of its participants. Perhaps best-known is his tale of two railway lines in competition with each other and suffering from excess capacity, whose only long-term solution is the construction of successively further railways lines to ensure full capacity utilization on railways lines already built.[2]

[1] Toporowski, 'A Kalecki Fable on Debt and the Monetary Transmission Mechanism', 2015.
[2] Kalecki, 'Stimulating the Business Upswing', 1933/1990.

Interest and Capital: The Monetary Economics of Michał Kalecki. Jan Toporowski, Oxford University Press.
© Jan Toporowski 2022. DOI: 10.1093/oso/9780198816232.003.0006

In the course of an exchange of views on the Greek crisis with Kalecki's student, Kazimierz Łaski, I passed on to him a fable of private debts in a Greek village being cleared through the circulation of a €100 note brought to the village by a German tourist, and returned to him at the end of the story. Łaski pointed out that the story was much older and had in fact been originally told to him by Kalecki when the two men were working together in the 1960s. I was able to reconstruct Kalecki's story from the fragments remembered by Łaski, adding to it my own explanatory remarks, to make the story comprehensible to the twenty-first century reader. The story is presented in the next section.[3] References to literary versions of debt processes are given in my original paper.

5.1 Kalecki's Fable

Following the death, in 1935, of the Polish military dictator Józef Piłsudski, his regime continued under a group of his military cronies, known as the 'colonels', who increasingly modelled their regime on that of Mussolini in Italy. One of the colonels, who was responsible for economic development, wanted to understand the economic principles behind government policies of economic recovery.[4] He called in Kalecki's colleague from the Institute for the Study of Business Cycles and Prices (*Instytut Badań Konjunktur Gospodarczych i Cen*) Ludwik Landau, to explain the principles behind the 'new economics'. Landau had just been fired from the Institute and was now working then at the national statistical office, Główny Urząd Statystyczny.[5]

[3] A humorous, Mexican version of the story is available on Youtube at https://www.youtube.com/watch?v=Aw6zsJBVMCM&t=42s

[4] Kazimierz Łaski thinks it may have been Roman Górecki (1889–1946), a lawyer who had joined Piłsudski's 'Legion', a militia formed to fight alongside the Austrian army in 1914. By 1926, just before Piłsudski's military coup against the civilian government, Górecki had been advanced to the rank of General. Shortly after the coup he was appointed head of the National Economic Bank (*Bank Gospodarstwa Krajowego*). Górecki's book, complete with hagiographic descriptions of Piłsudski and his chosen head of state Ignacy Mościcki, concludes its Introduction with the following summary of Polish economic policy:

'...the rational economic policy of the Government is based on three fundamental principles: (1) the maintenance of a stable currency based upon a balanced national budget and favourable trade balance. (2) The creation of conditions favourable to the process of internal capitalization (i.e., investment JT). (3) The adaptation of all elements of economic life to the new conditions brought about by the crisis.

> Experiments of every kind have been avoided, particularly the experiment of artificial 'manipulation of business conditions,' in the belief that only by means of simple, classic, orthodox methods can positive results be achieved. (Górecki, *Poland and Her Economic* Development, 1935, p. 17)

Górecki was Minister of Trade and Industry in the Polish Government from October 1935 to May 1936.

[5] See Kalecki, 'Ludwik Landau – Economist and Statistician', 1964, and Landau, *Wybór Pism* (Selected Writings), 1957.

Landau explained at length the principles of effective demand and credit cycles underlying levels of output and employment at any one time. The colonel had evident difficulty in grasping this. In a final effort to break through the colonel's incomprehension, Landau told the following story:

> In an impoverished Jewish shtetl in Eastern Poland, whose residents were mired in debt and living on credit, a wealthy and pious Jew arrived one day and checked into the local inn, taking care to pay his hotel bill in advance. On Friday, to avoid breaking the Sabbath injunction against carrying money, he handed over to the inn-keeper for safe-keeping a $100 note.[6] Early on Sunday, the wealthy and pious Jew left the inn before the inn-keeper had had a chance to return the banknote.
>
> After a few days, the inn-keeper decided that the wealthy Jew was not going to return. So he took the $100 note and used it to clear his debt with the local butcher. The butcher was delighted and gave the note for safe-keeping to his wife. She used it to clear her debts with a local seamstress who made up dresses for her. The seamstress was delighted, and took the money to repay her rent arrears with her landlord. The landlord was pleased to get his rent at last and gave the money to pay his mistress, who had been giving him her favours without any return for far too long. The mistress was relieved because she could now use the note to clear off her debt at the local inn where she occasionally rented rooms.
>
> So it was that the bank-note finally returned to the inn-keeper. Although no new trade or production had occurred, nor any income been created, the debts in the shtetl had been cleared, and everyone looked forward to the future with renewed optimism.
>
> A couple of weeks later, the wealthy and pious Jew returned to the inn, and the inn-keeper was able to return to him his $100 note. To his amazement and dismay, the wealthy Jew took the note, set fire to it at the paraffin lamp that was on the table, and used it to light his cigarette. On seeing the inn-keeper's dismay the wealthy Jew laughed and told him that the banknote was forged anyway.'

[6] The Polish currency, the złoty, had been placed on a dollar standard in 1934 at a rate of zł.5.26 to the US$. Efforts to maintain this parity included a restriction on the issue of banknotes. Hence the widespread use of informal credit and debt. The Polish writer Stefan Themerson related to the author how, faced with a shortage of banknotes and bank credit, Themerson's publisher in the 1930s Gebethner and Wolff had offered Themerson a wagon-load of coal in payment for royalties. Themerson refused this payment, and they finally agreed that Themerson would receive as payment a stay in a hotel in the Polish mountain resort of Zakopane, where the publisher had credit.

Landau finished his story and waited for understanding to take hold of the colonel. Beads of sweat appeared on the colonel's forehead, from the intellectual effort at comprehension. Finally, the colonel detected some explanation and exclaimed: 'Ah, I knew from the very beginning that there was something wrong with that Jew. Of course, the money was forged!'

Kalecki's conclusion from this was that unfortunately too many people think like the colonel, and very few people understand the story as we do.

5.2 Debt Payment Processes

This section interprets Kalecki's debt fable as demonstrating how debts may be serviced purely by financial transfers, without any income from the real economy. This interpretation challenges the classical theory of interest according to which the rate of interest is derived from the rate of profit in the economy.

Consider a group of mutually-indebted agents (MIAs) who have no income. These may be rentiers (with assets, in the form of debt claims against each other, but no income, apart from the interest on those claims), or retired persons holding such debt claims and owing money, but without any pensions. How can they make debt payments to each other? The answer, as the above fable shows, is very simple. Those who *receive* interest or debt payments can make payments from the interest or payments on debts that they have received. The rest can *sell* financial assets, in the form of the debt claims that they hold, in order to make their own debt payments. Obviously for such payments to be made, the system requires some minimum holdings of monetary assets (bank deposits), say $\acute{M}$.[7] If actual holdings of money or bank deposits, M, are less than $\acute{M}$, the MIAs have to depend on net revenue from real activities (surplus). Only in this sense is interest an actual deduction from a surplus generated in the real (non-financial), as affirmed by the theory of interest that prevailed in classical political economy, that the rate of interest is ultimately determined by the rate of profit in the economy.[8] From this classical

[7] Strictly speaking, the money or liquidity required to settle debt payment in this situation depends on three factors. First of all there is the actual sum of debts outstanding (in money terms). Secondly, there is the distribution of debts and debt claims among the MIAs. Total debts obviously equal total debt claims, but not for every agent, so that there will be some *net* debtors and some *net* creditors. Thirdly, there is the sequence over time of contracted debt payment (interest and principal repayment) commitments of the MIAs. In turn these depend on the term (short or long term) of the debts and the interest payments are annual, quarterly or weekly.

[8] This is further explained in Chapter 7 below.

view is derived the widely held view that interest must somehow be paid out of a surplus generated in the real economy. This link to current surplus is the foundation of the Wicksellian theory: that the money rate of interest may deviate from the rate of profit; that capitalists do not have bank deposits so that interest does not redistribute such deposits among capitalists, but takes those deposits out of circulation among capitalists; and therefore that the rate of profit places a ceiling on the interest that may be paid in an economy. It is this determination of interest by the rate of profit that Kalecki's fable challenged, by considering a situation in which the mutually-indebted characters in the story had no income, but were able to pay off their debts with a token money (the detail of its forgery is incidental to the financial circulation of money).

To test this supposed link between interest and income from non-financial activities we may consider a situation in which the circle of mutually-indented agents not only have no other income, except the interest that they may receive on their debt claims on each other, but also find that their holdings of money, M, are less than the amount $\acute{M}$ required to allow payments to be made to each other. In this situation interest payments cannot be made in full. What would our MIAs do now? They would sell the debt claims that they hold in exchange for money, to those MIA's who have money, and use that money to pay what they owe. In this situation, the velocity of circulation of money among the MIAs would increase, because it is now not only being used to pay interest, but it is also being used to buy and sell debt claims.

In a credit economy, commercial banks may ease the shortage of money by offering credit against the security of debt claims held by the borrower. With bank deposits acceptable as means of payment of interest, bank lending has the capacity to ease the shortage of money, but at the expense of increased borrowing by our MIAs, who now not only owe money directly to each other, but also to banks. However, the interest that they pay to their bankers is off-set by the interest that our MIAs may now receive on their bank deposits. Thus, the role of commercial banks is the creation of new debt claims. With each new bank debt claim an equivalent deposit is created (and hence an addition to M).

However, this mechanism requires a commercial banking system willing to grant, on demand, new credit against the value of debt claims. What happens if the MIAs jointly become net sellers of their debt claims. In that situation, the price of their debt claims will fall in relation to the interest that comes with ownership of the debt claim. This price will continue falling until, at some point, the yield on the debt claims will attract into the market for debt claims holders of money who will wish to obtain a generous income from holding debt claims rather than money. This will continue until the market for debt claims has absorbed enough money for the indebted to be able to service their debts.

However, the creation of new credit against existing debt claims, or the attraction of money into the market for debt claims is not a reliable mechanism, not least because holders of money stocks may be deterred from buying debt claims by the prospect that their purchase may not be sufficient to stem the fall in the prices of those debts. The markets for debts are the hunting grounds of speculators who buy debts in the conviction, not always borne out, of a rise in the value of those debts. This, after all, is the basis of Keynes's famous 'beauty contest' theory of financial speculation.[9] If the mechanism of selling off debt claims breaks down, then interest payments cannot be made. Keynes's Treasury rival, Ralph Hawtrey called this situation a 'credit deadlock', clearly in reference to the situation after the First World War, when the foreign debts of the Western powers were supposed to be paid from reparations paid by the government of Germany, which had been stripped at Versailles of its ability to pay those reparations.[10] He recommended that 'a credit deadlock which is impervious to cheap money may (thus) yield to treatment through open market purchases of securities' by the central bank. In Hawtrey's view such operations would make banks more liquid and therefore more inclined to lend.[11] But the same logic applies to direct purchases of debt claims in the event of a debt market breakdown, if net selling continues. Net selling by indebted agents requires a net buyer and, if commercial banks will not do this on behalf of their depositors, the central bank can perform this operation through its open market operations. We are familiar with this from the Quantitative Easing programmes that have been pursued by central banks in the United States, Europe, and Japan, since the crisis of 2008.[12]

[9] Keynes, *General* Theory, 1936, chapter 12.

[10] This contradiction in the financial policies of the Western Powers had been noted by Keynes in his critique of the Versailles settlements, *The Economic Consequences of the Peace*, 1920, chapters V and VI; see also Keynes, *A Revision of the Treaty being a sequel to The Economic Consequences of the Peace*, 1922, chapter VI.

[11] Hawtrey, *A Century of Bank* Rate, 1938, p. 256.

[12] This now introduces a fourth factor affecting the minimum money stocks or liquidity necessary to ensure debt payments, namely the class of debt and from which agent debt claims are purchased by the central bank, or the class of debt accepted as security against loans by commercial banks; and in turn the sequence by which the additional liquidity meets the contracted debt obligations of MIAs. This is not a random process, subject to shocks. These factors are given by the structure and distribution of debts inherited from the past at any one time. Ḿ- M is therefore determinate at any one time, even though the process of making debt claims liquid (selling them to the central bank, or to commercial banks, or borrowing against them from commercial banks) will modify the structures of debt and debt claims.

The analysis has reached the point where the debts of mutually-indebted agents with no non-financial income have been used to expand borrowing from commercial banks, and the liquidity of those banks is maintained by central bank to buying debt claims from commercial banks. These are the conditions for keeping the portfolios of MIA's sufficiently liquid for them to make payments on their debts to each other, directly or through commercial bank intermediation, or to the central bank. Over time, more interest is diverted among MIAs, through commercial banks, or paid to the central bank as opposed to other MIAs, as their debts pass into the ownership of the central bank. 'In the long run we are all dead'[13] and on decease our remaining debt claims may pass into the possession of commercial banks or the central bank to help write off debt claims against the deceased held by those commercial banks or the central bank.

5.3 Some Implications for Debt Management

Four features of this process, of maintaining payments on debts without drawing down on income from the real economy, warrant comment. First of all there is the growing intermediation by banks to maintain a level of money in the economy sufficient to allow payments to be made on debts by our MIAs with income other than the interest that comes with their ownership of debt claims. Agents who started off borrowing money from each other end up owing larger amounts of money apparently to banks but, indirectly, to other MIAs who hold bank deposits. These deposits are backed in bank balance sheets by debts owed to banks by MIAs who took out loans against the security of their initial debt claims against each other.

Secondly, there is the market in debt claims. Debt claims can only be used as collateral for additional bank loans if the debt claims can be sold into a market. Transforming debts into marketable securities is a procedure known as 'securitization'. Hyman Minsky was correct to point out that the function of securitization is to make portfolios of assets (in this case debt claims) more liquid.[14] Without such securitization, the system of debt would have collapsed if all MIAs had insufficient money to service their debts. Securitization allowed them to obtain such money, either by selling their debt claims to each other, or by obtaining credit from a bank secured against an asset or debt

[13] Keynes, *A Tract on Monetary Reform*, 1923, p. 80.
[14] Minsky, 'Securitization', 2008.

claim that the bank could sell if the borrower defaulted. Finally, securitization allows banks to maintain the liquidity of their balance sheets by selling the debt claims in their possession to another commercial bank or a central bank in exchange for reserves that can be used to settle payments between banks.

Thirdly, the analysis in the previous section explains how financial crisis arises because commercial banks stop lending and the central banks stop buying. Both of these breakdowns in the system were apparent during the 2008 crisis: the suspicion of collateralized debt obligations among banks and in securities markets, and the monetary policies of the central banks that were satisfied by interest rate movements, rather than by open market operations. Such operations (led by the Troubled Asset Relief Program in America) were only re-started after the crisis had taken hold, and quickly stabilized financial systems. Unfortunately by then the damage had been done to the private sector investment that determines the business cycle in market capitalism.[15]

The analysis leads directly to a paradoxical conclusion, namely that the answer to a debt crisis is more debt. This is paradoxical because the first two features discussed above, namely growing financial intermediation and securitization, are commonly associated with financialization, which is widely held to contribute to financial crisis. It is an irony of the literature on financialization that it seeks to constrain, or even eliminate, in the case of securitization, precisely those mechanisms that facilitate the avoidance of financial crisis. To a great extent this is because of a misreading of the 2008 crisis, which was indeed preceded by rising financing intermediation and securitization over an extended period. However, to focus merely on this trend is to overlook the failures in financial intermediation, in particular in the capital markets, and the difficulties of securitization that started in the 1990s, *before* the crisis itself.

Fourthly, and perhaps least apparent of all, is that in a situation of mutual indebtedness, the problem of payments on debt is essentially a transfer problem, i.e., how to ensure that there is enough liquidity in the portfolios of indebted parties to ensure that mutual debt obligations can be settled. This involves swapping assets (debt claims) for money among the indebted parties, or borrowing from banks (the resulting deposits being backed by banks' loans to indebted parties), or purchase of debt claims by a central bank. In any case, the financial assets that are created by debt (debt claims) remain within the system as a kind of 'inside' debt.

[15] Toporowski, 'The Crisis of Finance and the Crisis of Accumulation', 2016c.

This is not the case when debt is owed to someone who is 'outside' the system, i.e., when the creditor does not owe money to anyone else within the system so that, on receipt of debt payments, the 'outside' creditor merely takes the money and does not use it to make payments to anyone else in the system. To some degree this is the case with the 'central bank' in the system described in the previous section. But that central bank husbanded its resources for the greater good of the financial system, using the reserves that it can today create in order to buy debt claims from MIAs. Of course, the more of these debt claims that it buys, the more monetary resources it will take out of the system in the future, with payments on the debt claims that the central bank has purchased. This is why central banks need to maintain continuous open market operations to regulate the liquidity of the financial system. This is further discussed in the concluding chapter of this book.

A much more obvious case of 'outside debt' was the international gold standard. In that system gold was the ultimate monetary resource, but brought no return to its possessor, since the price of gold was constant. In that situation, the rate of interest was the only incentive for parting with gold. A central bank, mindful of its responsibility to issue only banknotes backed by gold, had only a limited capacity to buy in debt claims, and private creditors had even less incentive to plough back payments received into buying debt claims. There is a sense in which the gold standard made all debt into 'outside' debt, inhibiting the financial circulation of money. This was the background to the 'classical' theory of interest that tied interest to the rate of profit. This system, with its periodic banking crises when banks ran out of reserves, is the one that the more ardent critics of 'financialization' would have restored.

It was only with the development of fractional reserve banking and the widespread use of bank deposits as means of payment that a credit system emerged in which commercial banks could lend to create deposits, and central banks buy more freely.[16] By facilitating interest payments through financial circulation, the credit system finally released interest from its dependence on surplus, or income generated in the non-financial economy. As Kalecki's fable illustrates, once debt becomes 'inside debt', interest and payments on debt need only financial circulation for their prompt settlement. For the system as a whole, debts are truly 'fictitious capital' that may be settled with a forged banknote. The interest on fictitious capital may also be fictitious.

[16] This is recognized in De Cecco, *Money and Empire: The International Gold Standard 1890–1914* 1984, Hobson, *Gold Prices and Wages*, 1913, pp. 89–92, and Chick, 'The Evolution of the Banking System', 1986.

PART II

KALECKI'S MONETARY ANALYSIS TODAY

As the previous part showed, Kalecki's monetary economics was the major casualty of his revisions of his 'essays'. It meant that Kalecki did not leave any systematic account of money or monetary circulation in the economy, an account that might have tackled the monetary controversies of his time countering residual efforts to sustain the quantity theory of money in the face of assaults on it by the followers of Keynes and Wicksell. Kalecki restricted himself to going over monetary aspects of the business cycle that was the centre-piece of his macroeconomics, the determination of output and employment at any given time, and the monetary consequences of the financing that was necessary to remedy the deficiencies of capitalism, in its gross and unnecessary inequalities and the inefficiency of its use of labour.

His incidental interest in monetary economics means that Kalecki's monetary economics needs to be reconstructed in order to tackle the monetary controversies and issues that have arisen since his time. Since the failure of monetarism in the 1980s, monetary theory has largely reverted to Wicksellian orthodoxy, in which the classical theory of interest holds because the economic process is supposed to consist of arbitrage between the rate of interest and the rate of profit from real production. The return of liquidity of capital markets since the 1980s, amid increasing financial instability, highlights the absence of any theory of asset prices in Kalecki's analysis. The rise of a property-owning middle class and its financial operations highlights the starkness of a theory of distribution in which there are only capitalists and property-less workers.

This part outlines the foundations of Kalecki's monetary ideas, and places them in an institutional setting, before extending them into some twenty-first century controversies and issues. Chapter 6, on 'Capitalist Money', outlines the essential principles of Kalecki's monetary economics and their roots in the system of long-term finance. Chapter 7 examines in greater detail the 'classical' doctrine of interest and the reasons for Kalecki's rejection of it. Chapter 8, on 'Industrial without Financial Circulation', presents a reassessment of one of the major contributions to the 'circuit theory of money' that, in the Post-Keynesian literature, is perhaps the closest to Kalecki's monetary thinking, and uses this analysis to criticize some of the more classically inspired concepts of finance that have emerged with recent studies of 'financialization'. Finally, in this section, Chapter 9, 'The Transfer Theory of Government Debt' examines government finance and how Kalecki resolved the problem of deficit financing, by comparison with a distinguished predecessor, and how Kalecki's solution depends very much on his view of monetary circulation.

6
Capitalist Money

Kalecki's fragments on money are based on certain common principles. A common thread in those fragments is the idea that money is essentially credit money. This is of course widely accepted: The key distinction among monetary theorists is simply whether this credit money is state money, i.e., based on money issued by the state through its central bank's note issue monopoly and the rate of interest at which it lends the reserves from which banks create credit in a fractional reserve system; or whether credit money is a bank creation, because banks can create the bank deposits that are used as means of payment. Keynes's monetary analysis was based on a state theory of money and in general Post-Keynesians have followed Keynes, with theories of monetary endogeneity centred around the accommodation that the state's central bank must give to commercial banks in order to enforce its policy rate of interest. More structuralist Post-Keynesians regard monetary endogeneity as arising out of financial and monetary innovation. Kalecki understood the need for such accommodation and he regarded monetary innovation as arising out of the liquidity needs of capitalist businesses, rather than of banking.

The distinctive feature of Kalecki's monetary economics is that, for Kalecki, capitalist money is the money of capitalists. It is not the money of banks behaving as capitalists, and determining their supply of credit according to its profitability. Nor is it, as in Keynes, a state monopoly exercised through the banking system for the convenience of capitalists and wealthier consumers. On this foundation, Kalecki developed certain principles of his monetary analysis.[1]

6.1 Principles of Kalecki's Monetary Economics

There are certain fundamental principles that run through the fragments on money and monetary circulation in Kalecki's work. **The first and most**

[1] The summary provided here differs somewhat from the summaries provided in Sawyer, 'Money and Finance in Kalecki's Analysis', 2004 and the same author's 'Kalecki on Money and Finance', 2001 in that I try to highlight here the distinctive features of Kalecki's view, rather than its parallels with the views of other writers.

Interest and Capital: The Monetary Economics of Michał Kalecki. Jan Toporowski, Oxford University Press.
© Jan Toporowski 2022. DOI: 10.1093/oso/9780198816232.003.0007

important of these principles is his assertion that capitalist money is the money of capitalists. This money is thrown into circulation when capitalists undertake production and investment. Production and exchange concentrate money in the hands of the economically most powerful capitalists. In a developing country, those concentrations are shared with pre-industrial classes, merchants, money-lenders, and landowners. But the characteristic feature of capitalism is that money hoards accumulate in the balance sheets of capitalist firms, rather than in the pockets of pre-industrial ruling classes. In the modern economy capitalists hold money, or they acquire it when workers consume, or governments spend money.

The idea that, in a capitalist economy, money is capitalist money is therefore inherent in the nature of the dominant class under capitalism. The ownership of money—along with the ownership, more commonly observed by economists, of means of production—is what defines capitalists. This assertion is perhaps most obvious in Kalecki's famous definition of a capitalist: 'Many economists assume, at least in their abstract theories, a state of business democracy where anybody endowed with entrepreneurial ability can obtain capital for starting a business venture. This picture of the activities of the "pure" entrepreneur is, to put it mildly, unrealistic. The most important prerequisite for becoming an entrepreneur is the *ownership* of capital.'[2] By capital, here, Kalecki quite clearly meant 'money capital'. His famous working assumption that workers do not save or, in Joan Robinson's phrase 'workers spend what they get and the capitalists get what they spend'[3] amounts to a view that workers are monetarily passive. It is capitalists who, at any one time, can activate money in ways other than just buying consumption goods. With wage and salary differentiation, the velocity of circulation of money rises as incomes rise.[4]

A second principle concerns the origin of this money. In Kalecki's analysis, the source of money in a capitalist economy is process of production in a market (as opposed to a subsistence) economy, circulating money from capitalists who pay their workers and suppliers with money that they have in their reserves, augmented by money that they might borrow from their banks. Kalecki alluded to this macroeconomic circulation in his explanation of how profits arise from this circulation. In the first place it implies an equality between saving and investment (since the value of consumption accrues to capitalists who sell or produce consumption goods): '...the equality between savings and investment plus export surplus plus budget deficit in the general

[2] Kalecki, *Theory of Economic Dynamics*, 1954a, pp. 94–5.

[3] Robinson, 'Kalecki and Keynes', p. 341.

[4] Kalecki, 'Wage Bill and Cash Circulation', 1940b.

case—or investment alone in the special case [of a closed economy with no government—JT]—will be valid under all circumstances......investment, once carried out, automatically provides the savings necessary to finance it...If investment increases by a certain amount, savings out of profits are *pro tanto* higher.'[5] The automatic availability of savings to finance investment means that, as Keynes argued in his *General Theory*, the rate of interest is not required to equalize saving with investment (or the supply of loanable funds with the demand for investment finance).

Kalecki went on: 'if some capitalists increase their investment by using for this purpose their liquid reserves, the profits of other capitalists will rise *pro tanto* and thus the liquid reserves will pass into the possession of the latter. If additional investment is financed by bank credit, the spending of the amounts in question will cause equal amounts of saved profits to accumulate as bank deposits. The investing capitalists will thus find it possible to float bonds to the same extent and thus to repay the bank credits.'[6]

Thus capitalists acquire money because they make profits on production and exchange. The origin of this in Rosa Luxemburg's insistence that capitalists undertake production for the sake of monetary reward, rather than outright exploitation, is obvious. This conception of monetary circulation is very different to the standard textbook notion of monetary circulation that is the number of times a banknote or a coin changes hands in a given period, essentially a commodity, or fiat money concept. For Kalecki monetary circulation is about how money flows between social classes as money income,[7] giving a macroeconomic foundation to his monetary theory. In his 1933 'Essay on the Business Cycle Theory' an appendix on 'The Money Market' shows precisely how the business cycle is financed by accelerating the circulation of a quantity of money that, as a stock, stays the same.[8]

So much is obvious from Kalecki's theory of profits. But what determines the distribution of those profits, or monetary accumulation, among capitalist firms? The answer to this is given in Kalecki's *price theory*, according to which prices are a mark-up on the *direct* cost of production (labour and raw materials) with the size of that mark-up determined by the degree of monopoly or control over its markets that a given firm possesses.[9] This means that

[5] Kalecki, *Theory of Economic Dynamics*, 1954a, p. 50.

[6] Kalecki, *Theory of Economic Dynamics*, 1954a, p. 50.

[7] For example, wage increases that tend 'to increase the thriftiness of capitalists by causing a relative shift of income from rentiers to corporations'. Kalecki, *Essays in the Theory of Economic Fluctuations*, 1939a, p. 91.

[8] Kalecki, 'An Essay of the Business Cycle Theory', 1933.

[9] Kalecki, *Essays in the Theory of Economic Fluctuations*, 1939a, chapter 1.

monetary accumulation is distributed not in proportion to the value of production, as suggested by proponents of a uniform rate of profit across the whole economy, but is concentrated among the largest, most powerful firms. Since the end of the nineteenth century, these dominant firms are big, monopolistic corporations.

The process of concentrating monetary resources in the largest corporations is a feature of modern industrial capitalist economies. In the case of developing countries, the process occurs in a somewhat different way that is fundamental to Kalecki's development economics, but also reveals his thinking on the question of the activation of 'idle' funds. Developing countries suffer from an inelasticity of supply of basic necessities, in particular food, that may be observed even in the twenty-first century in the famines and inflation afflicting those countries. Any increase in employment results in higher wage revenue being spent on such necessities. Without an increase in their supply, their prices rise. Real wages fall and the money accumulates in the pockets of merchants, money-lenders, and landowners, as higher farm incomes are drained by higher rents. Those merchants, money-lenders, and landowners are the ruling classes that absorb the surplus of a pre-industrial economy. With the rise of industrial capitalism, more of the surplus is taken by industrial capitalists.

This approach to the price system in an economy is almost unique in economic theory. The standard textbook exposition treats prices as being important for determination of equilibrium between supply and demand in particular markets, i.e., consigning prices to the microeconomics part of economics that is supposed to provide correct insight irrespective of the money in the economy, while money along with monetary policy, is treated separately in a part that is macroeconomics. By contrast, Kalecki put forward a *monetary theory of prices*, in which the price system determines the distribution of monetary resources from production and trade among individual capitalists, or firms.

Alongside the acquisition of monetary resources through production and exchange is the acquisition of monetary resources through borrowing or financial operations. This is the subject of the next chapter.

In Post-Keynesian monetary thinking, perhaps the closest to Kalecki in respect of this view on the origin of capitalist's money has been the 'theory of the monetary circuit'.[10] This theory was put forward as an alternative both to general equilibrium theories of money (including the Neo-Classical synthesis

[10] See, for example, Halevi and Taouil, 'On a Post-Keynesian Stream from France and Italy: The *Circuit* Approach', 2002. The theory of the monetary circuit is further discussed in Chapter 8 below.

of Hicks and Tobin), and the state or banking theories of money that prevail among Post-Keynesians. However, there is one important difference between Kalecki's notion of money and that of the 'circuitists', namely that, in their efforts to demonstrate the endogeneity of credit supply, the starting point of 'circuit' theory are capitalists who have no money, and therefore have to borrow from banks. For Kalecki, the supply of money or credit is elastic precisely because capitalists, with the exception of those on the margins of capitalist production who lack money (and may even constitute the majority of capitalists),[11] start off with money capital which they can then augment with bank credit. This is fundamental because, as is argued in Chapter 7, the possession of money capital is what detaches the rate of interest, in a capitalist economy with a financial system, from the rate of profit, or the 'classical' theory of interest.

A third principle is that an increase in the money supply is not necessary to finance production and investment. A boom in business is marked by an increase in the velocity of circulation of already existing money in the accounts of capitalists. In his first account of the business cycle, Kalecki included an appendix on 'The Money Market' that showed how a boom is financed by the transfer of funds from the reserve accounts of capitalists to their current accounts: The value of the total balance sheet of the banking system stays the same through the boom.[12]

Here it may be helpful to make some comparison with the monetary theory of Keynes. Keynes laid out the principles of his monetary analysis in chapter 15 of his *General Theory* 'On the Psychological and Business Incentives to Liquidity'. Here, he introduced the key nexus of the demand for money, Keynes's 'Liquidity Preference' with uncertainty, and the novel part of that analysis in the *precautionary* and *speculative* demand for money (precautionary demand being due to uncertainty, and speculative demand being related to changes in the rate of interest, or bond prices). He wrote that:

> 'A change in M [the supply of money] can be assumed to lead operate by changing r [the money rate of interest], and a change in r will lead to a new equilibrium partly by changing M_2 [the speculative demand for money] and partly by changing Y [national income or output] and therefore M_1 [the transactions and precautionary demand for money]. The division of the new

[11] Steindl, 'Capitalist Enterprise and Risk', 1945, which Kalecki cited with approval (Kalecki, *Theory of Economic* Dynamics, 1954, p. 95).

[12] Kalecki, 'Essay on the Business Cycle Theory', 1933.

increment of cash between M_1 and M_2 in the new position of equilibrium will depend on the responses of investment to a reduction in the rate of interest and of income to an increase in investment.'[13]

This response of investment and income to the change in the rate of interest came to be known as the 'Keynes effect'. According to the proponents of the 'classical' theory, the 'Keynes effect' was supposed to justify deflationary policies to reduce wages, because this would increase the value of any given money supply. The increase in the supply of 'real money balances' would cause the 'real' rate of interest to decrease, and thereby stimulate investment.[14]

The novelty of this approach clearly motivated Keynes to provide some kind of explanation of how his new theory of the demand for money related to the quantity theory of money, which had featured as one of the mainstays of his *Treatise on Money*.[15] He therefore continued

> ...the income velocity of money is defined as...the ratio of Y to M_1. Thus, if V is the income-velocity of money,
>
> $$L_1(Y) = Y/V = M_1.$$
>
> There is, of course, no reason for supposing that V is constant. Its value will depend on the character of banking and industrial organization, on social habits, on the distribution of income between different classes and on the effective cost of holding idle cash. Nevertheless, if we have a short period of time in view and can safely assume no material change in any of these factors, we can treat V as nearly enough constant.[16]

Keynes then digressed into various institutional, conventional and psychological factors that may influence liquidity preference, and the role in it of monetary policy, until he came to his conclusion, where he stated the conditions under which the income velocity of money will be constant:

> In a static society, or in a society in which for any other reason no one feels any uncertainty about the future rates of interest, the Liquidity Function L_2 [the liquidity preference function that relates the speculative demand for money to changes in the rate of interest], or the propensity to hoard (as we

[13] Keynes *General Theory* 1936, pp. 200–1.

[14] In his 'The Lesson of the Blum Experiment' (1938/1990) Kalecki showed that the Keynes effect does actually happen.

[15] Keynes, *Treatise on Money*, 1930/1971b, chapter 24.

[16] Keynes, *General Theory*, 1936, p. 201.

> might term it), will always be zero in equilibrium. Hence in equilibrium $M_2 = 0$ and $M = M_1$; so that any change in [the money supply] M will cause the rate of interest to fluctuate until income reaches a level at which the change in [transactions demand] is equal to the supposed change in M.[17]

Kalecki's approach is exactly the opposite. Rather than interest rates and income fluctuating until the supply of money is equal to demand for it, in Kalecki there is no 'equilibrium' and the rate of interest and the velocity of circulation of deposits vary in response to a change in income or expenditure. Production is determined by demand, which can be limited by income. But, since production is undertaken by capitalists who are deemed to hold money, production cannot be frustrated by a shortage of money in the aggregate. Any increase in the money supply will merely depress the rate of interest; while, with a given money supply, any investment or growth in production can be accommodated by an increase in the velocity of circulation of that money. The rate of interest may bring the money markets in the financial system into equilibrium. But in the non-financial economy it is the velocity of circulation that adjusts to bring Keynes's transactions demand for money into equilibrium with the supply available to the non-financial public.

Kalecki postulated a positive relationship between the money market rate of interest and the velocity of circulation of money, viewed as the turnover of bank deposits, where the key factor was the 'marginal convenience of holding cash':

> ...the higher the short-term rate the greater is the inducement to invest money for short periods rather than to keep it as cash reserve. Or, to put it more precisely: transactions can be managed with a larger or smaller stock of money; however, a larger stock of money in relation to turnover means on the average a smoother and more convenient handling of transactions. The higher the short-term rate of interest the more expensive is this convenience as compared with the alternative of investing in short-term assets.[18]

[17] Keynes, *General Theory*, 1936, p. 209. Later, in chapter 21, on 'The Theory of Prices', Keynes defined the income velocity of money as 'The ratio between the quantity of effective demand and the quantity of money closely corresponds to what is often called the "income-velocity of money"; – except that effective demand corresponds to the income the expectation of which has set production moving, not to the actually realised income, and to gross, not net, income' (p. 299).

[18] Kalecki, *Theory of Economic Dynamics*, 1954a, pp. 73–4.

It is by drawing on the funds that firms have invested in short-term assets that those firms are able to finance investments and the growth of production without an increase in the money supply.[19]

This leads on to a **fourth principle of Kalecki's monetary economics, namely that the *monetary* function of fiscal policy is to mobilize the unused (uncirculated or 'idle') monetary balances of capitalists**, or the wealthy classes, to finance demand, or expenditure, in the real (non-financial) economy.[20] Taxes on profits and, in particular the capital levy on wealth that he favoured, if spent on government contracts with the private sector, or on public services, or on welfare payments, recycle these idle balances into current profits. For Kalecki the excess of liquid savings was a general problem, whether the money balances were held by households or firms. Government borrowing therefore does not need additional 'real' resources, but merely increases the circulation of existing 'idle' balances.

Steindl was later to show a particular version of this argument, in which household saving have their counterpart in the running down of firms' reserves or the 'forced indebtedness' of firms.[21] Taxation and the management of government debt should therefore aim also to stabilize the money capital that accrues through profits. The taxation of wealth is especially appropriate for debt management because it is a way of recycling that money capital as tax revenue, which is then returned to holders of government bonds. In aggregate the monetary reserves of the capitalists remain the same.

A fifth principle of Kalecki's monetary economics is the use of fiscal policy to stabilize that money capital, in situations where its excess may cause financial instability, in particular in developing countries prone to capital flight through the dollarization of savings. Wealth taxes not only reduce the amounts of money held in the asset portfolios of the rich. Where such wealth is illiquid (for example in the case of land) a wealth tax obliges owners of such wealth to hold liquid assets against future wealth tax payments. Kalecki argued that fiscal deficits should be a permanent feature of full employment policy. But the resulting accumulations of profits need to be taken off the

[19] See 'The Money Market' appendix to Kalecki' s 'Essay on the Business Cycle Theory'.

[20] Kalecki, 'The Maintenance of Full Employment after the Transition Period', 1945.

[21] Steindl, 'The Role of Household Saving in the Modern Economy', 1982. Steindl here exposed the true meaning of Kalecki's observation in 'A New Approach to the Problem of Business Cycles' (1950) that 'with the high level of income there is correlated a high level of savings, and that stream of new savings makes it possible to undertake investment without increasing indebtedness'. Dennis Robertson interpreted this as conceding that 'it is not so much investment which governs savings as savings which governs investment' (Robertson 'Thoughts on Meeting Some Important Persons', 1954/1966 p. 244). In fact, Kalecki never departed from the view that investment determines saving. In his 1950 article he had in mind the savings of firms, rather than savings in general.

money markets through the issue of long-term government bonds. Such bonds have fiscal advantages in fixing government debt costs, and reduced cash outflow in rolling over short-term bills. Their long term to maturity also ties up further liquidity in secondary markets for long-term securities.[22]

For Kalecki, the problem of financing economic development is not the question of where the government of a developing country may obtain the funds to pay for public works or industrial infrastructure, or how the 'savings' of rich countries may be made available to countries with inadequate 'savings'. Rather financing economic development is about how to immobilize the liquid assets that accrue to merchants, money-lenders and landowners in the process of economic development, in order to prevent the expenditure of those funds on luxury imports, or capital flight. This should be done through taxing away those assets, or immobilizing them with the issue of long-term debt.[23]

In the more industrially advanced capitalist economies Kalecki's theories of taxation and fiscal policy are more about how to mobilize these accumulations of 'idle' money to prevent them depressing economic activity because private investment, the usual capitalist way of recirculating accumulated profits, is inadequate. His fiscal strategy for full employment was to tax accumulations of money, or replace them with government debt to allow the government to put the money into circulation, since capitalists will not naturally do so. The money taken or borrowed by the government returns of course to capitalists as the government, or its employees and their dependents, spend the money.[24]

Kalecki's monetary economics extended to international monetary arrangements in the discussions before and after the Bretton Woods conference in 1944, although it is difficult here to separate Kalecki's own views from those of his chief collaborator in commenting on Bretton Woods, Ernst 'Fritz' Schumacher, or the other author of an 'Oxford Critique' of Bretton Woods, Thomas Balogh.[25] In general Kalecki favoured fixed exchange rates. But he saw the international monetary system as bedevilled by a problem of trade imbalances if countries tried to move towards full employment. Floating exchange rates would not achieve trade balance, but would impart a deflationary bias, as they had in the 1930s, exacerbating the problem of unemployment.

[22] Kalecki, 'The "Mysteries" of the Money Market', 1940a; Kalecki, 'A Theory of Commodity, Income and Capital Taxation', 1937; Kalecki, 'The Problem of Financing Economic Development', 1954b.

[23] Kalecki, 'The Problem of Financing Economic Development', 1954b.

[24] Kalecki 'A Theory of Commodity, Income and Capital Taxation' 1937, and 'Political Aspects of Full Employment' 1943/1990. This last paper offers brief but penetrating insights into the effects of fiscal policy on monetary circulation. Unfortunately these were taken out of some of the later editions. The full text is given in the original and in the first volume of Kalecki's Collected Works.

[25] Toporowski, *Michał Kalecki: An intellectual Biography Volume 2...*, 2018, pp. 127–36.

However, fixed exchange rates, even if adjustable to allow for misalignments, required adequate international reserves to be available to trading countries. For this reason, he preferred the Keynes Plan, to the White Plan. However, he considered the mechanisms put forward by Keynes for achieving trade balance, through charging interest on borrowing reserves as well as surpluses of such reserves, to be inadequate, and he considered Keynes's definition of international equilibrium in the form of balanced trade inappropriate for developing countries that need to import capital equipment. Development needs should be met by means of long-term loans while the surpluses of richer countries should be directed towards imports from countries with chronic trade deficits.[26] After the war Kalecki reiterated his view that full employment could not be sustained without adequate foreign currency reserves and long-term loans for deficit countries.[27]

6.2 Monetary Endogeneity in Finance

Kalecki's view that the 'idle' money balances of capitalists needed to be mobilized and thrown into circulation, and that this mobilization increases the velocity of circulation of money, led at least one observer, Harry Johnson, to conclude that Kalecki adhered to the quantity theory of money, according to which the rate of inflation is determined in some way by changes in the money supply. Johnson observed that 'on the one occasion on which I met him in Cambridge [in 1955 – JT]...Kalecki delivered a lecture on inflation that employed a simple quantity theory of money together with expectations about the future trend of prices—and which met with a reception from his former admirers so hostile that he was discouraged from publishing it'.[28]

The lecture was in fact a lecture on hyper-inflation. A revised version of it was published seven years later as 'A Model of Hyper-inflation'. The model was distinctive in presenting hyper-inflation as a temporary aberration in which the rapid conversion of money into goods, when money ceases to be an effective store of value, causes the velocity of circulation of money to accelerate. To illustrate this Kalecki used the famous Fisher equation in which the quantity of money multiplied by its velocity of circulation (the number of times its changes hands) is equal to nominal national income, that is the

[26] Kalecki and Schumacher, 'International Clearing and Long-term Lending', 1943.
[27] Kalecki, 'Mulilateralism and Full Employment', 1946/1990.
[28] Johnson and Johnson, *The Shadow of Keynes*, 1978, p. 159.

quantity of goods and services produced multiplied by the prices of those goods and services.[29]

Johnson's recollection of the lecture was not reliable and Kalecki's mathematics may have misled his audience. The article in which Kalecki published the lecture, made clear that the quantity theory was being applied to cases of hyper-inflation, rather than to the regulation of the price level in 'normal' times and a reliance on a stable velocity of circulation, so that changes in the quantity of money make for proportionate changes in prices. According to the article, 'in normal conditions the increase of the quantity of money in circulation results directly in a greater liquidity and lower velocity of circulation than an increase in prices...the consequent fall in the rate of interest will tend to increase investment and thus output and prices. But this effect may be small. The fall in the short-term rate of interest will normally affect but little the long-term rate of interest in short and medium periods, and this limits the effect upon investment in fixed capital. In any case the effect of the quantity of money on prices will be very indirect in character.'[30] He had pointed out in an earlier note for the United Nations that, in hyper-inflation, the monetary factor increasing the price level in hyper-inflation is the rise the velocity of circulation that occurs when people decide to hoard commodities instead of holding cash balances.[31]

The results of central bank quantitative easing since the 2008 have borne out Kalecki's analysis. In the absence of hyper-inflation, the increase in the money supply has indeed given rise to a reduction in the average velocity of circulation of that money. This reduction in lending has been widely attributed to a Keynesian 'liquidity trap', and this might be regarded as simply another way of saying that the velocity of circulation of money has fallen. However, there is one difference between Kalecki's argument and Keynes's liquidity trap hypothesis. For Keynes, the liquidity trap would arise if the central bank tried to push its policy rate of interest fell below some critical level.[32] For Kalecki, the reduction in the velocity of circulation may occur at any rate of interest. Keynesians would argue that this is simply the increase in the demand for money attendant upon a fall in the long-term rate of interest, as

[29] Kalecki, 'A Model of Hyper-inflation', 1962. See also Toporowski, *Michał Kalecki, Volume 2* 2018, pp. 199–202 and Łaski, *Lectures in Macroeconomics*, 2019 p. 84.

[30] Kalecki, 'A Model of Hyper-inflation', 1962.

[31] Kalecki, 'Introductory Remarks on Inflationary and Deflationary Processes', 1949.

[32] 'There is the possibility...that, after the rate of interest has fallen to a certain level, liquidity preference may become virtually absolute in the sense that almost everyone prefers cash to holding a debt which yields so low a rate of interest. In this event the monetary authority would have lost effective control over the rate of interest...' Keynes, *General Theory*, p. 207.

measured by the market yield on bonds (their nominal rate of interest or coupon rate, divided by the price of the bonds). But this long-term rate is not the same as the rate of interest in the money markets.

Like Post-Keynesians today, and unlike monetarists who regard the money supply as being issued by the state, or its agent the central bank, Kalecki saw the supply of money as endogenous, or emerging from economic or financial processes that are independent of government control. In that earlier note he identified two sources of 'additions to the money supply'. One of them was 'the financing of budget deficits' and the other was 'expanding bank credit to business'.[33]

For Post-Keynesians, money is endogenous because the central bank *has* to supply whatever reserves commercial banks desire, if the central bank is to function as a lender of last resort, or control short-term interest rates. An alternative Post-Keynesian view is that endogeneity is a 'structural' result of financial innovation.[34] However, an older view of endogeneity that was more familiar to Kalecki was the notion that bank credit money was created and regulated not through the interaction of commercial banks with central banks, but from the lending activity of banks with their customers.

The notion that bank advances create deposits was well known in the 1930s. It was originally put forward by Hartley Withers and was taken up by the political economist J. A. Hobson who pointed out that most of this credit was advanced not on the security of some future revenue that would be obtained by investment in factories and machinery, but on the basis of a much more immediately priced (even if, in Marx's view, 'fictitious') security of financial collateral: 'We have spoken of bankers and financiers as the makers of credit. But we have also recognized that the chief financial material out of which they make it is the stocks and shares and other certificates of value which represent the capital created by the saving and investing classes.'[35] Financial assets make especially good security for loans because there is always a market from which to obtain a money value for that

[33] Kalecki, 'Introductory Remarks on Inflationary and Deflationary Processes', 1949.

[34] There is, by now, a huge literature on this. But the key texts are Kaldor's, *The Scourge of Monetarism*, 1982, Moore, *Horizontalists and Verticalists*, 1988, Smithin *Controversies in Monetary Economics*, 2003, chapter 5; Chick and Dow, 'Monetary Policy with Endogenous Money and Liquidity Preference' 2002, and Chick, 'The Evolution of the Banking System and the Theory of Saving, Investment and Interest', 1986.

[35] Hobson, *Gold Prices and* Wages, 1913, p. 89. Withers put forward the view that loans create deposits in his book *The Meaning of Money*, 1909. See also Chapter 5 above.

security. It was Hobson's and Withers' discovery that the British banking system was readily advancing loans, and creating deposits that could be used as means of payment, in other words as money, against long-term securities, that put paid, in Hobson's, if not in Withers' (or even Keynes's at that time) view, to the gold standard and the quantity theory of money. According to that theory, the restriction of the banknote issue to the amount of gold reserves in the banking system, was supposed to keep prices stable. In fact, the monetary system had innovated to substitute a credit supply, for capitalists with financial assets to put up as collateral, for the inelastic banknote issue.

Nowadays economists would say that this is merely the same as the notion of monetary endogeneity, according to which the money supply is somehow determined by the needs of trade and business. But on the whole, the long-term securities that are used to leverage up the supply of credit have disappeared from the monetary analysis. The severely 'real' Neo-Classical analysis considers only real (i.e., fixed capital) as possible collateral, 'shocked' by productivity and other supply changes.[36] In any case, monetary endogeneity based on financial collateral poses difficulties for financial economists operating with models that have highly reduced financial systems. The model then has to explain how credit cycles or crises may occur where monetary endogeneity is presumed to supply credit more or less on demand. With highly reduced financial systems, changes in credit are attributed to 'shocks' that are either 'real', or difficulties that arise on bank balance sheets. In recent models such difficulties are held to arise because of 'illiquidity' which a central bank may relieve.

For example, in a recent paper Gregory de Walque, Olivier Pierrard, and Abdelaziz Rouabah have a representative firm that borrows and a representative household that lends. Two banks with endogenous balance sheet decisions, one a net lender, the other a net borrower on the interbank market (operated by two firms). That interbank market is dependent on monetary policy liquidity injections, and difficulties arise if those injections do not arrive on time or are too small. But the (undifferentiated and representative) firm does not hold liquid assets, making it very different to the large firm, which

[36] Kiyotaki and Moore, 'Credit Cycles', 1997; Bernanke and Gertler suggest 'shocks' in the form of changes in 'net wealth', which renders ambiguous changes in the value of collateral (Bernanke and Gertler, 'Agency Costs, Net Worth and Business Fluctuations', 1989).

Kalecki described.[37] Even before the 2008 crisis made such studies fashionable, Charles Goodhart collaborated with various colleagues to model how illiquidity may give way to default. This is generally in the context of Dynamic Stochastic General Equilibrium models, where 'shocks' occur that expose the illiquidity of banks that have engaged in maturity transformation.[38] The relief of illiquidity by central open market operations, buying securities in exchange for reserves, is obvious. But it has also reinforced a Keynesian, 'state money' notion of monetary endogeneity. With this has come a view that looks at the banking system as it was in the mid-nineteenth century, rather than the more complex financial system at the heart of which are the financial operations of capitalist business, rather than the inter-bank operations of banks, with liquidity viewed as the *financial* circulation of money, rather than the reserve transfers of banks.

Keynesians and Post-Keynesians have in general followed Keynes in embracing *state* theories of money derived from the historic grant from the state to the Bank of England, or other banks of issue, of monopoly powers over the money supply in the form of banknotes. Hence the focus of recent Post-Keynesian theory on the interaction of the central bank and the banking system.[39]An older generation of Post-Keynesians regarded the link with financial asset markets as important. But this is because they attached importance to the Keynes's speculative *demand* for money, rather than because financial assets affect the *supply* of credit.[40] The other branch of Post-Keynesian monetary thought, based around the theory of the monetary circuit is discussed in a later chapter.

There is no doubt that Kalecki was well aware of the practice of banks making advances on the basis of financial collateral. He noted this as the way in which the financier Ivar Kreuger operated, until he ran out of collateral and committed suicide in 1932.[41] This technique of expanding the supply of credit is also mentioned in Kalecki's later observations on the financing of full employment. Here, Kalecki supposed that the government, finances its fiscal

[37] De Walque, Pierrard, and Rouabah, 'Financial (In)Stability, Supervision and Liquidity Injections: A Dynamic General Equilibrium Approach', 2010.

[38] Goodhart et al., 'A Risk Assessment Model for Banks to Analyse Financial Fragility', 2005; Goodhart et al., 'A Model to Analyse Financial Fragility', 2006; Hőrman and Schabert, 'A Monetary Analysis of Balance Sheet Policies', 2015. A more general and more critical discussion is provided in Goodhart et al., 'Macro-Modeling, Default and Money', 2019.

[39] Moore, *Horizontalists and* Verticalists, 1988; Wray, 'Money', 2013.

[40] e.g., Kahn, 'Some Notes on Liquidity Preference', 1954/1972.

[41] Kalecki, 'Ivar Kreuger', 1932/1996. See also Toporowski, *Michał Kalecki, Volume 1*, 2013, pp. 22–3.

deficit, by paying its suppliers with short-term bills. The recipients of these bills either hold them as savings, or sell them to their bank in exchange for bank deposits, *which banks create for the purpose of buying the bills.* If the rate at which the banks discount the bills starts to rise (the price of the bills in terms of bank deposits falls) then the central bank can always force an increase in the discount rate by issuing bonds and using the proceeds to buy in the bills.[42]

There is an important difference between a state theory of money in a banking system, as postulated in the *General Theory* of Keynes, and in some of the literature cited above, and a credit theory in a financial system which this chapter argues is the monetary theory of Kalecki. In the state money-banking view, a change in the rate of interest gives rise to arbitrage through the purchase or sale of real assets. This is the foundation of Keynes's theory of interest, and his policy of the 'euthanasia of the rentier', which was supposed to force capitalists into real investment because a profit could be earned on the margin between the expected return on investment (Keynes's'marginal efficiency of capital') and the cost of borrowing the money to finance the investment.[43] This was the interpretation of Keynes that was taken up in the 'Neo-Classical Synthesis' of J. R. Hicks and James Tobin.[44] In the Post-Keynesian interpretation of Keynes, this arbitrage channel through real investment is frustrated by uncertainty and 'liquidity preference' leading, in the extreme case, to a liquidity trap.[45] In the Neo-Wicksellian orthodoxy that rules today, changes in the rate of interest are supposed to give rise to arbitrage between consumption today and consumption in retirement, that are then supposed to determines saving and investment.[46]

Kalecki rejected the notion that the rate of interest, whether the short-term rate or the long-term one, affects the dynamics of the real economy. The part of monetary endogeneity that interested him was the ability of businesses to

[42] Kalecki, 'Political Aspects of Full Employment', 1943/1990.

[43] Keynes, *General Theory*, 1936, pp. 375–7.

[44] Hicks, 'A Suggestion for Simplifying the Theory of Money', 1935; Tobin, 'A General Equilibrium Approach to Monetary Theory', 1969.

[45] E.g., Davidson *Money and the Real World*, 1978, chapters 10 and 11. Davidson's account is interesting because although he recognizes the distinction between the short-term rate of interest and the long-term rate, and adheres to Keynes's view that it is the long-term rate that is critical for investment, he still holds onto the Wicksellian notion that it is the arbitrage between the rate of interest and real investment that is critical for the economy.

[46] Woodford, *Interest and Prices*, 2003.

use their monetary and financial resources as collateral for loans, thereby giving them preferential access to credit. The endogeneity of credit supply within a complex system of credit and debt allowed Kalecki to go further than Keynes in rejecting the classical theory of interest, whereby interest is somehow related to, or derived from the rate of profit. In the remainder of this section this argument is expanded in the context of recent monetary controversies. The third section of this book discusses the implications for monetary policy of this rejection.

7

The Classical Theory of Interest

A Critical Note

> There is, I am convinced, a fatal flaw in that part of the orthodox reasoning that deals with the theory of what determines the level of effective demand and the volume of aggregate employment; the flaw being largely due to the failure of the classical doctrine to develop a satisfactory and realistic theory of the rate of interest.[1]

As argued in the previous chapter, Kalecki rejected the idea, derived from classical political economy and maintained through the monetary theory of Wicksell to today's 'New Consensus' on monetary policy, that the rate of interest affects the real economy by inducing arbitrage in productive activities that become more or less profitable with a given rate of interest. In this way, monetary theory and policy are still tied to the classic Ricardian theory of interest, in which the rate of interest is determined by the industrial rate of profit. Subsequent chapters in this book address the monetary policy that derives from this classical theory.

There are almost as many versions of the classical theory as there are monetary economists. This chapter uses as the exemplar of this theory the one that has been put forward in a recent book by Anwar Shaikh, *Capitalism, Competition, Conflict, Crises*. The book may be taken to represent much of the recent literature that is rooted in classical political economy. Like any economic theory, it should be viewed in the context of the conditions which make this theory true. The classical theory of money applies under special assumptions to a very particular capitalist economy in which the monetary sector or banking are external to capitalist production. However, when credit is endogenous to capitalist production, the rate of interest is no longer governed by the rate of profit in the real economy, and the rate of profit of the banking sector does not depend on the actual rate of interest. In the modern capitalist economy, credit is endogenous to the system of production and

[1] Keynes, 'Poverty in Plenty', 1934.

Interest and Capital: The Monetary Economics of Michał Kalecki. Jan Toporowski, Oxford University Press.
© Jan Toporowski 2022. DOI: 10.1093/oso/9780198816232.003.0008

distribution. In this more general case, debt and interest have the function of redistributing income, but are unrelated to the rate of profit from production.

It should be pointed out that this chapter does not represent Shaikh's book, or even its core argument. The chapter uses the Shaikh version of the classical theory of interest as the starting point for a critique of that theory. This chapter describes the banking system in which the classical theory of interest holds true and then explains how, in the credit system that emerged with capitalism, that classical theory of interest does not hold. It is then possible to argue that debt and interest perform a purely distributional function in a credit economy. Contrary to the classical view that the rate of interest is determined by the rate of profit, the rate of interest in a capitalist economy is unrelated to the rate of profit from production around which Shaikh builds the analysis in his book.

7.1 The Classical Theory of Interest

By the classical theory of interest is meant the view that the rate of interest is governed by the return on investment undertaken using borrowed funds: a rate of interest higher than this would find no demand for loans, because no capitalist would be able to earn a profit from new investment; a rate of interest lower than the return that may be obtained from real capital investment would find capitalists taking out additional loans to undertake new investments. This was expressed by David Ricardo: 'the rate of interest... [is] regulated by the profits on the employment of capital, and not by the number or quality of the pieces of metal, which are used to circulate its produce'.[2] In this way the rate of interest determines the level of production, employment (in the case of labour reserves) and investment because that rate marks the limit to which production and investment can profitably be pushed by profit-maximizing capitalists. In the classical theory, this limit is set because the interest paid on his loans is a deduction from the profit of the capitalist. In Neo-Classical theory this link with the marginal productivity of capital is reinforced by the notion that the rate of interest is the opportunity cost of any real investment.

In Anwar Shaikh's book (and in classical economics generally, following the abolition of the Usury Laws), the rate of interest is an exogenous factor, introduced after the determination of production and distribution in a classic,

[2] Ricardo, 'The High Price of Bullion', 1810, pp. 88–9.

Sraffian way, with an input–output matrix showing the combinations of labour and produced inputs necessary for final production. Real wage rates and rates of profits are inversely related, in the Sraffian or Neo-Classical (but not Kalecki's) theory of wages. In Shaikh's book, a process of 'real competition' equalizes the rate of profit across all industries. The rate of profit of banks is equal to the common rate of profit minus operating costs. The process of real competition between capitals brings the rate of profit of banks into equality with the common rate of profit throughout the real economy.[3]

As first enunciated by David Ricardo, it is the rate of interest that is 'ultimately and permanently governed by the rate of profit'[4] rather than the other way around. By the end of the nineteenth century, Eugen von Bőhm-Bawerk could write authoritatively that 'while the concept of Loan interest is exceedingly simple, that of Natural interest [i.e., profit] requires more close definition'.[5] In Neo-Classical theory, following Alfred Marshall, it is the rate of interest that causes capitalists to invest and vary production so that the marginal productivity of capital is brought into line with that rate of interest.[6] Marshall's view remains the conventional wisdom guiding current monetary policy that considers the rate of interest to be a key variable in determining the equality of saving and investment. Marshall's concept of the relationship between investment and interest then found its way through Keynes's circle into Post-Keynesian analysis. In this way, the classical theory of interest retains its influence today.[7]

7.2 Capitalist Credit and Finance

The classical theory may be brought into sharper relief by comparing it with Kalecki's theory of interest, highlighting the fundamental distinction between

[3] 'The loan interest rate directly regulates capitalist accumulation through its role as the benchmark against which the general rate of profit can be measured. But it also determines the bank rate of profit itself. Bank revenue consists of interest receipts on loans,...and bank profit...is the difference between bank revenue and operating costs.' Shaikh, *Capitalism Competition, Conflict, Crises*, p. 448. A similar approach may be found in Kahn, 'Notes on the Rate of Interest and the Growth of Firms', 1971, although Shaikh does not cite this work.

[4] Ricardo, Principles, 1817, p. 297.

[5] Bőhm-Bawerk, *Interest and Capital*, 1922, p. 8.

[6] 'My position is that the mean rate of discount is governed by the mean rate of interest for long loans; that again is determined by the extent and the richness of the field for the investment of capital on the one hand, and on the other by the amount of capital seeking investment...Equilibrium is found at that rate of interest for long loans (and the corresponding rate of discount for short loans) which equates supply and demand.' Marshall, 'Minutes of Evidence' to the Royal Commission on the Values of Gold and Silver, 1887, p. 51. See also Wicksell, *Interest and Prices*, 1936, pp. 138–41.

[7] '...the size of the gap between the rate of interest...and rates of profit is a material factor in the rate of growth of companies...' (Kahn 'Notes on the Rate of Interest and the Growth of Firms', 1971, p. 230).

that theory of interest and the classical theory of interest. *In the Kaleckian theory of interest, changes in the rate of interest are non-neutral in respect of income, but neutral in respect of expenditure*: a rise/fall in the rate of interest increases/decreases gross income, and transfers income from net debtors to net creditors, but does not change the overall volume or composition of consumption or investment. *In the classical theory of interest, changes in the rate of interest are neutral with respect to income, but non-neutral with respect to expenditure.* Income remains determined by the real resources available for production and exchange; while changes in the rate of interest affect the allocation of those resources between consumption and saving, and hence the volume of investment.

The classical theory of interest supposes a situation in which money is a commodity produced separately from the rest of production and distribution (that determines the respective rates of profit and wages). In the case of Marx, the production of gold is included in the sector producing means of production, and therefore using labour and having a rate of profit that corresponds to Ricardo's and Shaikh's rate of profit.[8] More generally, though, the determination of bank profit and interest advanced above would be true in an economy that uses gold as money, where the bank has purchased or produced the gold in the past (so that the cost of the gold had come out of past revenue) and now lends the gold out to capitalists. The bank's total revenue now includes all the interest revenue that it receives on such loans. From that interest revenue the bank's operating (office) expenses are deducted to produce a profit for the owners of the bank. This would also be true of a credit economy in which banks paid no interest to its depositors or bond-holders, so that all the interest on its borrowing was available to pay operating costs and distribute to shareholders.[9]

Put like this, it is immediately obvious why Ricardo's and Shaikh's capitalists carry on investing in the real economy: because they cannot earn any money on their bank deposits and other financial assets. This is indeed the

[8] Marx, *Capital Volume* II, 1974, pp. 473–7.

[9] In his comments to an earlier draft of this chapter, Anwar Shaikh has pointed out that, in his book, zero interest on deposits applies only on demand deposits, but not on savings deposits. If that is the case, then the interest on those savings deposits needs to be deducted from gross bank revenue, in calculating bank profits. Moreover, the interest paid by banks needs to be added to the income of depositors who, in a classical world in which workers do not save, would be capitalists. See comments below at the start of section 7.3. Kahn, whose 1971 paper anticipates much of Shaikh's analysis, postulated an equity-financed real sector in which the dividend rate on equity is held to be equivalent to the rate of interest.

'euthanasia of the rentier' (as already anticipated by Marx).[10] However, these are highly unusual circumstances and it is doubtful whether even in Ricardo's time banking outside London, where he worked, operated like this. It is true that gold production can be given a separate industrial sector. But in a capitalist economy, the banking sector cannot be treated separately from the system of production and distribution. If it is so treated, for the sake of exposition, then interest and debt cannot be treated as a drain on capitalist income, since capitalists either receive interest or derive profits from selling goods and services to recipients of interest who are neither industrial capitalists not workers. Historically, capitalist banking and finance was always more like a 'credit club' of capitalists. The origins of capitalist credit lie in the discounting of bills by 'merchant' or 'country' banks who were originally merely capitalists in possession of sufficient money hoards to be able to use them to buy, at a discount, the IOUs of their business associates.[11] This is implicit in Marx's analysis of money and interest, and was later made explicit in Kalecki's first exposition of capitalist financing.[12]

This inter-capitalist credit and debt is what distinguishes capitalist credit from its predecessors in usury and traditional money-lending in pre-capitalist societies, or the sovereign debt of the absolutist state within which merchant capitalist credit first emerged. The focus in monetary economics on money as a medium of exchange obscures the key distinguishing feature of capitalist credit, namely that it redistributes money hoards among capitalists, rather than exploiting the rural poor or buying pensions from the state.[13] In a capitalist economy, money comes into exchange through the expenditure of capitalists' money on production, and not as a conventionally, or even legally, accepted token of value in exchange.

The operations of banks as a credit club of capitalists are the foundation of monetary endogeneity. Capitalists have assets, including financial assets like bills, bonds, shares and government paper, that they can post as security of loans, and those loans create deposits.[14] It is this financially collateralized

[10] 'If an untowardly large section of capitalists were to convert their capital into money-capital, the result would be a frightful depreciation of money-capital and a frightful fall in the rate of interest; many would at once face the impossibility of living on their interest, and would hence be compelled to reconvert into industrial capitalists.' Marx, *Capital Volume* III, 1970, p. 378.

[11] Niebyl, *Studies in the Classical Theories of* Money, 1946, chapter 3.

[12] See Chapter 6 above and Kalecki, 'Essay on the Business Cycle Theory', 1933, pp. 93–8.

[13] It is the neglect of the distinction between capitalist credit and debt and pre-capitalist debt, and the income and balance sheet implications of that distinction, that confuses long-term (econometric) studies of debt, such as Reinhart and Rogoff, *This Time It's Different*, 2008.

[14] Withers, *The Meaning of* Money, 1909; Robertson, 'Theories of Banking Policy', 1928. 'We have spoken of bankers and financiers as the makers of credit. But we have also recognized that the chief financial material out of which they make it is the stocks and shares and other certificates of value

lending, rather than the provision of government reserves, as postulated by most Post-Keynesians and reiterated by Shaikh,[15] that makes the supply of credit determined by demand, or the ability of capitalists to provide collateral.

The proper test of the classical theory of interest is therefore against this kind of capitalist finance, rather than gold production. As a first approximation to reality, let us, for the sake of simplicity, leave aside the government and foreign sectors, and assume that workers are true proletarians, whose only asset is their labour power. This gives a 'pure' capitalist economy in which the only banking is the 'pure' capitalist credit club. Banks operate holding the deposits of capitalists and advancing loans to them. Banks receive interest from the loans that they advance. But they also pay interest on the funds that are deposited with them. *The profits of the banks are the margin between deposit and lending rates of interest multiplied by the value of the balance sheet of every bank, after deducting the operating costs of each bank.*[16] *Bank profits are therefore unrelated to the level of the rate of interest itself.*

However, it should be pointed out that the profits of the financial sector make no difference to profits overall in this capitalist economy: the margin between deposit and lending rates received by capitalists engaged in banking business is obtained at the expense of the profits of non-bank capitalists; the costs of banking business (premises, staff) constitute demand for the output of the non-financial sector and in this way returns to non-bank capitalists a part of their profit that those capitalists hand over to bank capitalists under that margin between borrowing and deposit rates of interest.

In this sense, bank expenses may be subsumed under Investment spending (insofar as those expenses are a necessary part of investment) or Capitalists' Consumption (insofar as they are merely the discretionary extravagances that are nowadays associated with financial business) in Kalecki's well-known profits equation.[17]

which represents the capital created by the saving and investing classes. It is thus the growth of the forms of saving which take these financial shapes that enables the increased credit to emerge from the financial factories. All such modern saving can furnish material for the creation of more credit.' Hobson, *Gold, Prices and Wages*, 1913, p. 89.

[15] Shaikh, *Capitalism Competition, Conflict, Crises*, p. 613.

[16] 'The rate of interest that is paid on deposits is always somewhat lower than the rate charged by banks on loans. The difference between these two rates remunerates the bank...' Wicksell, 1936, p. 139.

[17] The theory may be summarized as follows. In a closed economy, with no government, in a given period, total income (Y) is equal to the sum of profits plus wages (W + P), which in turn is equal to Consumption plus Investment (C + I). Y – C = I = Saving. Saving may be divided into the saving of workers (S_w) and the saving of capitalists (S_c). Similarly, Consumption may be divided into the consumption of workers (C_w) and the consumption of capitalists (C_c).

Profits are therefore equal to $S_c + C_c$. S_c is equal to total Saving or Investment minus S_w ($I - S_w$). Total Profits ($S_c + C_c$) therefore equal to $I + C_c - S_w$. See Kalecki, 'A Theory of Profits', 1942b.

The more fundamental doctrine of the classic theory of interest is the link between interest and the gross profits of capital. This too can be examined from the 'capitalists' credit club point of view. A literal reading of Marx and the classics suggests that *current* interest is paid out of *current* profits. In fact, at any one time capitalists hold loans, and they also hold deposits and bank shares accumulated from past profits. It is out of the total accumulation of profits that interest is paid. But the interest received by capitalists adds to their income. In our 'pure' capitalist economy, the total value of those deposits and bank shares is equal to the total value of the loans in the banking system. If rates of interest are zero, banks make no profit and the capitalists' net income is the profit that they make from production. If interest rates rise, the net income of the capitalists is unchanged: as a class they now pay interest. But their interest income, including the dividends received on their bank shares, has also risen by the same amount. How do they pay that higher interest? They do so by using the deposits that they have in the banking system. Hence, in Kalecki's theory of interest, it is the velocity of circulation of deposits, rather than the volume of business investment, that varies in proportion to the rate of interest on money.[18]

What if the capitalists do not have enough deposits to pay a really exorbitant increase in interest rates? In a credit system they can borrow more, by pledging assets as security against loans, and this corresponds to an increase in their deposits. Providing that banks are accommodating, capitalists will borrow as much deposits as are necessary to maintain interest and debt payments. From those interest and debt receipts they can repay debts.

It follows that current industrial profits are not, as the classical theory asserts, the sole source of the means of payment that capitalists have with which to settle their financial obligations. Capitalists have savings, and may borrow against the assets that they possess. This can be illustrated by considering the ultimate Ricardian–Marxian (à la Grossman, perhaps) case where aggregate profit is equal to zero, but interest remains stubbornly positive. Of course this does not mean that no capitalists are making a profit, merely that the profits of some capitalists are balanced by the business losses of other capitalists. Any profits in the banking sector from the margin between lending and deposit rates would be at the expense of overall losses among non-bank capitalists.

In this situation of overall zero profits, capitalists still have deposits (from accumulated past profits and borrowing) and loans from the bank intermediaries.

[18] Kalecki, 'The Short-term Rate of Interest and the Velocity of Cash Circulation', 1941b.

Interest on that borrowing can be paid from deposits held by capitalists who owe interest. Capitalists with credit balances will therefore receive interest income. The higher is the rate of interest, the higher will be the interest paid, and received by capitalists. Bank deposits will be redistributed from net debtor capitalists to net creditor capitalists. What happens when, as a result of successive deposit redistributions, net debtors start to run out of bank deposits to pay interest on their borrowing? In that case, providing they have assets to post as collateral, they can borrow to pay interest, or else borrow without security. The expansion of loans increases also the supply of deposits. As new deposits are redistributed from net debtors to net creditors, the net creditors accumulate the new deposits, which the net creditors can use to repay their loans. The only circumstance that can prevent the continuing servicing of financial liabilities in this way is not the failure to generate a profit in production and trade, but a refusal of banks to lend more to net debtors.

The classical theory of interest asserts that capitalists must engage in production and productive investment in order to generate the income that they must pay as interest. The theory does not hold because, in a capitalist economy, capitalists hold savings. Ultimately, through the intermediation of banks, capitalists are indebted to each other. The deposits corresponding to the loans must be in the system and some of those deposits will be available to make interest payments. With a sufficiently elastic credit system, capitalists may pay any amount of interest to each other, and will then receive that same amount of interest (from which to pay interest in future). In practice, of course, the distribution of credits and debts are not the same so that capitalists will be either net creditors or net debtors to each other. Interest and debt are thus ways of redistributing their income among capitalists. They do not require production or investment to generate the profits out of which interest may be paid.[19]

7.3 Capitalist Credit Extended

In the previous section, it was argued that in a capitalist economy in which production is undertaken for profit, the savings that capitalists have out of their profits may be used to pay interest. With only capitalists and (non-saving)

[19] The process by which this happens is described in Chapter 5 above. Wicksell, who conceded that capitalists hold bank deposits (Wicksell, *Interest and Prices*, 1936, pp. 138–9), did not draw the logical conclusion from this that those capitalists then also receive interest on those deposits in addition to their income from production and trade, in other words, that interest cannot reduce the aggregate profits received by capitalists.

workers in the economy, the banking system is in effect a credit club of capitalists. With their own savings and access to credit, there is no necessity to pay interest solely out of current profits, except in the marginal cases (small enterprises perhaps) where capitalists have no savings. Accordingly, there is no necessary correspondence between the rate of interest and the rate of profit. However, despite being a staple of classical economic analysis, the assumption of a 'pure' capitalist economy, in which there are only capitalists and workers, is somewhat abstract. In this section the model of a pure capitalist economy is modified by successive approximations to a more realistic analytical framework to show, contrary to the view of Shaikh and the classics, that bank profits are not determined by the absolute level of the rate of interest, and that the rate of interest is unrelated to the rate of profit.

As a second approximation, the business cycle may be incorporated into this analysis. Shaikh observes the empirical finding first put forward early in the nineteenth century by Thomas Tooke, and later also noted by Wicksell, and which Keynes referred to as Gibson's Paradox.[20] This is the observation that nominal interest rates rise and fall with prices (and not inversely, as is assumed by the monetary policy consensus today). Accordingly, we should expect capitalists' income from financial operations and assets, their interest income, also to rise in a boom, to some degree because more payments, in relation to operating profit (the difference between sales revenue and direct costs of production) are diverted into interest payments to other capitalists through the banking system as the boom proceeds and interest rates rise. On the one hand the velocity of circulation of demand deposits used as means of payment increases, as rising interest rates make depositors reluctant to keep idle funds in zero-interest demand deposits. On the other hand, the capitalists' income from financial assets increases, with rising interest rates. It then becomes debatable whether the profit that the theoretical capitalist is supposed to be maximizing is the operating profit of his enterprise, the net income of the enterprise's productive activities or investment in particular years, or the profits of his enterprise *including* his net claims on other capitalists.[21]

Taking the system as a whole, we know that those net claims on other capitalists sum to zero (each claim is another capitalist's liability), and classical

[20] Keynes, *A Treatise on Money Volume* II, 1930/1971, p. 198.

[21] Marx observed, adhering to the classical theory, observed that '...even when operating with his own capital...[the individual capitalist] necessarily considers the part of his average profit which equals the average interest as fruit of his capital as such, set apart from the process of production; and as distinct from this portion singled out as interest, he considers the surplus of the gross profit as mere profit of enterprise.' Marx, *Capital Volume* III, 1970, p. 378.

and Neo-Classical theory tell us that the aggregate net profit is equal only to the sum of operating profits. But do the individual capitalists know this and, from the point of view of the microeconomics of the firm, is it this operating profit that they are maximizing, or their operating profit plus their credit and interest claims on each other? Shaikh's and the classics' solution of a banking and financial sector separate from the system of real production and distribution does not really allow for the intermediary function of modern credit. The interest that banks receive is largely passed on to their depositors, bond-holders, and shareholders. But in a 'pure' capitalist economy, those depositors, bond-holders and shareholders are other capitalists. Interest and debt may therefore vary the distribution of profit more than influencing the level of production.

In practice, the credit system is of course more complicated. As a third approximation to reality, it is obvious that the capitalists' 'credit club' is itself stratified. On its margins are capitalists who have no financial assets that they can use as collateral against borrowing. These capitalists, mostly small and medium-sized enterprises, are the ones that most correspond to the 'classical' capitalist: borrowing to generate a surplus from production out of which to pay interest and repay loans. Net creditors are concentrated among corporations,[22] and net debtors among small and medium-sized enterprises. The credit system therefore redistributes income from these smaller enterprises to corporations, much as the price system in general redistributes the overall flow of profits to large monopolists. However, smaller businesses, while accounting for the bulk of private sector employment in most countries, undertake only a small proportion of fixed capital investment, the vast bulk of which is conducted by large corporations. This stratification therefore even further reduces any link between the rate of interest and real production and investment.

As a fourth approximation there is now in most countries, next to the capitalists' credit club, a middle-class credit club, constituted around and inflated by the residential housing market. The middle class is here defined by its ownership of assets, principally housing, through whose market the middle class borrows and redistributes bank deposits, paying interest to each other (with appropriate margin deductions for the financial intermediaries). On the margins of this household credit club is the portion of the working class that

[22] Obviously a debt-financed company with real assets cannot be a net creditor. To be a net creditor, a company has to have share capital in excess of its real assets. See Toporowski, 'Notes on Excess Capital and Liquidity Management', 2008.

remains proletarian in being without assets and that least engages with the credit system.[23]

A key implication of the classic theory of interest is that all debt involves a transfer out of the (productive) economy. Shaikh follows the recent financialization literature in attributing to the rise in gross household debt and debt service payments a growing debt burden on household.[24] The problem with taking gross debt as the indicator of financial stress is that it does not distinguish situations of genuine financial stress, where households face rising debt payments without any increase in income or liquid assets, from situations where debt increases, but is hedged with liquid assets, so that the drain on income is just the margin between income from those assets and the cost of the debt. Most of the debt service payments of the household sector are transfers between households, even if mediated by banks, rather than out of the households sector as a whole. Net debt transfers have, inevitably, been much smaller. This presents a more complex picture than that suggested by the figures on gross indebtedness in any economy. Those transfers between households due to *net* interest and debt/deposit payments need to be analysed, rather than drawing conclusions from gross debt and gross debt service payments that largely reflect transfers of income on debt contracts derived from the exchange of residential property among better off households.

As a final approximation to reality, it is necessary to include government borrowing,[25] and credit transactions abroad.[26] These add more complexity to

[23] Toporowski, '*Why the World Economy Needs a Financial Crash*', 2010, chapter 12.

[24] Shaikh, *Capitalism Competition, Conflict,* Crises, pp. 735–6. See also Godley, 'Seven Unsustainable Processes', 2000; Wolff, 'Recent Trends in Household Wealth in the United States: Rising Debt and the Middle Class Squeeze – An Update to 2007', 2010; Dodig, Hein, and Detzer, 'Financialisation and the Financial and Economic Crises', 2016.

[25] These too should be seen as redistributive mechanisms. The theory of Ricardian Equivalence, which Shaikh does not discuss, can only, like the classical theory of interest, be true in an economy in which the monetary sector is external to the system of production and distribution. In a modern credit economy government debt is simply a commitment to redistribute income from tax-payers to government bond-holders. The flaw in the theory of Ricardian Equivalence is its failure to account for the receipt of future interest and debt repayments that a given government debt implies. A suitable tax on bond-holders should make any government debt manageable. Government debt causes problems when bond-holders are foreign residents and thus the beneficiaries of its redistribution are outside the tax jurisdiction of the government, or when that debt is in foreign currency. See Chapter 9 below.

[26] Keynes's 'bancor' project was to be essentially a credit club of governments who kept foreign exchange transactions as book-keeping transfers between themselves using interest rates and exchange rates to manage trade disequilibria. When the actual International Monetary Fund was set up the restriction of the scope of this credit club provided the opportunity for the replacement of the government credit club with the commercial international bank credit club for international transactions (see Chapter 4 above). It is this commercial credit that now governs the international monetary system. Shaikh's book considers the purchasing power parity theory of exchange rates and he evaluates critically the theory of comparative advantage in foreign trade. But the breakdown of the Bretton Woods system is attributed to 'neo-liberalism' rather than the failings of the international monetary arrangements set up at Bretton Woods (Shaikh, *Capitalism Competition, Conflict, Crises*, 2016, chapter 11).

the redistribution of income that credit, debt, and interest contracts generate in a credit economy. But they do not change the fundamentally redistributive character of credit, debt and interest.

7.4 Conclusion

Shaikh's is but the latest attempt to revive the classical theory of interest. This follows from his prior exposition of a theory of production and distribution, which leaves only room for money as an external sector that, through the rate of interest, gives the 'benchmark' rate to which the rate of profit conforms by the process of 'real' competition (of capitals) that equalizes rates across industries. Shaikh's exposition arouses little controversy because the minds of successive generations of economists have been marinated in the classical theory ever since the first merchant capitalist approached one of his moneyed fellows for a loan and promised that his venture would earn a return in excess of the interest cost; through to modern times when the sophisticates of *haut finance* can enlarge without contradiction upon the significance of their trade. But modern credit has only a tenuous influence on production and investment, that influence being largely due to the respect given to Ricardo's theory at the expense of serious consideration of the conditions under which it holds true. Credit and interest in a capitalist economy are contracts to redistribute bank deposits. And if they redistribute bank deposits then it is from net debtors to net creditors rather than from all debtors to some undefined 'rentiers' external to the process of production and distribution. Those net debtors that exist on the lower margins of the business and household credit strata, whose net incomes may be reduced by their debts, are usually marginal to the process of paying interest and debt. It is not the income or profit generated in production that determines the ability to pay interest, but liquidity.

Shaikh argues his case by showing logically that the rate of profit of banks is determined by the rate of interest, and that the rate of interest is brought, by a process of 'real competition' or arbitrage, to equal the rate of profit. However, this is based on special assumptions. This chapter shows that, more generally, bank profit is equal to the margin between banks' revenue from their assets minus their payments on their liabilities, that is their interest margin, rather than the rate of interest (with appropriate deductions for their operating costs), and the rate of interest is in general unrelated to the rate of profit.

8

Industrial without Financial Circulation?

Credit and Distribution in the Theories of Augusto Graziani and Michał Kalecki With Some Remarks on Financialization

As argued in previous chapters, Kalecki's economic analysis is a monetary analysis, showing how money circulates through the processes of production and distribution. In this respect it comes close to the monetary analysis of a school of thought in economics that has devoted itself to putting forward 'the theory of the monetary circuit'. The affinity between Kalecki's analysis has been recognized by many 'circuitists'. A key author has been Augusto Graziani. In his book *The Monetary Production Theory* he provided a rich analysis of the use of credit in capitalist production, showing the endogeneity of such credit and giving new insights into the use of credit as money. The theory suggests a credit system, inflated by loans for production and investment and deflated by loan repayments. Incomes in the form of profits and wages are recorded in such money. A key part is played by workers' saving, and this results, in Graziani's approach, in a problem of interest monetization, or how capitalists can acquire the money with which to pay interest. The chapter shows that this difficulty disappears once it is recognized that capitalists own financial assets and bank deposits, as Kalecki argued.

The discussion of credit circulation then moves on to examine the more recent 'Neo-Kaleckian' theories of financialization that highlight the indebtedness of workers to capitalists, as a factor reducing workers' incomes and increasing the share of profits. As in the theory of Graziani, a key part is played by inter-class debt relations between capitalists and workers. However, it is argued here that the distribution of credit and debt among capitalists themselves and, on a smaller scale, among workers themselves, is a more significant influence on the distribution of income between those classes.

Interest and Capital: The Monetary Economics of Michał Kalecki. Jan Toporowski, Oxford University Press.
© Jan Toporowski 2022. DOI: 10.1093/oso/9780198816232.003.0009

8.1 The Finance of Production

Augusto Graziani was a pioneer and leading scholar of the 'circuit theory of money', one of the more serious attempts to break away from thinking about money in terms of simple insights drawn from every-day exchange transactions and commonplace deposit and loan operations. His theory was an effort to break away from the Post-Keynesian preoccupation with monetary endogeneity arising out of central bank operations with banks, to return the theory of money to its roots in capitalist production. This is perhaps the greatest achievement of circuit theory. Yet, circuit theory as constituted in Graziani's most advanced version of it, his Federico Caffè Lectures on The Monetary Theory of Production, comes to paradoxical conclusions over the ownership of financial resources and eventually to difficulties in the theory of interest. This chapter explains the most fundamental of these problems by way of comparison with the ideas of Michał Kalecki and applies the conclusions from this to more recent accounts of financialization.

In his Introduction to the published version of his Lectures, Augusto Graziani related the ideas in the circuit theory of money not only to its obvious precursors in the work of Bernard Schmitt and Alain Parguez in France, Hajo Riese in Berlin, and, further back, Knut Wicksell and Hans Neisser. The theory in particular rejects a Walrasian approach to general equilibrium, in which money is found only in exchange after production. A specific inspiration is of course Keynes, but the Lectures also acknowledge the influence of Kalecki and Post-Keynesian monetary theory.[1]

In his Introduction to the Lectures, Graziani gave a 'synthetic explanation' of how credit comes into the system:

> *Step one:* A decision is taken by the banks to grant credit to firms, thus enabling them to start a process of production...[2]

The credit is used to pay the costs of production. In the course of the production process it finds its way into the pockets of workers who provide labour, and other firms that supply other inputs into production. In Step three of the

[1] See 'Introduction' in Graziani, *The Monetary Theory of* Production, 2003b; also Halevi and Raouil, 'On a Post-Keynesian Stream from France and Italy', 2002. A more comprehensive view of the background to Graziani's monetary thought is provided by Riccardo Bellofiore in 'Monetary Economics after Wicksell', 2005.

[2] Graziani, *The Monetary Theory of Production*, 2003b, p. 27; a somewhat shorter account is provided in Graziani, 1989.

process, commodities produced are sold, consumer goods to workers, and investment goods to other firms. 'The money that wage earners spend in the commodities market, as well as money spent in the financial markets on the purchase of securities, flows back to the firms, who can use it to repay debt. To the extent that bank debts are repaid, an equal amount of money is destroyed....Once the initial bank debt is repaid and the money is destroyed, the monetary circuit is closed.'[3]

With remarkable modesty, Graziani pointed out in a footnote that 'It is debatable whether the description of the circulation of money as a monetary circuit is implicitly present in Keynes's thought', citing a number of his own works and those of other circuitists in support of the Keynesian connection, but also the American Post-Keynesian Jan Kregel as opposing such a link.[4]

However, a curious role is played by workers saving:

> As soon as the firm starts operating,...the credit initially granted is totally turned into wages. At the end of the process, the firm being granted the initial credit is in debt to the banking system, while wage earners are creditors of the bank...

As already cited above, 'the money that wage earners spend in the commodities market, as well as money spent in the financial markets on the purchase of securities, flows back to the firms, who can use it to repay debt. To the extent that bank debts are repaid, an equal amount of money is destroyed. To the extent instead that wage-earners use their money to increase their own cash balances, an equal amount of money remains in the form of bank debt and wage-earner's credit towards the banks.' The latter bank debt is that of capitalists.

Graziani went on to explain that if workers spent all their money on consumption, or purchased securities, then firms (which might issue the securities) would get back the money needed to repay their bank debt:

> If wage-earners spend their incomes entirely – whether on the commodity market or on the financial market – firms will get back the whole of their monetary advances and will be able to repay the whole of the principal of their bank debt. In this way, as some would say, the circuit is closed 'without

[3] Graziani, *The Monetary Theory of* Production, 2003b, pp. 27–30.
[4] Graziani, *The Monetary Theory of* Production, 2003b, p. 27. Kregel, 'Shylock or Hamlet', 1986. Victoria Chick, 'Lost and Found', 2005, also criticizes the idea that circuit theory is Keynesian.

> losses'. If instead wage earners decide to keep a portion of their savings in the form of liquid balances, firms are unable to repay their bank debt by the same amount. As a consequence, at the end of the production cycle the money initially created will not be entirely destroyed. If banks are now intending to finance a new production cycle equal to the preceding one by granting the same finance, the total money stock will be increased: precisely it will be equal to the wage bill plus the new liquid balances set aside by wage earners at the end of the previous cycle.[5]

In this way, the role of workers' saving is to place firms in debt to their workers, whether through the workers' liquid balances in the bank, whose counterpart is firms' bank debt, or through the workers' holding of securities, issued by firms in order to repay debt.[6]

The part played by workers' saving leads Graziani to a fundamental difficulty over the question of where the money comes from to pay interest. Graziani put the problem as follows:

> It is self-evident that since the only money existing in the market is the money that banks have lent to the firms, even in the most favourable case, the firms can only repay in money the principal of their debt and are anyhow unable to pay interest. In order to get the money needed to satisfy their interest payments, the only thing they can do is to sell part of their product to the banks, which is tantamount to saying that interest can only be paid in kind. A parallel solution, not widely different in substance, is reached if the banks buy equities issued by the firms. The presence of a government sector would not make things easier. A government deficit might bring to the firms the money necessary to pay interest to the banks; but a government debt towards the central bank would remain pending. There seems to be no way out: either a debt equal to the interest payments remains unsatisfied, or interest is paid in kind.[7]

This was not an incidental observation. Graziani was here returning to a theme which he had taken up almost half a century earlier. In a 1965 discussion of the Harrod Domar growth model he had argued that 'In the position of equilibrium, the social rate of return to capital, which…is constant over

[5] Graziani, *The Monetary Theory of* Production, 2003b, pp. 30–1.

[6] This last kind of funding of debt is further discussed in Graziani, 'The Investment Decision in Keynes's Thought', 2002.

[7] Graziani, 'The Investment Decision in Keynes's Thought', 2002, p. 31.

time, is equal to the rate of increase of money income...divided by the propensity to save.'[8] In other words, to maintain a constant rate of profit, the economy must expand at a constant rate in relation to the propensity to save. There cannot be a static economy with a constant rate of profit.

8.2 The Kalecki View of Credit

In Graziani's credit analysis investment is just another form of production, and is financed in the much the same way.[9] Kalecki presented an alternative view of credit, in which the investment of firms may be financed from their own resources, or from bank borrowing:

> ...the equality between savings and investment...(is) independent of the level of the rate of interest...(I)nvestment, once carried out, automatically provides the savings necessary to finance it...(I)f some capitalists increase their investment by using for this purpose their liquid reserves, the profits of other capitalists will rise *pro tanto* and thus the liquid reserves will pass into the possession of the latter. If additional investment is financed by bank credit, the spending of the amounts in question will cause equal amounts of saved profits to accumulate as bank deposits.[10]

However, Kalecki insisted that ownership of financial resources is the precondition for being a capitalist, and therefore any requirement for initial finance was solely a problem of small companies, rather than the corporations that dominate production and investment. In his words:

> Many economists assume, at least in their abstract theories, a state of business democracy where anybody endowed with entrepreneurial ability can obtain capital for starting a business venture. This picture of the activities of the 'pure' entrepreneur is, to put it mildly, unrealistic. The most important prerequisite for becoming an entrepreneur is the *ownership* of capital.[11]

[8] Graziani, 'Equilibro generale ed accumulazione di capitale nel sistema Paretiano', 1965, p. 77.

[9] See Graziani, *The Monetary Theory of* Production, 2003b, pp. 71–2; also Graziani, 'Finance Motive', 2003a.

[10] Kalecki, *Theory of Economic* Dynamics, 1954a, p. 50.

[11] Kalecki, *Theory of Economic* Dynamics, 1954a, pp. 94–5.

In Kalecki's analysis, the banking system, in addition to its function as a clearing house for payments, serves as a credit club for capitalists as well as for workers. The net interest receipts or payments for each capitalist in a given period depend on the amount, maturity and interest rates on the debt or monetary instruments, or financial obligations, in its balance sheet.[12] An increase in equity transfers such monetary instruments in the form of bank deposits into the possession of a capitalist from another capitalist or a collective saving institution, or a rentier paying for the new shares with a bank deposit; or even from a hedge fund that may be using the shares as security for a bank loan. Production as the sole purpose of bank advances is incidental to financial operations in banking systems based on collateralized lending that, at the margin, ensures that there is enough credit in the system to pay for current production and investment.[13]

8.3 Inter-class Credit and Debt

In practice, the existence of an elastic credit system means that there is no limit to the amount of interest that capitalists may pay each other. Their formal gross income (gross profits) rises by the amount of interest that they receive from each other as they increase their payments of interest to each other. The Ricardian notion that interest reduces net profit is only true of outside debt, such as the amounts that capitalists as a whole may borrow from workers as suggested by Graziani.[14]

It may be useful here to illustrate this with a more analytical comparison of the respective theoretical claims of Graziani and the recent school of 'financialization' theorists, who adhere to Ricardian theories of debt and profit-led growth, namely that debt is a liability outside the social class of the borrower.[15] As will be shown, the theories of Graziani and the circuit theorists, as well

[12] Toporowski, 'Notes on Excess Capital', 2008.

[13] See Withers, *The Meaning of Money*, 1909 and Hobson, *Gold, Prices and Wages*, 1913.

[14] 'The rate of interest, though ultimately and permanently governed by the rate of profit, is however subject to temporary variations from other causes' (Ricardo, 1817, p. 297). Incidentally, the independence of interest from net profits is the reason why the rate of interest can only have a marginal effect on the business cycle, as Kalecki argued. The margin of net debtors whose expenditure may be constrained or expanded by a rise or fall of interest rates is off-set by the rise or fall in the expenditure of net creditors whose income is increased or reduced by that rise or fall in interest rates. If the net creditors and net debtors are engaged in financial operations, then the interest rate elasticity of expenditure in the economy is zero and interest rate changes have no effect on the overall volume of production in the economy. See Chapter 7 above.

[15] Hein, *The Macroeconomics of Finance-Dominated Capitalism*, 2012a, Stockhammer, 'Financialization', 2012.

as some 'Neo-Kaleckian' financializationists, attach major, but differing, importance to the credit and debt relations between capitalists and workers. These inter-class debt relations are supposed to have played a major part in the financial crisis of 2008 and the subsequent economic stagnation, in particular in Europe. To understand the limitations of the two positions requires a brief excursion into the theory of the determinants of profits.

The view common to Graziani, Kalecki, and the financialization theorists is that income is created by expenditure, and this relationship is expressed (but not wholly explained) by the national income identity between income and expenditure. In an open economy with government, in any given period, total income (Y) is equal to consumption, plus investment (I) plus government expenditure minus tax revenue (G – T) plus the foreign trade and income surplus (X – M).

With two classes in the economy, capitalists and workers, whose households consume and save, so that capitalists' net (after payment of interest) profits are either consumed (C_c) or saved (S_c), and workers wage income is either consumed (C_w) or saved (S_w). Implicit in this is a three-sector system of production of wage goods, luxury or capitalists' consumption goods, and investment goods. From this can be derived the famous Kalecki profits equation whereby the total of profits is equal to the sum of investment, the fiscal deficit, the foreign surplus, plus capitalists' consumption minus workers' saving:

$$\text{Total profits} = I + (G - T) + (X - M) + C_c - S_w. \qquad (8.1)$$

This equation gives us the total value of capitalists' profits, after they have paid (or received) interest on their borrowing (or credit balances). In order to obtain a complete picture of the economy, and break down those total profits among the individual capitalists or firms, it is necessary to introduce two systems of redistribution. First of all there is the network of prices in the economy. In addition to their commonplace function of making supply equal to demand in individual markets, prices also function to detail the distribution of total profits among individual capitalists and firms.[16] The second system is the redistribution of liquidity by means of interest and debt.

[16] This is the important function of the price system in the theory of Kalecki as well as in Marx. It should be noted that in Marx and Kalecki, capitalist profits cannot be derived in a mercantile way from buying cheap and selling dear. Buying cheap and selling dear are how the process of making a profit appears to the individual (merchant) capitalist. However, it is a fallacy of composition to extend this reasoning to society as a whole. In a society of capitalists and workers, capitalists cannot as a whole sell a higher value to their workers than they pay them. Hence, the Kalecki profits equation, Equation (8.1) above, is necessary to show how profits as a whole are monetized, but not how they are distributed among individual firms and capitalists. See López and Assous *Michał Kalecki*, 2010, p. 197.

From the above equation (8.1) it is easy to derive an equation for the ratio of profit to wage income, or the profit share, in terms of the expenditures that are necessary to provide for income flows in money terms. This is:

$$\frac{I+(G-T)+(X-M)+C_c-S_w}{C_w+S_w} \qquad (8.2)^{17}$$

in which the numerator represents the expenditures that generate profits, and the denominator represents wages.

Now it is clear that the Graziani concept of credit advanced by workers to finance production by capitalists is not the same workers' saving as given in equations (8.1) and (8.2) above. In Graziani's analysis, the credit is merely the means of payment that capitalists use to pay for labour, and that returns to capitalists when workers buy their wages goods.[18] S_w merely represents the residual of that means of payment (or net saving) that workers as a whole retain at the end of a given period. This relationship can be used to show how changes in prices, in particular in the price of labour, affect distribution. Assuming that there is excess capacity in the sector producing consumption goods, if workers are given a pay rise that is spent on consumption, C_w rises. *Profits in absolute terms do not fall, but the share of profits relative to wages falls.* The distribution of profits changes, with a shift in profits from the investment goods and capitalist consumption goods sectors, which are paying higher wages, to the capitalists in the wage goods sector. If workers are given a pay rise that is wholly saved, then *profits in absolute terms fall, and the share of profits relative to wages falls.* In terms of Graziani's theory, capitalists' indebtedness to workers increases.

This raises the question of the function of debt and credit in the economy. Graziani and the financialization theorists take contrasting positions on this. In Graziani's theory workers advance credit to capitalists; in the view of the financialization theorists capitalists advance credit to workers. In both approaches to the analysis, inter-class debt is pivotal. As mentioned above, in Graziani, credit is used as a means of payment. Since we are operating in a

[17] In the Bhaduri and Marglin 1990 paper that initiated the 'profit-led growth' research agenda, Equation (8.2) is presented as a profit margin that capitalists can increase or decrease 'in the long run'. This contrasts with Kalecki's observation, 'Now, it is clear that capitalists may decide to consume and to invest more in a given period than in the preceding one, but they cannot decide to earn more' (Kalecki, *Theory of Economic Dynamics*, 1954, p. 46). Kalecki was also sceptical of whether different considerations could apply in the long run: 'In fact, the long-run trend is only a slowly changing component of a chain of short-period situations; it has no independent entity...' Kalecki, 'Trend and the Business Cycle', 1968.

[18] Graziani, *The Monetary Theory of Production*, 2003b, pp. 31–1.

credit economy it is necessary to have in our notional capitalist economy a banking and financial system that intermediates credits and debts in the economy. The account ledgers kept in the financial system serve a similar function to the price system in determining the distribution of total profits and wages among individual capitalists and firms, and among individual workers. The system of intermediation therefore consists of a network of credit and debt contracts between capitalists, in which the interest and payments merely redistributes liquid reserves and existing profits among capitalists; and a network of credit and debt contracts between workers, on which the interest and payments merely redistributes existing wage income among workers.[19] Since we are here concerned with the effect of debt on the distribution of income between capitalists and workers we may for the sake of simplicity ignore here credit and debt relations with the government and the foreign sectors. The ledger system makes it possible to examine the intra-class indebtedness of capitalists to each other, the intra-class indebtedness of workers to each other, and the net debt of workers to capitalists, that is the excess of workers' debt over their claims on each other.

It is now possible to consider the conditions under which debt may increase the profit share. The literature on financialization emphasizes that falling wage income forces a resort to debt in order to maintain consumption standards and that debt is an obligation to capitalists.[20] However, from the model outlined above it is obvious that, in a situation of falling wage income, workers have more than one option in financing a stable level of consumption. In the first place workers are likely to save less than in the current period. Secondly they may run down savings accumulated in previous periods. Thirdly they may borrow from other workers. All of these would allow a stabilization of workers' consumption at the cost of a reduction in workers' net saving, S_w. As indicated in Equation (8.2) an increase in profit share is likely as S_w is reduced, increasing the numerator and reducing the denominator of the wage share equation. However, that increase in the profit is not because of workers' indebtedness to capitalists, or their indebtedness to rentiers. Capitalists overall are receiving the same amount of money because workers are spending the same amounts on their consumption and capitalists are spending the same amounts on investment and their own consumption.

[19] The process by which debt redistributes income is vividly illustrated by Kalecki in his fable of money circulating among mutually indebted inhabitants of a poverty-stricken village. See Chapter 5 above.

[20] Stockhammer, 'Financialisation', 2012; Hein, *The Macroeconomics of Finance-Dominated Capitalism*, 2012a.

However, capitalists now have lower labour costs. The borrowing by workers from other workers would institute debts and claims that would then merely redistribute wage income in the future but, as indicated above, not increase or decrease in net terms (after interest payments) the income of workers. Workers lending money to other workers directly or through the banking system would receive interest and repayments of the loans. The gross income of workers as a whole would be increased by the interest received on the debts to them of other workers, and reduced by the interest that they would pay to each other. Overall then, the net income of workers still depends on the wage rate and would be more or less unaffected by such borrowing, the margin between borrowing and lending rates being largely accounted for by the wages of workers employed in financial intermediation.

At the margin, however, it is possible that workers will realize their claims on capitalists from earlier saving, or borrow from capitalists.[21] In that case the borrowing and running down of credit with capitalists, still reduces net workers' saving, and the effect on the profit share is the same as in the previous case where workers are borrowing from each other. The amount of money received by the capitalists producing consumption goods will be unchanged. But the capitalists producing investment goods, and luxury goods for capitalists' consumption, will have their profits increased because their labour costs have been reduced by the amount of the reduction in wages.

It follows that the change in the respective wage or profit shares in total income, as well as the change in workers' indebtedness, is, in this example, the result of a fall in the wage rate. The 'Neo-Kaleckian' financialization approach, however, views the rise in indebtedness as the *cause* of a rise in the profit share. As has been argued above, this cannot come about through workers increasing their borrowing from other workers because this merely redistributes workers' income or savings to other workers. If however workers' net borrowing from capitalists' increases, because workers' consumption is increasing (either directly financed by borrowing from capitalists, or because workers whose loans to other workers have been repaid spend the repayments on consumption) then the denominator in Equation (8.2), showing total workers' income stays the same (workers' consumption has risen by the same amount as workers' saving has fallen). But the profit share rises with the fall in workers' net saving, because more of the money paid by capitalists to their

[21] Kalecki mentioned destitute American workers in the Depression borrowing from sympathetic retailers. According to him economic recovery was unlikely to be consumption-led because any growth in wage income was likely to be spent on repaying informal debts with retailers (Kalecki, 1934).

workers returns to the capitalists in payment for consumption goods, rather than because workers have been borrowing from each other or from capitalists.

This can be illustrated and summarized by examining what happens to the circulation of credit in a simple, reduced form balance sheet of a banking system that has liabilities in the form of deposits of workers and capitalists and, on its asset side, loans to workers and capitalists:

Balance Sheet of the Banking System

Liabilities	Assets
Deposits of workers	Loans to workers
Deposits of capitalists	Loans to capitalists

In the financialization view, workers are obliged by the falling wage share to take out loans from the banking system. The assets of the banking system thereby increase with such loans. Corresponding to them are now deposits which the poor workers use to buy consumer necessities. In the process of buying those necessities, the deposits pass into the possession of the capitalists who are producing those necessities, swelling the deposits that capitalists have in the banking system. The financialization view is that over time the deposits that correspond to this 'forced' borrowing of workers increase as workers recurrently resort to borrowing to make ends meet, or to finance housing or their purchase of otherwise 'public' goods such as education.[22]

However, as the analysis of Graziani shows, the capitalists who sell those necessities to the impoverished workers do not just keep those deposits, accumulating their claims on workers. With the exception of their profit margin, they spend the deposits on producing those necessities which the workers are buying with borrowed money, because it is only by producing and exchanging wage goods with the indebted workers that the capitalists can acquire their bank deposits. In this way, the deposits that workers are forced to borrow largely return to the workers, to be recycled again through the production process. In this way, on the deposits side at least, the balance sheet of the banking system would tend to converge on its original proportions of distribution between workers and capitalists. On the assets side, the underpaid workers now employed to produce wage goods, and their employers who receive payment for those wage goods may use the deposits that they receive

[22] This I take to be the view of Lapavitsas, *Profiting without Producing*, 2013.

in exchange for wage goods to repay their debts, or accumulate them as a hedge against their debts, or use them to buy additional goods. In this latter case, output and employment will grow further. Thus the borrowing of destitute or low income workers generates production from the proceeds of which workers receive incomes out of which they may repay their debts.

It may be noted here that if unemployment and economic stagnation are due to under-consumption, a clear inference from the financializationists' studies of household debt,[23] then workers' indebtedness must surely be an effective means of combatting underconsumption. The only substantial difference between this kind of household debt-financed consumption and debt-financed fiscal stimulus is that the government should, in theory, have less difficulty than workers in managing its debt (unless it has the misfortune to be in the European Monetary Union). The contradiction between under-consumption that is supposed to be due to workers' indebtedness, and the demand injected into the economy by the spending of indebted workers (whereby capitalists acquire the deposit counterparts of the workers' debts) is a fundamental inconsistency in financialization theory.

Graziani has credit used as means of payment, with credit of workers as claims on indebted capitalists. Neo-Kaleckian financializationists have capitalists' credit as claims on indebted workers. However, in a capitalist economy, credit and debt are simply channels for redistributing income, rather than creating net new incomes. A fundamental principle of Keynesian or Kaleckian economics, accepted by Keynesians, circuitists and Neo-Kaleckians, is that expenditures create incomes, and not the other way around. Accordingly, changes in the profit share are the result of changes in expenditure with only marginal effects of inter-class debt relations, represented by changes in the relatively small element of net workers' saving. As a result, the focus on credit transfers and debt contracts between classes can reveal very little about debt structures as a whole, and the debt structures that brought about recent financial crises.

Riccardo Bellofiore sums us the argument in this section neatly in perceptive observations on Luxemburg and Kalecki:

[23] 'The debt-led consumption boom...in Greece, Ireland and Spain (led to)...negative financial balances (as a share of nominal GDP) of the private household sector and thus increasing private household debt...with the corporate sector being in surplus in all countries of this group except Spain' (Hein 'The Crisis of Finance-Dominated Capitalism in the Euro Area', 2012b). Much of the statistical evidence for rising household debt is the result of a hasty conclusion that household debt is workers' debt, whereas a significant share of household debt in most countries is the debt of unincorporated (small) businesses. See Steindl, 'The Role of Household Saving in the Modern Economy', 1982.

> ... expenditures within the capitalist firm sector are an internal family matter, and pose no problem at all. The same is true for the money wage bill: even though it flows from the capitalist class to the working class, if workers spend all their income, as Kalecki assumes in his first approximation, this initial finance goes safely back in its entirety to firms as a whole (the same would be true if all workers' savings went into the financial markets).[24]

This is correct. But the resulting circulation of money among firms is not 'an internal family matter' but depends on the market processes of commodity exchange, in which all classes participate, and the financial processes of the money and financial markets, in which the participation of firms and their bankers may influence the business investment that determines capitalist dynamics. The participation in those financial processes of worker and middle-class households may influence the prices of the assets that those households use as security for their borrowing. But their debts and the turnover of the financial portfolios can have little effect on capitalist dynamics as long as their margin of saving absorbs changes in their income to ensure that consumption is maintained at previous levels. Without fiscal intervention, the intra-capitalist circulation of money depends on capitalist expenditure.

8.4 Conclusion

Augusto Graziani was a pioneer in developing a theory of money in which banks create credit that is used in production. His starting point of capitalists without financial resources provides a poor foundation for corporate finance and leads the analysis into difficulties over the monetization of interest. Kalecki's analysis was more securely grounded in corporate finance and the theory of interest and may lead to a better circuit theory of money, in which the circulation of deposits among capitalists (as payment for investment goods and capitalists' consumption goods) is the monetary counterpart of capitalist profits.

This *intra-class* circulation of deposit money among capitalists is the key to economic dynamics, because the *inter-class* circulation of (deposit) money between workers and capitalists is simply the routine of workers' consumption. Financialization theorists, who follow Ricardian socialists in attributing poverty and unemployment in capitalism to deficient consumption by

[24] R. Bellofiore, 'Luxemburg and Kalecki', 2014, p. 98.

workers (low real wages), find the *inter-class* debt of workers to capitalists logically congenial to their outlook. But in a capitalist economy in which production is undertaken for profit, this inter-class debt is incidental (endogenous) to capitalist dynamics. Kalecki's monetary insight, that the intra-class circulation of money among capitalists is the key to the profitability of their undertakings, is more profound.

Kalecki's approach disposes of Graziani's paradox of the workers as creditors to the capitalist system, in favour of a much more plausible capitalist ownership of financial resources. It also resolves in a neat, even classical way, Graziani's difficulty over the payment of interest. Banks in Kalecki's analysis intermediate between capitalists, and only insignificantly between capitalists and workers. In this situation interest becomes a purely distributional variable. Capitalists that earn a surplus in the form of a bank deposit pay a portion of the surplus to other capitalists who are in credit with the banks. Capitalists therefore pay interest to themselves. The solution is classical, because Kalecki's view of interest is the same as Marx's view of the interest: a portion of the surplus that functioning capitalists pay to money capitalists or the redistribution of surplus among capitalists. But in Kalecki's case, the rate of profit overall is not reduced by the potential interest and debt payments that capitalists may make to each other via the banking system. The system of credit and debt in a capitalist economy is therefore a system for redistributing bank deposits, rather than reducing the profits of capitalists as a class. By contrast, Neo-Kaleckian financialization treats finance as gross interest and debt payments as deductions from net income, and hence as usury, rather than as a system for redistributing income within classes with only marginal shifts in net debt payments between the classes.

9

The Transfer Theory of Government Debt

What Keynes Learned from Kalecki

In 1944, the Oxford University Institute of Statistics published a book on *The Economics of Full Employment*. In the book was a paper by Kalecki called 'Three Ways to Full Employment', and a copy of the book was sent to Keynes. Keynes was impressed by Kalecki's proposal for financing full employment, where Kalecki put forward a transfer theory of debt. Keynes should not have found this quite so original because this way of analysing debt had been put forward in 1917 by Hartley Withers. Regarding debt as a transfer problem highlights the logical flaw in current thinking along lines of 'Ricardian Equivalence', confusing 'inside' or domestic debt with 'outside' debt. The transfer approach to debt also highlights the need for central open market operations to ensure the financial circulation of money.

This paper was originally written as its author's tribute to the work of Sheila Dow, an undogmatic Post-Keynesian and one of a handful of economists who understands banking because she does not cover up the gaps in her knowledge with 'assumptions'.

9.1 Financing Full Employment

In 1944, the Oxford Institute of Statistics prepared a set of studies, under the title *The Economics of Full Employment*. Michał Kalecki, at that time working in the Institute, contributed a chapter entitled 'Three Ways to Full Employment'. The three ways were deficit spending on public investment and social welfare, financed by borrowing, stimulating private investment, and by redistributing income from those on higher incomes to households on lower incomes.[1]

Kalecki reiterated his previous arguments that a fiscal deficit always finances itself, in the sense that the spending ensures that funds accrue in

[1] See Chapter 3 above.

Interest and Capital: The Monetary Economics of Michał Kalecki. Jan Toporowski, Oxford University Press.
© Jan Toporowski 2022. DOI: 10.1093/oso/9780198816232.003.0010

bank accounts, where they may be drawn upon to finance the government borrowing. The problem is merely an inter-temporal one of securing the funds for the government before they arrive in the bank accounts. But this is made easy by the fact that the capitalists who hold bank accounts have money in them in the first place. The rate of interest would not rise as long as the central bank expanded commercial banks reserves sufficiently to allow commercial banks to maintain their cash ratios. If the rate of interest on government bonds started to rise, then the government could always switch its financing to shorter term bills. In this way, as with the wartime fiscal deficit, the government borrowing could continue without affecting the rate of interest. Wage pressure on prices of consumer goods could be regulated by a combination of price controls, subsidies, and income tax. Concerns about the 'burden' of the National Debt could be met by servicing it from the proceeds of a capital levy, or a tax on profits with the amounts of fixed capital investment deducted from the profits liable to tax. This last Kalecki called a modified income tax that would have a neutral effect on output and employment.

The capital levy idea cannot have failed to appeal to John Maynard Keynes, working on government finances in the British Treasury. In the footsteps of David Ricardo, Joseph Schumpeter, John A. Hobson, and Otto Bauer, Keynes had been a long-standing advocate of a capital levy.[2]

Kalecki found the regulation of private investment to be the most problematic way of securing full employment. The optimal amount of such investment was the amount that would keep productive capacity growing with the level of consumption and total expenditure. However, investment is the least stable part of expenditure in an economy. It was therefore unlikely to be regulated by tax allowances, or the rate of interest, where the relevant long-term rate of interest is relatively stable, indicating only a very weak relationship between the central bank's rate of interest, which is short-term, and the level of private investment. Both tax allowances and cuts in the rate of interest would require cumulative reductions to maintain their effect so that, in time, a government would be unable to reduce interest rates or taxes any further. Another way may be to use public investment to augment and stimulate private investment. But such public investment depends on social need and, if that need is not there, it may be preferable to subsidize consumption with welfare payments. The problem with relying on private investment is that it also adds to

[2] '...the scientific, expedient...rational, the deliberate method' of financing government debt, Keynes, *A Tract on Monetary Reform*, 1923, p. 65. See also Balogh, 'The Unimportance of a Capital Levy', 1944. Despite its title, Balogh's article is in fact about the unimportance of *objections* to the capital levy from J. R. and Ursula Hicks, and Nicholas Kaldor.

productive capacity. Excess capacity emerges, because the rate of investment required to maintain full employment is less than that required to maintain full capacity utilization. In this situation excess capacity will tend to depress investment.

Relying on private investment to achieve full employment was, in Kalecki's view, a 'fundamental error'. 'The proper role of private investment is to provide tools for consumption goods, and not to provide enough work to employ all available labour...Both public and private investment should be carried out only to the extent to which they are considered useful. If the effective demand thus generated fails to provide full employment, the gap should be filled by increasing consumption [by subsidizing consumption and welfare payments] and not by piling up unwanted public or private capital equipment.'[3] There was moreover 'a technical but important disadvantage', relative to government expenditure, of using private investment to secure full employment. 'Government spending can never fail to achieve immediately the desired employment if it is on a sufficient scale, because it generates effective demand directly. The effects of stimuli to private investment depend, however, on the reaction of entrepreneurs, and it is quite possible that when they are in a very pessimistic mood they may not respond even to considerable inducements. This may happen, for instance, if they do not feel confidence in the political situation.' Private investment, therefore, cannot be regarded as a 'satisfactory' policy for achieving full employment.

The third way of achieving full employment is by redistributing income to achieve higher consumption by taxing higher incomes and subsidizing, with welfare payments, those on lower incomes. The tax on higher incomes would have to be 'modified' by allowing deductions for business investment, so that the redistribution does not adversely affect private investment. The redistribution would result in a more equal distribution of income after tax. Such redistribution was likely to meet with much stronger opposition than the policy of deficit financing. It may therefore be necessary to reinforce redistribution with deficit spending by the government.

Kalecki noted two further distributional aspects of full employment. Wage bargaining, he argued, would have a different role in a regime of full employment. With the economy operating at full capacity, maintaining demand at the level of the output of consumer goods may require taxation to be higher than planned for under a policy of fiscal stimulus. Prices could be kept constant by price controls. The other aspect concerned the distribution of income

[3] Kalecki, 'Three Ways to Full Employment', 1944/1990, pp. 52–3.

between profits and wages. Price controls would have the effect of redistributing income from profits to wages, by increasing real wages. Here too, price controls may need to be supplemented by increased taxation on higher incomes. This will also mean 'linking up trade union bargaining with general economic bargaining' over price controls.[4]

Kalecki concluded that the most reliable way of securing full employment was by a combination of deficit financing and redistribution through taxes, subsidies, price controls, and welfare payments. At the same time, it would be necessary to ensure that private investment provided sufficient capacity for demand, given full employment and labour productivity. Private investment could be encouraged by making fixed investment deductible against tax, or by replacing income tax by wealth taxes, which will have no effect on the profitability of investment. Such incentives to investment could be supplemented by public investment, for example, in slum clearance.[5]

Keynes, who had urged in his *General Theory* 'the socialisation of investment'[6] as a solution to the problem of unemployment, was impressed. He wrote to Kalecki to thank him for the book. 'Your own contribution seems to me most striking and original, particularly pages 44–6; also most beautifully compressed. It is a great comfort to read something so short and so much to the point. I am very much taken with your modified income-tax [i.e., the tax on profits]. It will be alleged, I am afraid, that the difficulties of transition would be excessive, since it would mean that a new business might have next to no tax to pay for years, which would appear to give it a great competitive advantage. Nevertheless, there is, I think, a good answer to this, and such criticisms, which would be certain to arise, would be based on a fallacy.'[7]

9.2 'Inside' and 'Outside' Debt

Pages 44–6 in Kalecki's essay were where Kalecki advanced the idea of the National Debt as not 'a burden to society as a whole because in essence it constitutes an internal transfer' and proposed a wealth tax, or a tax on profits from which investment could be deducted. Kalecki clearly had in mind debt issued in the domestic currency, in the fiscal jurisdiction of the government.

[4] Kalecki, 'Three Ways to Full Employment', 1944/1990, pp. 56–7.
[5] Kalecki, 'Three Ways to Full Employment', 1944/1990, pp. 57–8.
[6] Keynes, *General Theory*, 1936, p. 378.
[7] Letter of J. M. Keynes to M. Kalecki dated 30 December 1944 in Keynes *Collected Writings Volume XXVII*, 1980b, pp. 381–2.

Such *inside* debt needs to be distinguished from *outside* debt owed to residents in a foreign country.[8] The most salient difference between the two kinds of debt concerns their effect on the financial resources of a country. *Internal* debt conserves financial resources, because the counterpart of the government's liability is the asset held by residents who are owed money by the governments. Such government debt merely requires regular transfers of money from taxpayers to holders of government bonds in the form of interest and agreed repayments. By contrast, *external* debt drains the financial resources of the economy: these liabilities of a government are assets for foreign residents and interest and repayments are therefore transfers from tax-payers in the economy to residents outside the country.

The distinction between internal and external debt highlights the ingenuity of Keynes's and Kalecki's proposals for a capital levy to pay for the servicing of government debt. The National Debt, in Kalecki's approach, is a system for redistributing monetary resources from tax-payers in general to the smaller, wealthier group of government bond-holders (although today, in the twenty-first century, a significant proportion of governments bonds are held on behalf of the less wealthy in pension funds and insurance companies). Such transfers are in general regressive, because tax-payers in general have more modest incomes and wealth than bond-holders. However, a tax levied on capital wealth, or a wealth tax, to pay for servicing the government's debt, would reverse this regressive transfer, by making the transfer from wealthy tax-payers to wealthy bond-holders. Since the asset counterpart of government debt is wealth, a capital levy effectively mobilizes the monetary assets of the wealthy to pay interest to the wealthy and repay bonds held by them. Kalecki had already argued for that in his earlier paper on 'Political Aspects of Full Employment', pointing out an additional advantage of this financing, that it does not affect the incentive to invest.[9] Similarly the tax on profits, with deductions for investment, would not reduce the returns from investment. In an article he wrote at around the same time, Kalecki observed that

> ...it is possible to devise special taxes for financing the interest on National Debt that will render its increase harmless in the sense that it will have no repercussions on output and employment; that therefore it is not necessary to consider the reduction of the budget deficit as such to be an important problem of war finance; and that a regime under which budget deficits

[8] '...we need to understand...why Ricardian equivalence fails', Cecchetti, 'Comment', 2012, p. 135.
[9] Kalecki, 'Political Aspects of Full Employment', 1943/1990.

> would be used whenever necessary to maintain full employment does not involve insuperable difficulties.

After some calculations of interest on the debt, Kalecki went on 'It may be objected to this calculation that, since a large part of the National Debt is in the form of floating debt [or short term Treasury bills—JT] the future "burden" of it would be higher if the short-term rate of interest increased after the war.... To that it may be replied that the short-term rate of interest may be easily controlled by the Government in combination with the Bank of England. There is thus no reason to expect its rise in the future as compared to its present level.'[10]

Kalecki then considered the kind of financing that would be required to neutralize any effect that an increase in Government debt may have on economic activity. The ideal kind of financing was by means of a capital levy equal to the interest payable on the debt: '...a special annual tax on all private capital (inclusive, of course, of Government securities). A rise in the National Debt will increase the amount of the capital tax to be collected, but will at the same time increase the interest-yielding assets in private possession, which would not have come into existence if the budget had been balanced. The capitalists as a body gain by an increase in the National Debt as much in interest as they lose in capital tax...'

> ...The current income after payment of capital tax of some capitalists will be lower and of some higher than if the National debt had not increased, but their aggregate income will remain unaltered and their aggregate consumption will be not likely to change significantly. Further, the inducement to invest in fixed capital is not affected by a capital tax because it is paid on any type of wealth. Whether an amount is held in cash or Government securities or invested in building a factory, the same capital tax is paid on it and thus the comparative advantage is unchanged.[11]

Kalecki clearly had in mind a tax on *net* wealth, because he continued: '...if investment is financed by loans it is clearly not affected by a capital tax because it does not mean an increase in wealth of the investing entrepreneur. Thus neither capitalists' consumption nor investment is affected by the rise in the National Debt if the interest on it is financed by an annual capital tax.'

[10] Kalecki, 'The Burden of the National Debt', 1943a.
[11] Kalecki, 'The Burden of the National Debt', 1943a.

Kalecki went on to show that, with a very unequal distribution of income, with the majority of wealth-owners having only wealth in the form of their housing, there is only a marginal loss in tax revenue if smaller property holdings are exempted from the capital tax. He pointed out that allowing the capital tax to be deducted from income before payment of tax would still leave the tax from a given amount national income unchanged: a rise in the National Debt would still bring in to the government the same revenue in income tax, because the increase in the capital tax (due to the increase in National Debt) would be exactly the same as the increase in interest income of wealth-owners.[12]

This argument is no more obvious for being expressed so simply by Kalecki. A reader familiar with accounting conventions will immediately object that the rise in National Debt is not an increase in private wealth, because private wealth-holders have, in purchasing the newly-issued government bonds, handed over to the government bank deposits to the value of the increase in National Debt. This is so, of course, at the moment of issue. But if the government uses the bank deposits that it has received in payment for the bonds, or the bank deposits that the government receives in payment of wealth taxes, to pay interest to bond-holders, then the money returns into the possession of those bond-holders. If the government uses the bank deposits to pay for public administration, public services, welfare payments or public investment, the money likewise, if less directly, returns to wealth-owners.[13] Despite its temporary passage through the accounts of the government's finance ministry and its beneficiaries, who will spend their incomes buying goods and services from business, the money's ultimate destination remains the pockets of the wealthy who bought the bonds. After its circulation, capitalist money returns to its owner. In this sense it is truly capitalists' money (see Chapter 6 above). A capital levy to pay government debt abbreviates that circulation to ledger transfers between the government and the wealthy.

Kalecki then argued that, if it is not possible to introduce a wealth tax, much the same kind of financing, with similar distributional effects, could be obtained from an income tax levied on unearned income, or income from property. This would reduce the returns from investment in fixed capital. But this penalty would be removed if firms were allowed to deduct from their profits in a given period investments in that period. He concluded that '…to keep down the Budget deficit in war-time in order to reduce the increase in

[12] Kalecki, 'The Burden of the National Debt', 1943a.
[13] Kalecki, 'A Theory of Commodity, Income and Capital Taxation', 1937.

the National debt ceases to be the primary objective of war finance. And, if to maintain full employment in peace time requires budget deficits there is no reason to be scared by the rising National Debt.'[14]

9.3 The Withers Connection

Kalecki's analysis of internal government debt as a system of income transfers, rather than just deductions from income, should not have come as any surprise to Keynes. The analysis had been put forward 27 years earlier by the distinguished economic journalist and editor of *The Economist* magazine, Hartley Withers, in a set of lectures on 'Public Finance' that Withers gave at the London School of Economics during an earlier war, in February and March 1917. Withers had already distinguished himself as a monetary economist with his book *The Meaning of Money*, published in 1909. In this book, he first enunciated the principle that, in a credit economy, bank deposits come into banks through banks' loan advances, rather than through public deposits of money. According to Schumpeter, this 'was considered as a novel and somewhat heretical doctrine'.[15] But it found its way into Keynes's *Treatise on Money* and was espoused by his colleague at Cambridge, Dennis Robertson.[16]

Keynes was also impressed by Withers' 'masterly account of the English financial system' for the United States Senate Commission that, in 1911, was preparing the establishment of the US Federal Reserve.[17] But, apart from using this account of the British financial system, and *The Meaning of Money*, in his Cambridge lectures, there is no evidence that Keynes knew of Withers' lectures in public finance, which were published in 1917, under the title *Our Money and the State*. Indeed, with the exception of the chapter dealing with the National Debt, the book is rather conventional. But it is also singularly free of the hostility towards government expenditure and debt that one would expect of an economic journalist of his generation (Withers was born in 1867) and an editor of *The Economist*.

This absence of fiscal conservatism may have been Withers' patriotic contribution towards the financing of the First World War. But it was also rooted in an unusually comprehensive view of monetary circulation: Withers' clear

[14] Kalecki, 'The Burden of the National Debt', 1943a.

[15] Schumpeter, *History of Economic Analysis*, 1954, p. 1111.

[16] Keynes, *A Treatise on Money in 2 volumes, Volume I*, chapter 2; Robertson, *Banking Policy and the Price Level*, 1926.

[17] Keynes, *Collected Writings Volume XI*, 1983, p. 368.

recognition in the lectures that when the government taxes the population in order to finance its expenditure, it is creating income for the public. The government draws on the monetary resources of the subscribers to its bonds; returns that money to the public in the course of expenditure; draws on that money again in the form of taxation to pay the interest cost of the bonds; returns those taxes to the holders of the bonds in the form of interest on those bonds; before drawing on the monetary resources of the public through taxation again to repay the bonds, returning that money to the subscribers of the bond. In this way, 'the view that borrowing at home puts the burden [of current expenditure] on posterity is a delusion…whatever posterity pays, it pays to itself'.[18] In the case of government borrowing in the form of what were known as *consols* (or 'consolidated funds', which were perpetual bonds) payment continues indefinitely: 'the interest charge will continue to be a burden to the citizens as a whole and an income to the heirs of those who originally subscribed.'[19]

A consequence of this is that the national debt is not 'net wealth', that is the 'existence of a national debt, held by the citizens, does not affect the wealth of the nation as a whole. The wealth of a nation consists of its material assets in the way of industrial plant, agricultural estates and stock, houses, roads, railways, canals, and so on, and its holding, if any, of foreign investments, and its income consists of the annual produce of these material assets as organized and worked as a going concern by the nation's brains and sinews.'[20] However, the debt does involve a transfer of incomes. On the one hand 'the system has this advantage in a community in which wealth is unequally distributed, that it enables those who have a margin of income above the necessaries of life to pay for whatever be the object that the Government wants without at the time feeling any poorer, because they get a security that makes them think they are actually richer. If taxation is equitably imposed they will afterwards be taxed to pay themselves interest in proportion to the amount that they ought to have put into the loan when appealed to by the Government.' However, '…if those with a margin, who can save without serious discomfort, take up all or the greater part of the loan, and then taxes are imposed on all, whether they have a margin or no, then the system of financing Government spending by loan tends to accumulate more and more wealth in the hands of those who are well off'.[21]

[18] Withers, *Our Money and the State*, 1917, pp. 45 and 35.
[19] Withers, *Our Money and the State*, 1917, p. 40.
[20] Withers, *Our Money and the State*, 1917, p. 41.
[21] Withers, *Our Money and the State*, 1917, pp. 40–1.

Perhaps because of this income transfer from the general mass of tax-payers to the smaller minority of wealthy bond-holders, Withers did not recognize any reluctance in the financial markets or among the wealthy to lend money to the government. Implicit in his (and perhaps Kalecki's) argument is the notion that the regressive redistribution of income that is effected by government debt requires more progressive taxation. The logical conclusion of such reasoning is Kalecki's capital levy to pay the annual costs of servicing the government's debt: reducing the redistribution of income effected by government debt to a redistribution entirely within the class of the wealthy, that is, making the wealthy pay the cost of servicing the debt owed to the wealthy. Withers' analysis suggests why even the prospect of having to pay taxes may not deter the enthusiasm of the wealthy for more government bonds. If they recognize that their tax liability is increased by government debt, they will buy even more government bonds: Their tax liability will not increase, because their total wealth has not increased (they have merely swapped money for bonds), but their *after-tax* income will rise, providing the government bonds pay a sufficient interest margin over the rate of interest on bank deposits. (Withers here is taking the view that the money raised by the bonds is not returned to the wealthy when the government spends that money, whereas Kalecki knew that the money ends up through the market process with the wealthy.) The reaction against government borrowing was more likely from taxpayers rather than bond-holders: 'High taxes, due to a big debt charge produced by home borrowing, will only go out of one pocket into another, but the taxpayers will not all recognize this, and if they are not also debt-holders it will not console them if they do.'[22]

Withers concluded that it may be too easy for governments to finance expenditure by borrowing, and recommended as a progressive financing system that borrowing should only be undertaken where it was not possible to finance by means of taxation:

> A well-informed and benevolent despot, with a perfectly docile people, would see that if there is money in the country that he can get by borrowing he can also get it by taxing if he sets about it in the right way, and that by doing so he not only cheapens the war by reducing his subjects' demand for goods which competes with that of his War Minister, but also makes industrial recovery in peace more rapid and hearty, by the absence of after-war taxation. All the money that he wanted for war he would just take from his

[22] Withers, *Our Money and the State*, 1917, pp. 47–8.

people in taxes as the war went on, without going through the cumbrous process of borrowing it from them and afterwards taxing them to pay themselves back. But in order to do so he would have to be able to rely on a truly equitable system of taxation, which would curtail the power even of the richest to waste money on things that are not really needed at a time of national crisis, without taking food out of the mouths and clothes off the backs of those who are hungry and ill-clad.[23]

So far, Withers was lecturing/writing about 'internal' or domestic debt. His view of external debt was more critical. In his view, foreign borrowing wherever possible should be avoided because, in contrast to domestic borrowing, it drained financial resources, by redistributing income from domestic sources, via taxation, to foreign holders of government bonds. Borrowing abroad was only worthwhile if it promoted economic development:

Borrowing abroad, except for reproductive purposes such as railway building, is so evidently 'bad business' that it is only done by Governments of economically backward countries, or by Governments which are impelled into this course, against their will, by the force of circumstances, as happened to ours in the present war.[24]

9.4 Debt as Real or Monetary Claim?

An ambiguity remains in the Withers' exposition, as to whether government debt is a claim on *real* resources (a deduction from the real output of the economy) or merely a claim on the monetary resources of the economy. In some passages, he regarded debt charges as being claims on the money in the economy (e.g., the phrase above about 'high taxes, due to a big debt charge produced by home borrowing, will only go out of one pocket into another') while at the same time regarding it as a claim or the real output of the economy ('…debt-holders, without making any further effort, get for all time, as long as the loan is outstanding, a large slice of the nation's revenue, which has to be found out of its annual produce'.[25]

[23] Withers, *Our Money and the State*, 1917, pp. 48–9.
[24] Withers, *Our Money and the State*, 1917, p. 50.
[25] Withers, *Our Money and the State*, 1917, p. 42.

There is no doubt that 'external debt' that Withers warned against is a claim on real resources, in the sense that borrowing from abroad then requires income from abroad for servicing its interest and repayment. That income, as Withers pointed out, can only be obtained from: either investments abroad, e.g., using foreign borrowing to invest abroad, what might be called today a perfect 'hedge' for the borrowing, but of little economic use to a government or a country unless the foreign investment entails buying equipment from that country, as Withers noted; or by exporting goods and services abroad to generate the foreign currency to repay the foreign borrowing.

With internal debt, the situation is more complicated. Withers explained the sources of government debt finance as follows:

> When we subscribe to the loan we either do so out of money that we borrow...or by drawing down our bank balances, in which case, unless we have been stupid enough to keep unnecessarily big ones, we shall save to replenish them. If we save we have so much less to spend on our own comforts and amusements, or so much less to invest in other directions, from which we should have received interest and repayment that would not have come out of our pockets. So by subscribing we hand over our money...[26]

Here Withers reveals himself as one of Keynes's 'Neo-Classicals', that is someone who still believes that the financial system intermediates between 'saving' and investment (but who differ from the 'classicals', according to Keynes in believing that 'saving and investment can be actually unequal').[27] Withers also shows himself unaware, at this point, that the money which the government takes in exchange for the issue of bonds, is put back into circulation through government expenditure and, in Kalecki's analysis, ends up back in the pockets of the capitalists. So there is no reason to believe that the amount of money available to take up government bond sales is limited to saving out of current income.

But this is also the same Withers who had earlier argued that bank loans, rather than saving, create deposits and, in the following chapter of *Our Money and the State*, went on to argue for the quantity theory of money, that the price level in the economy is determined by the quantity of money because the velocity of circulation of that money may be taken to be constant.[28]

[26] Withers, *Our Money and the State*, 1917, p. 38.

[27] Keynes, *General Theory*, 1936, p. 177. To give Withers his due, at the time Withers was writing, Keynes himself was a 'Neo-Classical'.

[28] Withers, *Our Money and the State*, 1917, pp. 55–6.

Perhaps Schumpeter was right in paying him a double-edged compliment, describing the London *Economist* as being part of 'the most valuable part' of a 'vast literature' on credit and banking, despite it being 'written by...financial writers...who knew all about the facts, the techniques and the current practical problems of banking, but who cared little about "principles"—except that they never failed to refer to established slogans—and cannot be said to have had any very clear ideas about the institutional trends they beheld'.[29]

Despite his confusions over 'the established slogans' and the 'institutional trends' which he was observing, Withers was in advance of academic opinion in his time. The academic oracle of his time, in the discipline of economics, was Arthur Pigou, who in 1908 had succeeded Alfred Marshall as Professor of Political Economy at the University of Cambridge. In wartime and after, Pigou commented extensively on the financing needs of the First World War. A brief comparison of his war finance analysis with that of Withers shows how acute was the latter's understanding of financial circulation and how far ahead of its time.

Pigou's radicalism came in his advocacy of progressive taxation and paying off the national debt by means of a capital levy. However, he considered financing the war effort by borrowing in the conventional way in which it is still presented a century later, as a transfer of resources from future generations to the present generation. This was because those resources were real rather than financial and his chain of reasoning proceeded from entirely non-monetary and non-financial considerations of the marginal utility of income in different classes of income. Already before the war, he had argued for higher taxes on those receiving higher incomes because the marginal utility of money for a wealthy person is lower than it is for a person who is poor. Accordingly, total welfare in society may be increased by taxing the rich and transfer payments to the less well off.[30] During the First World War, he put forward this view as a reason for financing the war with higher taxes on the wealthy, rather than taxing articles of common consumption which would reduce the real incomes of the poor.[31] Since the cost of the war was clearly beyond the fiscal resources that could obtained through taxation, Pigou advocated borrowing to be paid off after the war by taxing wealth, or a capital

[29] Schumpeter, *History of Economic Analysis*, 1954, p. 1110. Schumpeter's view also applied to Withers' better-known predecessor at *The Economist*, Walter Bagehot.

[30] Pigou, *Wealth and Welfare*, 1912.

[31] Pigou, *The Economy and Finance of the War*, 1916.

levy. However, after the war, he came to the view that such a levy may discourage the business investment necessary for economic reconstruction.[32]

While considerations of real income are of course important for wage-earners, whose real incomes constitute the major share of aggregate demand, Pigou's analysis of war finance was limited by his confining the distributional effects of war finance to a 'real welfare' sphere of economic activity, separate from the monetary financial system. Withers provided more insight precisely because he kept war finance in the sphere of monetary and financial circulation. Kalecki's major contribution was to see that government expenditure that was not financed by taxation accrued to capitalists' profits accounts. Bond-financed expenditure is a way of turning over those financial resources in the real economy. Taxing this wealth makes that government expenditure much more financially sustainable than general taxation.

9.5 Conclusion

There is no evidence that Kalecki was aware of Withers' fiscal analysis. However, there are similarities in their common view of government debt as 'inside' debt, merely redistributing the monetary resources of society. What they both had in common was a background in business and financial journalism that gave the the two men a grounding in monetary and financial practice that few academic economists have today. Both of them recognized debt as being a way of accelerating the velocity of the financial circulation of money, even if Withers did not quite realize that this meant that debt was less of a claim on real resources.

For his part, Keynes was very aware of the transfer problem in international debt that, along with the gold standard, dominated international economic diplomacy in the inter-war period.[33] However, he appears not to have considered domestic debt in the same light. This is a pity, because the transfer theory of debt points to a 'pure monetary' theory of interest, in which interest is the relative price of different kinds of financing, the *slope* of the yield curve, as opposed to the level of the curve at some standard maturity, reflecting the different liquidity of the various kinds of financing according to their maturity. This was what Keynes was working towards in his 1937 controversy over

[32] Arthmar and McLure, 'Pigou on War Finance and Welfare', 2017.
[33] Keynes, *Collected Writings Volume XVIII*, 1978.

the rate of interest.[34] As argued above in Chapter 7, this approach to the theory of interest is in contrast to the classical theory of interest that links interest to the rate of profit.

The difference between the classical and the transfer approach is essentially about where the money comes from to pay interest and repay loans. In the transfer approach, the money to pay interest and repay loans comes from existing money hoards: In the case of government debt, taxpayers run down their money hoards to pay the government, which in turn returns the money to holders of government bonds. The amount of money held by 'the public' has not changed; it has simply been redistributed or transferred from the pockets or (as Keynes and Kalecki would have it) the portfolios of taxpayers to the pockets or portfolios of bond-holders. By contrast, in the classical theory, the public are deemed not to hold money, but have to sell commodities in order to raise the money to pay the taxes. But even in that situation, the money raised returns to holders of government bonds. Interest here is, in effect, a Ricardian rent that comes out of the surplus currently generated from production. In Withers' words, writing as 'classical' who appears to have what he had written a few pages earlier, '...the interest we shall have to provide out of our annual production of goods and services...we shall have to work harder to provide for our own wants'.[35]

Would the classical theory still apply if the money holdings of tax-payers were insufficient to pay the taxes required to defray the interest and repayment costs of government debt? To some degree the classical theory would hold. But then a market would have to be found with the monetary resources to buy the commodities being sold to pay taxes. This may be the case if taxpayers (including firms and banks) do not have the liquid assets necessary to pay their taxes. However, in the case of wealthy individuals and institutions this is not the case. In this situation the commercial banking system and the central bank have a very specific function in maintaining the liquidity of the assets portfolios of the wealthy: the commercial banks by creating bank deposits through lending against the security of other assets in those portfolios; and the central bank by buying in securities in exchange for the reserves that the commercial banks may need to support their lending.[36]

The transfer approach to government debt shows that its sustainability is reinforced by a progressive tax system that levies the taxes necessary for the

[34] Keynes, *Collected Writings Volume XIV*, 1973, pp. 201–33.

[35] Withers, *Our Money and the State*, 1917, p. 51.

[36] '...a credit deadlock which is impervious to cheap money may (thus) yield to treatment through open market purchases of securities' by the central bank. Hawtrey, *A Century of Bank* Rate, 1938, p. 256.

servicing of government debt on wealthy individuals, firms and financial institutions. The more progressive is the tax system, the less is the drain of government debt on current income. The banking system plays its part in advancing credit to maintain the monetary hoards that are transferred in the process of debt payments and creating, through securitization and buying government debt, the debt securities that the central bank can buy in maintain the liquidity of banks. In this respect financialization is good.

The transfer approach to debt also brings clarity where the discussion on government debt confuses 'inside' debt, where debt is simply a commitment to transfer money in the future from taxpayers to bondholders, with 'outside' debt, which drains monetary and financial resources, output and income. Under the gold standard, such confusion was to some degree understandable, because the gold for debt repayments had either to be mined at some cost, or imported in exchange for exports. In this situation, it was easy to mistake what, for an individual, may be 'outside' debt but which, for an economy as a whole, is merely a transfer of existing monetary resources. Certainly the transfer approach reveals the logical inconsistency in Robert Barro's doctrine of 'Ricardian Equivalence', in which government debt is assumed only to effect transfers from future generations to current generations, rather than 'from posterity to posterity' (as Withers put it).[37]

A similarly 'outside debt' approach is taken Luigi Pasinetti in two influential papers, in which he put forward an equality between the rate of growth of the economy and the rate of interest as the threshold between debt rising in relation to GDP (if the economic growth rate is below the rate of interest), or falling debt (if the economic growth rate exceeds the rate of interest).[38] Within the Ricardian model of production and distribution in which Pasinetti works, all debt is of course 'outside' debt. But this is not the case in the real world. Inside debt operates much more, as Thomas Piketty has argued, to concentrate wealth, although this happens irrespective of whether or not the rate of interest is greater or less than the rate of growth, and is more related to the incidence of taxation or private debt.[39]

The transfer approach not only reveals the confusion over 'inside' and 'outside' debt. The approach also has important implications for the theory of money. A staple of Post-Keynesian monetary theory is that money is held

[37] Barro, 'Are Government Bonds Net Wealth', 1974.

[38] Pasinetti, 'The Social Burden of High Interest Rates', 1997; Pasinetti, 'The Myth of Folly of the 3% Deficit/GDP Maastricht Parameter', 1998. See also Halevi, 'Luigi Pasinetti and the Political Economy of Growth and Distribution', 2016.

[39] Piketty, *Capital in the Twenty-First Century*, 2013.

because of uncertainty, and finance exists because money is being held. The transfer approach to government debt shows that, in our credit society with central banking regulating liquidity, monetary accumulations are held because payments need to be made on debt, and uncertainty arises over the returns from debt, as opposed to money, because the returns from debt depend on particular (financial) circulations of money. In these circumstances, money is held because of finance, and uncertainty arises because of money.

PART III

THE SCOPE AND FUNCTIONS OF CENTRAL BANKING

As argued in the previous two parts of this book, Kalecki was sceptical of the influence of central banking over the business cycle, because he regarded the cycle as essentially determined in the first instance by business investment; in the second instance by the fiscal policy of the government. Even inflation, which economists have traditionally viewed within the scope of monetary policy, because it affects 'the value of money', Kalecki regarded as being due to 'real' factors, such as resource or capacity constraints, or institutional factors, such as the class struggle that affects the wage rate. The only monetary influence on inflation was the exchange rate. Inflation only became a 'monetary phenomenon' in a situation of hyperinflation. But even here the 'money supply' was deemed to come from credit expansion by commercial banks, or through the deficit financing of the government. Central banks, in his view, could affect the reserve position of commercial banks and this would affect interest rates. But the reserve position of the non-financial businesses that undertake actual (real) investment is more important in determining how much of that investment may be undertaken without financial risk.

Kalecki rejected Wicksellianism, or the doctrine that there is a reliable relationship between investment and the rate of interest. The more important factor was liquidity. This improves spontaneously in a boom when capital is turned over more rapidly (the velocity of circulation of money rises). But in a recession, when the turnover of capital declines (Keynes's 'liquidity preference' increases), there is a crucial role for central in assuring the liquidity of banking and financial markets, so that the government and business are not hampered in the financial operations that they require for public and private sector expenditure. This part examines how central banks maintain the liquidity of banking and financial markets.

Chapter 10 on 'Central Bank Open Market Operations' explains how central banks can manage the liquidity of banks and financial markets. Chapter 11 on 'The Structure of Central Bank Operations' examines how those operations are essentially determined by the structure of the financial system in which they are conducted. The logical consequence of this structural dependence is that monetary policy comes to be determined by conditions in the financial system, rather than by conditions in the economy outside the financial system, or how the central bank would like to see that economy evolving. This is explained in the 12th, concluding chapter of this book.

10
Central Bank Open Market Operations

At the start of the twenty-first century, central banks were organized around committees that set official (short-term) interest rates. The theoretical rationale for this was a Neo-Wicksellian doctrine that the rate of growth and inflation is determined by the difference between money market rates of interest and the 'natural' or 'equilibrium' rate of interest, which is supposed to be the marginal return on capital, or the return on business investment. If the money market rate is higher than the 'natural' rate, firms will not invest, the economy will fall into recession, and the rate of inflation will fall. If the money market rate was lower than the 'natural' rate, then business investment would cause the economy to grow and inflation to rise. The Neo-Wicksellian doctrine was enunciated most commonly as a monetary policy framework of 'inflation-targeting'. Because the 'natural' rate of interest cannot actually be observed (it is a hypothetical return at any one time that will immediately change with any change in economic circumstances), an econometrically constructed, 'synthetic', natural rate could be constructed, as that rate of interest that will secure a given target rate of inflation. This then became the 'natural' or 'equilibrium' rate of interest. Central banks could then vary their official rates of interest from this equilibrium rate in order to keep the rate of inflation on target.

This concentration on trying to effect economic outcomes by manipulating the rate of interest, as a key price in the overall system of prices, was at the expense of central bank open market operations. These operations had been critical when monetary policy was guided by monetarist principles that emphasized (actually exaggerated) the ability of the central bank to influence economic outcomes by manipulating the amount of reserves in the banking system. When monetarism failed to work, in the 1980s, because it proved impossible to control credit in this way, and inflation fell despite rising bank reserves, monetary policy moved towards using an official rate of interest to control inflation, effectively abandoning open market operations.

Open market operations are the buying and selling of securities, foreign currency, or financial instruments, by the central bank. They are called open market operations because they are usually conducted by the central bank's trading desk placing orders to buy or sell in markets for those securities,

Interest and Capital: The Monetary Economics of Michał Kalecki. Jan Toporowski, Oxford University Press.
© Jan Toporowski 2022. DOI: 10.1093/oso/9780198816232.003.0011

foreign currency, or financial instruments. These operations are undertaken on the initiative of the central bank. This distinguishes open market operations from discount operations, undertaken on the initiative of commercial banks that sell securities to the central bank in order to obtain reserves to give themselves a more liquid asset portfolio.[1]

Open market operations are one of the ways in which central banks make their policy effective, whether that policy is to control the level of reserves or credit in the economy, or the rates of interest at which commercial banks lend or take deposits. Historically, as indicated below, open market operations have been used when other instruments such as changes in the rate of interest have failed. However, their potential tends to be underestimated, perhaps because the effects of such operations depend on the complexity of the financial system in which those operations are conducted.

10.1 History

It is common to date the start of open market operations to an almost accidental discovery by the US Federal Reserve in 1922. The Federal Reserve had been active in supporting member banks with extensive loans during the First World War to commercial banks, whose cash ratios had fallen because the issue of banknotes had not kept up with inflation and the high level of economic activity. The loans proved to be a profitable part of Federal Reserve banks' balance sheets as the Federal Reserve increased its discount rate on cessation of hostilities, when the wartime ban on gold exports was removed. However, by 1921, the United States was in severe depression, which discouraged lending (and borrowing) at a time when America's trading partners were experiencing similar difficulties, complicated by hyperinflation and the trading of their currencies below their parities with gold, in which most of their wartime debts were denominated. In this situation, American exporters and bankers required foreign payments in gold or the few currencies (such as the Swiss Franc) that remained on the gold standard. An inflow of gold into the United States allowed US banks, in particular the New York commercial banks, to repay their loans from the Federal Reserve. The Federal Reserve Discount Rate had peaked in 1922 at 7 per cent (a rate last seen in the crisis of 1907, that precipitated the establishment of the Federal Reserve in 1913 with

[1] See Toporowski, 'Open Market Operations: Beyond the New Consensus', 2006.

a mandate to provide an elastic currency) after which it was rapidly and significantly reduced to 4.5 per cent.[2]

Faced with a squeeze on the Fed's interest income, as its loan portfolio contracted, the Reserve banks decided to diversify their portfolios by buying government securities. Repayments of Fed loans increased. It was the newly-established Statistics Department of the New York Fed that alerted the Federal Reserve to the fact that member banks were repaying their loans from the Fed with the reserves that they were receiving in payment for the government bonds that the Fed was buying. Significantly, too, loan repayments were not concentrated in the regions where the local Federal Reserve was buying government bonds, but were geographically dispersed, so that bond-buying in Kansas City might give rise to loan repayments in Chicago or New York. The conclusion was drawn that buying of government bonds affected the credit system in the whole country, rather than just the local market in which the buying was taking place. In other words, that open market operations had *systemic* effects.[3]

The result of this discovery was a decision by the Governors of the Federal Reserve in March 1923 to establish the Open Market Committee of five Governors as a Committee of the Federal Reserve Board. Open market purchases of securities in 1927 had the desired effect of bring an inflow of gold into the United States.[4] The regional Federal Reserve Banks resisted central control of their respective securities purchases and sales and arguments over their powers to determine the assets in their balance sheets continued through until 1935, when the Banking Act effectively abolished the separate portfolios of the individual Federal Reserve Banks. Furthermore, while the open market purchases had little effect on the total reserve position of the member banks of the Federal Reserve system, they did cause interest rates in the inter-bank market to fall. Similarly, sales of securities would tend to raise interest rates: '...the Reserve System almost got into the habit of bringing about desired changes in interest rates by open market operations – a sale of securities for raising rates, and a purchase of securities for lowering rates. The official Discount and Acceptance Rates would then be moved to match (and consolidate) the movement of interest rates.'[5]

The Federal Reserve's 'accidental' discovery of open market operations was perhaps learning by what was then the youngest of key central banks in the

[2] Hawtrey, *Monetary Reconstruction*, 1926, chapter V.
[3] Burgess, 'Reflections on the Early Development of Open Market Policy', 1964.
[4] Hawtrey, *The Art of Central Banking*, 1933, pp. 289–90.
[5] Sayers, *The American Banking System*, 1948, p. 73.

international monetary system. The older central banks, with experience of the gold standard going back to its establishment in the middle of the nineteenth century, had been trading in securities, if not operating explicit open market operations for many decades, if not centuries, before the American discovery. Hawtrey noted that, before the abolition of the Usury Laws in 1833, '…when the Bank of England was experimenting in the control of credit, but discount policy was still shackled by the usury laws limiting interest 5 per cent, the Bank's chief reliance was on the purchase and sale of securities in the market'.[6]

Indeed, the Bank of England, as other central banks before the twentieth century, had been established explicitly to assist with funding the British Government, with the privilege of issuing banknotes against the government bonds that they held. Needless to say, these responsibilities entailed transactions in the securities held in the Bank portfolio. In his impertinent *Proposals for an Economical and Secure Currency* of 1816, David Ricardo had noted that, on the 5 January 1797, the Bank of England held bonds ('funds yielding interest') to the value of just over £15 million. In the following year, this had increased to £18,951,514. By 1799, the amount of these bonds had increased to £21,912,683. In the following year, the bonds had been reduced slightly to £20,883,128, before rising again in 1801 to £22,522,709 and, in 1802 to £24,319,247 and so on. This therefore constituted a substantial portion of the Bank's portfolio, and its profits were augmented by the sums that the Bank was paid for managing the debt of the British, Irish, German, and Portuguese governments.

Once the Usury Laws were abolished, exaggerated powers of economic and financial control were attributed to changes in the rate of interest. However, the rate of interest proved to be a not always helpful or effective instrument of monetary control, and least so when the ruling policy doctrine that emerged in the nineteenth century required a quantitative, rather than price, restriction on the banknote issue to the amount of gold reserves available to back that issue. The currency theorists who proved, initially at least, to be most influential, were of the opinion that the rate of interest would be sufficient to sustain that gold link, through some kind of an international specie-flow adjustment in response to interest rate differentials. But this was confused with arguments over the supposed role of the rate of interest in determining the equilibrium between saving and investment.[7]

[6] Hawtrey, *Monetary Reconstruction*, 1926, p. 142.

[7] Corry, *Money, Saving and Investment in English Economics 1800*–1850, 1962; Hawtrey, *The Art of Central Banking*, 1933, p. 136.

The result was the Bank Charter Act of 1844, which gave the Bank of England the monopoly of the note issue in England and Wales, but tied that note issue now to gold reserves. The Act was a watershed in the practice of central banks and was widely discussed and emulated as the gold standard emerged to become the mechanism for international banking transactions. Its significance for open market operations lay in the effective abandonment of trading in securities in order to provide liquidity for markets in longer-term securities. With the discount rate proving to be sluggish in effecting the inflow of gold reserves, open market operations were subordinated to the task of controlling the note issue. By then, in any case, the Bank of England was operating in the discount market, trading securities with much shorter-term maturities.

The discount market was, until recent times, the effective money market in London. This reflected not only the way in which banking developed in Britain, with country banks managing their cash positions by discounting their bill holdings with the London discount houses. The discount houses themselves would, in times of cash shortage, turn to the Bank of England to discount trade bills and Exchequer or Treasury bills. The practice had been established at the end of the eighteenth century that the Bank of England would discount such bills. But the Bank's ability to make a market in them was constrained at the time by the usury laws (limiting interest to a maximum of 5 per cent). After the abolition of those laws, the Bank's operations were limited by the need to keep its note issue within the bounds of its gold reserves and the fiduciary issue, and Bank Rate, the rate of discount on Treasury bills became its main policy instrument. The Bank would therefore alleviate modest cash shortages on a routine basis unless an obvious and compelling payments emergency arose in the discount market.[8] Open market operations were restricted because Bank Rate seemed to offer an effective instrument of monetary control.

But Bank Rate made better press headlines than it delivered in practice and open market operations were brought back as it gradually became standard practice for central banks to buy securities in order to alleviate the effects on commercial banks, or discount houses in London, of an outflow of gold. Walter Bagehot in his classic *Lombard Street*, published in 1873, had noted the Bank of England's practice of buying securities in a 'panic' to alleviate cash shortages among banks and merchants, and famously encouraged this operation.[9] The preferred securities tended to be short-term, for the simple

[8] Hawtrey, *The Art of Central Banking*, 1933, pp. 117–22.
[9] Bagehot, *Lombard Street*, 1873, p. 52.

reason that they were less subject to fluctuations in their price. By the end of the nineteenth century, open market operations had become a way of enforcing the Bank's policy rate of interest, the Bank Rate. Selling securities was referred to as 'making Bank Rate effective', at a time when the inter-bank market of the commercial banks operated using Treasury Bills. Keeping the money markets 'short' of liquidity obliged commercial banks to sell securities to the Bank. In this way, open market operations came to be not so much an alternative to interest rate policy as much as a necessary supplement to such policy.[10]

By the twentieth century, central banks in Europe used open market operations to off-set such outflows or even just to bring market rates of interest back to the central bank's official or preferred rate.[11] In the 1930s, after the abandonment of the gold standard, when reduced interest rates failed to stimulate an economic period it became common to blame the burden of debt for this failure in monetary policy. Ralph Hawtrey called it 'credit deadlock', or what Irving Fisher called 'debt deflation', a situation in which economic activity is frustrated by excessive debt which makes firms unwilling to borrow even at low interest rates. Hawtrey then recommended that 'a credit deadlock which is impervious to cheap money may (thus) yield to treatment through open market purchases of securities' by the central bank. Such operations would make banks more liquid and therefore more inclined to lend.[12] But, as noted above, it is the liquidity of entrepreneurs, rather than the liquidity of banks, that is crucial for financing enterprise. Richard Sayers was later to note that, in the United States, '...In the years 1930–1933, the Reserve Banks pushed their open market purchases far beyond the point of off-setting gold losses and creating a marginal surplus of funds which would cause open-market rates to fall away. At a time when there were large gold imports, the system actually added some two thousand million dollars to its security portfolio.' As a result '...member banks acquired enormous excess reserves...they were unable to extend their assets appreciably (indeed the outlet for ordinary business loans seemed to be diminishing) and the excess reserves position lasted through the remaining years of peace.'[13]

[10] Sayers, *Central Banking after Bagehot* 1957, pp. 49–52; Sayers *Bank of England Operations 1890–1914*, 1936. Hicks suggested that the Bank of England exceeded its official mandate in this regard (Hicks, 'Monetary Theory and History – An Attempt at Perspective', 1967, p. 168).

[11] Hawtrey, *Currency and Credit*, 1934, pp. 55–6. See also Sayers, *Central Banking after Bagehot* 1957, chapter 5.

[12] Hawtrey, *A Century of Bank Rate*, 1938, p. 256. See also Sandilands, 'Hawtreyan "Credit Deadlock" or "Keynesian Liquidity Trap"?', 2010.

[13] Sayers, *The American Banking System*, 1948, pp. 74–8.

The scope and scale of the operations varied between countries according to custom, the structure of banking markets, and statutes of the central bank. The Banque de France, for example, was not allowed until 1938 to use open market operations to control credit, but could use them for 'smooth out' the flow of reserves to banks.[14] Similarly, the central bank of the Netherlands, De Nederlandsche Bank, was restricted in its open market operations until 1937, and subsequently by a shortage of Treasury bills. Nevertheless, according to one authority, the Bank was responsible for one major innovation that was to have a lasting effect on later open market operations, the repurchase agreement, first used by De Nederlandsche Bank in December 1956,[15] although this priority is disputed.[16]

The history of open market operations confirms their use usually as an alternative to interest rate policy, when that policy cannot be used, and as a supplement to such policy when it appears to be ineffective, as hinted at by Hawtrey. Thus, in the two and a half decades or so following the Second World War, when interest rates were controlled by central governments rather than central banks, open market operations were extensively used by central banks for the purposes of credit control, and to control exchange rates (through open market operations in foreign currency). This was noted by the British Radcliffe Committee on the Working of the Monetary System. In his evidence to the Committee, Richard Kahn urged the purchase and sale of securities of short- and long-term securities in order to control the whole yield curve, rather than just the money supply, or the short-term rate of interest.[17]

The emergence of the Euro-markets of unregulated transactions in credit and foreign currency in the 1960s, made control of credit and exchange rates increasingly difficult, as well as casting doubt on the wisdom and usefulness of open market operations whose effects beyond the immediate counterparties of transactions were becoming less and less predictable. This was the background to the publication by the Bank of England of *Competition and Credit Control* that recommended a move towards the use of market mechanisms including more targeted open market operations.[18] The discussion

[14] Wilson, 'France', 1962a, pp. 48–51. [15] Wilson, 'The Netherlands', 1962b, p. 227.

[16] In his *Treatise on Money* Keynes noted that, before the First World War, '"open market policy" in the modern sense was virtually unknown. The Bank of England would occasionally supplement its bank-rate policy by the sale of consols for "cash" and their simultaneous repurchase for "the account" (anything up to a month later) which was an indirect way of relieving the money market of the equivalent quantity of resources for the unexpired period of the stock exchange account' (1930/1971b, pp. 204–5).

[17] Kahn, 'Memorandum of Evidence Submitted to the Radcliffe Committee', 1972.

[18] Bank of England *Competition and Credit Control*, 1971; Goodhart, 'Competition and Credit Control', 2014.

was the prelude to a period of banking and financial crisis in which, as with the recent crisis, central bank activity was concentrated on securing financial stability.

By the 1980s, monetarist theory provided the ruling doctrine of central bank operations. In the view of the theory's chief exponent at the time, Milton Friedman, open market operations had a special place in the control of the money supply: the sale of securities reduced commercial bank reserves and a stable credit multiplier ensured that the total amount of credit in the economy would be set by the amount of those reserves. The sale of securities to a commercial bank would be paid for by a transfer from that bank's reserve account at the central bank to the central bank, which would then cancel those reserves. The purchase of securities would be paid for by the creation of reserves that are credited to the reserve account of the commercial bank that sells those securities. The effect on commercial bank reserves is the same, whether the central bank buys from a commercial bank or from a customer of a commercial bank. In the latter case, the purchase price is credited to the commercial bank's reserve account at the central bank, and the commercial bank credit the same amount to its customer's account. In the case of a sale, the customer's account is debited with the amount that the commercial bank transfers from its reserves to the central bank. For Milton Friedman, open market operations were the way to regulate the money supply.[19]

The classic statement of monetarist central bank practice, Goodfriend and King urged that open market operations be used to supply reserves to the banking system, which could then allocate those reserves through the money market. If discount window assistance is provided, it should be sterilized, that is the central bank should sell in the open market the assets that it had bought through the discount window. In this way the overall reserve position of the banking system is kept constant, and the central bank in effect sells assets on behalf of the distressed bank. However, this procedure is considered to be inferior because it requires the central bank to monitor and supervise the bank to which assistance is being provided. Goodfriend and King contrast this 'monetary policy' with 'banking' by which unsterilized assistance is provided.[20]

Open market operations therefore reached a peak when central banks adhering to this reserve position doctrine sold securities in an attempt to

[19] Friedman, *A Program for Monetary Stability*, 1959. See also Bank of England, 'The Bank of England's Operational Procedures for Meeting Monetary Objectives', 1983.

[20] Goodfriend and King, 'Financial Deregulation, Monetary Policy, and Central Banking', 1988. For a later view, see Goodfriend, 'The Phases of US Monetary Policy 1987–2003', 2003.

regulate the level of reserves in the banking system.[21] A brief period of exchange rate targeting between 1986 and 1991, following the Plaza Accord of 1986, was marked by a reversion of open market operations to transactions in foreign currencies.

Since the 1990s, the policy doctrine directing central bank operations has centred upon the central bank's policy rate of interest as the key instrument of monetary policy. Initially it was felt that this needed to be reinforced by open market operations to ensure that the supply of reserves met demand in the money market at an equilibrium rate of interest that was the central bank's preferred rate. However, it was quickly realized that the official rate could be enforced more effectively simply by maintaining a narrow enough 'corridor' between the deposit and lending rates for reserves at the central bank. In the practice of the European Central Bank this was done through 'standing facilities' for commercial banks to deposit and borrow reserves with the central bank at its official rates. These facilities allow commercial banks to borrow reserves from the central bank, or to place excess reserves on deposit at the central banks. Standing facilities are a way in which commercial banks can influence *at their discretion* the balance sheet of the central bank, since decisions to use standing facilities are made by commercial banks, rather than a central bank.

By the early years of the twenty-first century, open market operations for the purposes of enforcing the policy rate of interest had been virtually abandoned by central banks. The notable exception of Japan, where the Bank of Japan has been buying securities since the turn of the century in a desperate effort to stave off deflation,[22] and the developing countries, where open market operations in convertible currencies are used to stabilize exchange rates that have a large influence on the domestic price level.[23]

10.2 Open Market Operations Today

In conducting open market operations it is sometimes useful to distinguish between 'outright' purchases and sales of securities, and 'reverse' purchases, or 'repos' or reverse sale agreements with participants in the money market.

[21] Bindseil, 'The Operational Target of Monetary Policy and the Rise and Fall of the Reserve Position Doctrine', 2004a. See also Goodhart, *Money, Information and Uncertainty*, 1975, pp. 156–60.

[22] See Stenfors and Toporowski, *Unconventional Monetary Policy and Financial Stability*, 2020 and Doi, Ihori, and Mitsui, 'Sustainability, Inflation and Public Debt Policy in Japan', 2007.

[23] See Levy-Orlik and Toporowski, 'Open Market Operations in Emerging Markets', 2007.

A reverse purchase agreement, for example, involves the purchase of risk-free longer-term securities, for example government bonds, for which payment is added to the reserves held at the central bank of the counterparty bank. The agreement then specifies the sale of those securities back to the counterparty bank after a certain period. In the European Central Bank's practice this was initially two weeks, but is now one week. The difference between the purchase and sale price is in effect the rate of interest on the temporary addition to its reserves that the counterparty bank now obtains. This rate of interest on repurchase agreements ('repos') became the official rate of the European Central Bank, the Bank of England and most European central banks during the 1990s. These open market operations may be repurchase agreements, providing reserves to counterparty banks, or they may be reverse sale agreements, reducing the reserves of banks.[24]

For central banks, repurchase agreements have the attraction that reserves supplied are not supplied as loans to counterparty banks but are exchanged for top quality assets from banks' portfolios. Their other attraction is that they allow central banks to inject (or withdraw) reserves over a fixed time horizon. This temporary accommodation offers central banks a way of acceding to any current requirement for reserves from commercial banks, without commitment to provide such reserves in the future. Such a commitment to provide all necessary reserves in the future is considered to remove the incentive to sound bank management that a reserve system is supposed to provide. According to the Bank of England '...an efficient, safe and flexible framework for banking system liquidity management...should retain incentives for banks to manage their own liquidity actively and prudently'.[25]

Once repurchase agreements are in operation, then obviously their effect on the money markets is the net outstanding amount at any one time. So if there are weekly repurchase agreements, the central bank's manager responsible for money market operations decides, when the agreements expire, whether to renew them, or increase or decrease their amount. An increase in the amount of purchase agreements (or decrease in sales agreements) would supply additional reserves. A decrease in purchase agreements outstanding (or increase in sales agreements) would reduce bank reserves.

The other kind of open market operations are the outright purchases and sales of securities without commitment to sell or buy back the securities

[24] There is an excellent guide in Osiński and Sławiński, *National Bank of Poland and Open Market Operations*, 1995.

[25] Bank of England, 'Reform of the Bank of England's Operations in the Sterling Money Markets', 2004, p. 218.

bought or sold. These are longer-term portfolio operations of central banks, and may include central bank issues of their own paper, for example, the short-term Euro notes that are issued by the Bank of England.

Outright purchases and sales of securities or foreign currency are undertaken with a view to changing the asset portfolio of the central bank, and hence providing reserves to the banking system, or reducing those reserves until such time as the central bank wishes to change its reserve provision. Reverse purchases ('repos') (or sales) involve entering simultaneously into an agreement with the selling (buying) bank to sell (or buy) back the securities at a fixed later date. Repos therefore provide (or reduce) reserves by a fixed amount for a fixed period of time. The price difference between the purchase and resale of the securities therefore constitutes the discount equivalent to the rate of interest on the reserves sold (or bought). Repos thus allow central banks to fix the period of time for which the reserves are provided.[26]

From the 1990s onwards, the Bank of England and subsequently the European Central Bank have used the repo rate as their policy rate, in the belief that this facilitated control over the rates of interest in the inter-bank market, without significantly affecting the liquidity of the markets in the longer-term securities that were the subject of these operations.[27] However, the response of central banks to the banking and financial crisis in 2008 was a dramatic switch to outright purchases, targeted in large measure at improving the liquidity of markets for long-term securities. As repo rates approached zero without significant effect in reversing the onset of deflation, the US Federal Reserve, the Bank of England, and on a more modest scale the European Central Bank, bought large quantities of securities at or near the bottom of the market. This has allowed the central banks to earn capital gains as the market recovered due to their injection of liquidity.[28] But central banks operate with thin capital so that these operations have left central bank balance sheets looking remarkably similar to those of hedge funds. Between 2007 and 2015, the balance sheet of the Federal Reserve expanded by a factor of five to nearly a quarter of US GDP. By comparison, the European Central Bank's assets have increased by around 50 per cent, the assets of the Bank of Japan have increased from 20 per cent of Japanese GDP to nearly 60 per cent of GDP. Perhaps most extraordinary among European central banks, the assets of the Swiss National Bank, which had committed itself to a fixed

[26] Bindseil and Würz, 'Open Market Operations', 2007.
[27] Toporowski, 'Open Market Operations', 2006.
[28] Fawley and Neely, 'Four Stories of Quantitative Easing', 2013; Bank of England, *The Bank of England's Sterling Monetary Framework*, 2015.

exchange rate against the Euro, rose from 17 per cent of Swiss GDP in 2007 to nearly 80 per cent of Swiss GDP before it abandoned the peg against the Euro in January 2015.

10.3 Conclusion

Following the financial crisis, central banks were forced to resume responsibility for the liquidity of the financial system. This meant a revival of open market operations. But for all their success in renewing liquidity in banking and capital markets, these 'extraordinary measures' of central banks have failed to revive economies. The conventional wisdom among central bankers is that this failure is because of a breakdown in the 'monetary transmission mechanism' that is supposed to go from central bank rates of interest, through money market rates of interest, to asset prices and expectations and, eventually to the saving and investment decisions that are assumed to be influenced by these short-term rates of interest. This conventional wisdom could be maintained in the early years after the financial crisis, when it was obvious that the money markets had been devastated by the collapse of banks like Lehman Brothers in the United States, or Northern Rock and the Royal Bank of Scotland in the UK. But after a decade of making the markets liquid through repeated buying of long-term securities, it is clear that something else is wrong. And that something else lies in corporate finance, and the reluctance of business to undertake investments. As Keynes and Kalecki noted in the 1930s, capitalism is suffering a crisis of under-investment that central banks cannot repair.

11
The Structure of Central Bank Operations

Kalecki was aware that maintaining a level of government expenditure sufficient to make the economy operate efficiently at full capacity, that is with full employment of the labour force, had monetary implications, in particular because it would require deficits in the government budget. Those deficits, in turn, would need financing in such a way as to maintain monetary and financial stability. Hence he favoured 'funding' deficits, with long-term bonds, and open market operations (buying and selling securities) by the central bank to keep interest rates stable. Such operations were to include purchases and sales of securities along the yield curve, including trading combined into what has come to be known as 'operation twist', namely the sale of short-term bills, using the proceeds to buy long-term bonds in order to bring down the market yield or rate of interest on long-term bonds.[1]

In 1943, Kalecki gave a brief theoretical explanation of this: '...Government borrowing policy determines within certain limits the long-term rate of interest', because 'the ratio of long-term assets to short-term assets + cash' determines the 'risk margin' required from borrowers. Kalecki went on:

> If the Government borrows a part of the amounts required on long-term at a certain fixed rate and the rest on short term—as was in fact the case during this war—the long-term rate is actually fixed by the Government. This is, however, only the case if this rate is chosen so that the Government is able to sell *some* amount of its long-term issues. If the Government long-term rate of borrowing is so low that nobody is prepared to lend at this rate, the Government must finance all the Budget deficit by floating debt. It loses then the control of the long-term rate unless it is prepared to borrow short over and above the deficit requirements and buy long-term securities from the public.[2]

[1] After the long-term rate of interest has been reduced, new bonds can be issued at the lower rate of interest to repay the maturing bills. See Ehlers, 'The Effectiveness of the Federal Reserve's Maturity Extension Program—Operation Twist 2', 2012.

[2] Kalecki, *Studies in Economic Dynamics*, 1943b, pp. 45–6. 'Floating debt' was the term used at that time for debt in the form of short term bill issues that had to be refinanced at whatever was the current

Interest and Capital: The Monetary Economics of Michał Kalecki. Jan Toporowski, Oxford University Press.
© Jan Toporowski 2022. DOI: 10.1093/oso/9780198816232.003.0012

However, monetarist doctrines focused the attention of policy debate solely on the money creation of central banks and more recently the short-term rate of interest. The role of central bank operations in the financial markets was thus reduced to its monetary, rather than financial aspects such as the influence on long-term interest rates.

11.1 Theory beyond Practice

As was noted in the previous chapter, open market operations were widely advocated at the time of the Radcliffe Committee on the Working of the Monetary System, at the end of the 1950s. However, thereafter, knowledge of these kinds of financial operations was lost to academic discussions, and confined to central bank officials and bankers who conducted such manoeuvres. The academic economists who provide the macroeconomic rationale for aspects of government policy took up the Modigliani–Miller theorem, that the capital structure of a firm does not affect its value[3] to show that financial operations along the yield curve are only possible if markets are incomplete, and growing exchange rate difficulties seemed to indicate that financial market development was in the process of completing the required market set. An implication of the theorem is that issuers of debt are indifferent to the term structure of that debt, and Franco Modigliani went on to argue that a 1961 operation to lower the market yield (interest to price ratio) on the US government's long-term debt did not affect the long-term rate of interest.[4]

At around the same time, another distinguished Keynesian economist James Tobin touched upon a pre-war American controversy about the scope for monetary policy by the, supposedly independent, Federal Reserve, when US Treasury was managing the sale of government bonds:

> There is no neat way to distinguish monetary policy from debt management, [both] the Federal Reserve and the Treasury…are engaged in debt management in the broadest sense, and both have powers to influence the whole spectrum of debt……The Federal Reserve cannot make rational decisions

rate of discount, or Bank Rate, at the time of issue. This passage was removed in subsequent revisions of Kalecki's chapter on the long-term rate of interest.

[3] Modigliani and Miller, 'The Cost of Capital, Corporation Finance and the Theory of Investment', 1958.

[4] Modigliani and Sutch, 'Innovations in Interest Rate Policy', 1966; Modigliani and Sutch, 'Debt Management and the Term Structure of Interest Rates', 1967. See also Ehlers, 'The Effectiveness of the Federal Reserve's Maturity Extension Program—Operation Twist 2', 2012.

> of monetary policy without knowing what kind of debt the Treasury intends to issue. The Treasury cannot rationally determine the maturity structure of the interest-bearing debt without knowing how much debt the Federal Reserve intends to monetise.[5]

The pre-war controversy was the view enunciated in the 1930s by Henry Simons that there was no point in having monetary policy conducted by the central bank separately from the policy effected by the Treasury (see below). From the monetarist perspective, Milton Friedman had long been advocating a solution to the institutional dilemma in the form of a monetary constitution to set an annual increase in the money supply as an obligation of the government.

Tobin's concession to monetarism was an acknowledgement that shortening the maturity of public debt improves the liquidity of the banking system and therefore may stimulate aggregate demand.[6] This contrasts with what may be called the 'funding' view of Keynes and Kalecki that the issue of long-term debt was necessary to regulate the amount of money in the financial markets in order to keep the long-term rate of interest stable. Tobin went on to advance a portfolio balance theory of monetary policy in which the macroeconomic effects of debt operations came to be concerned with portfolio rebalancing at the point of debt sale,[7] rather than what happened to the money acquired by the government through a bond issue, i.e., whether it went into general expenditure to accrue, unevenly, into wealth portfolios, or financial operations going more directly into those portfolios.

New Classical economics reinforced a tendency to reduce monetary operations to manipulations of saving decisions. With the doctrine of Ricardian equivalence came the idea that the government cannot influence the long-term rate of interest, because any increase or decrease in government borrowing is met by an increase or decrease in saving.[8] The New Keynesian reaction to New Classical doctrines brought forward a case that nominal rigidities may make monetary policy effective in the short run. But as developed by Michael Woodford, the New Keynesian analysis of monetary policy, the possibility of 'incomplete' markets that afforded scope for open market operations disappeared. Woodford has consistently argued that illiquidity may not arise in the financial markets, so that changes in the price of stocks of any

5 Tobin, 'An Essay on the Principles of Debt Management', 1963.
6 Tobin, 'An Essay on the Principles of Debt Management', 1963.
7 Tobin, 'A General Equilibrium Approach to Monetary Theory', 1969.
8 Barro, 'Are Government Bonds Net Wealth?', 1974.

particular maturity cannot be affected by changes in supply or demand. In that situation, open market operations are irrelevant to the setting of interest rates, except as 'signalling' to the markets of the central bank's intentions. But, since there are other, cheaper, more obvious and unambiguous ways of communicating with the markets, such operations remain redundant.[9] By implication the 'funding' view of Keynes and Kalecki cannot influence the markets.

Explaining varying degrees of liquidity in different parts of the financial system by an appeal to incompleteness of markets, or 'frictions', may convince in academic discussion. In practice, those who conduct central bank operations are doing so in a financial system with a particular structure. Those operations are therefore tailored to that structure and not to any particular model. The remaining part of this chapter examines how open market operations have functioned, and even dysfunctioned, because of the debt structures in which those operations have taken place.

11.2 The Structure of the Financial System and the Structure of Operations

The standard textbooks of monetary economics and banking suggest open market operations as merely another instrument in the 'tool-box' that central bankers bring to their work in monetary policy, bank supervision and so on. However, as the history of open market operations reveals, context is everything in understanding what such operations do, what they can do, and how we understand what is being done. Whatever their purpose, the context determines the scope and effectiveness of open market operations, and the degree to which the views of Keynes and Kalecki remain valid. This justifies a consideration of those broader factors that affect open market operations.

A key determinant of the scope and effectiveness of open market operations is the structure of the financial system. The standard distinction that is commonly made is that between bank and capital market systems.[10] Bank systems were common until recently in continental Europe and East Asia.

[9] Eggertsson and Woodford, 'The Zero Bound on Interest Rates and Optimal Monetary Policy', 2003; Curdia and Woodford, 'The Central-Bank Balance Sheet as an Instrument of Monetary Policy', 2011. The New Keynesian position on open market operations, in the light of quantitative easing, is examined in Zampolli, 'Sovereign Debt Management as an Instrument of Monetary Policy', 2012.

[10] See Allen, 'Stock Markets and Resource Allocation', 1995; also Mayer and Vives, 'Introduction', 1995.

In such systems, banks lend to household and commercial customers for both short and long-term and hold the loans on their balance sheets, even extending them by agreement with their customers. Markets for long-term securities exist in such systems. But the securities traded in them are largely government paper, and the commercial banks themselves make markets in the securities issued by the largest corporations.

In bank systems, open market operations are restricted by the smaller size of the capital market, although this smaller size means that central bank buying and selling of securities has much bigger impact. At the same time, commercial banks may be much more dependent on liquidity provision by the central bank because their loan book is much less liquid than are the loan books of banks in capital market-based systems. Typically, commercial banks in bank systems ease their liquidity by trading government securities among themselves, and availing themselves of discount facilities at the central bank. But the greater stability of bank systems tends to facilitate the planning of liquidity in commercial banks with less resort to hedging of liquidity and therefore a reduced need for central bank open market operations when that hedging breaks down.

Capital market systems are usually identified with the financial systems of the United States, Great Britain and the countries whose financial systems have been formed in the image and likeness of their English-speaking counterparts. As their name suggests, these systems have much more active capital markets. These allow commercial banks to manage their liquidity more effectively by holding large quantities of negotiable securities. Capital market systems are nowadays supposed to be more efficient than bank systems because market in loans facilitate 'price discovery'.[11] However, an older view from Lavington regards the liquidity of the secondary market, or the market for 'old' securities as it used to be called, as the key factor determining activity in the financial system.[12] The liquidity of the secondary market in turn determines prices in that market, and the prices in that market are the prices at which borrowers may issue new securities.[13] Accordingly open market operations are deemed to play a much more important in regulating the activity of the capital market systems.

In addition to overlooking a number of other important features of financial systems, the commonly made dichotomy between bank- and

[11] Hasbrouk, *Empirical Market Microstructure: The Institutions, Economics and Econometrics of Securities Trading*, 2007.

[12] Lavington, *The English Capital Markets*, 1921, p. 225.

[13] Keynes, *A Treatise on Money Volume 1*, 1930/1971a, pp, 222–3.

market-based systems ignores the appearance in many countries of conglomerate banks, that is banks that are members of conglomerate industrial groups. By pooling the liquidity of the companies in the conglomerate, the companies can economize on financial resources. By cross-shareholding, owners of conglomerates can retain control while maximizing outside share capital employed in the conglomerate. Because of their industrial activities, conglomerates would appear to offer a ready transmission mechanism of central bank monetary policy internalising that mechanism to provide more direct impact on those industrial activities. However, the conventional wisdom among bank regulators disapproves of bank conglomerates because of their lack of transparency and undiversified asset portfolios. Nevertheless, the predominance of such conglomerates in the industrial and commercial business of developing and emerging market countries, most notably in East Asia, may be a factor in limiting open market operations in those countries to foreign currency securities and government paper.[14]

Different financial systems are not just immutable traditions, 'havens of familiar monetary practice'[15] specific to particular countries and hallowed by the routine business of generations past. Financial systems themselves have evolved, and with them have evolved the open market operations of central banks and their predecessors. The principal factor in this evolution has been evolution of financial trading.

The earliest central banks, those of Sweden (the Sveriges Riksbank established in 1668) and of England (established in 1694) were established specifically to manage the debt of their respective governments, in return for their right to issue banknotes. It is therefore not surprising that their trading of securities concentrated on government paper, as well as paper issued by the companies chartered with trading concessions by the government, such as the East India Company. At the time these were private banks with the distinction among banks of having limited liability.

Their business rapidly developed and changed with the proliferation of trade and the bills of exchange that merchants used to finance trade. In the Netherlands, De Nederlansche Bank was established in Amsterdam, rather than in the capital, because Amsterdam rather than The Hague was the commercial centre. London became a crucial centre for trade in such bills because the Bank of England's privilege of note issue allowed the bank greater

[14] In this respect, the operations of the Bank of Japan are exceptional. These are discussed more extensively in Stenfors and Toporowski, *Unconventional Monetary Policy and Financial Stability*, 2020.

[15] Oliver Sprague, an advisor to the Government of the United States and the Bank of England in the 1930s was referring to the gold standard in League of Nations (1930).

discretion in the discount trade than the 'accommodation' that other banks, limited by their reserves of gold and Bank of England notes, could offer. At the same time, the short maturity (up to three months) of commercial and Treasury bills meant that any 'fiduciary' note issue to discount bills could be rapidly cancelled when the bills were paid up on maturity. The reflux of bank notes in the discount trade was the basis of the Real Bills Doctrine according to which, the note issue to buy bills could not be inflationary.[16] The Currency School proceeded by a critique of this doctrine. The inflationary fears of that School, which come down to us today as the doctrines of monetarism, have their roots in the credit practices of the merchants of the City of London and the discount business of the Bank of England.[17] However, the question of the maturity of the instruments traded by the central bank has an important influence on the scope and effectiveness of open market operations. This is further discussed in the following section.

The third watershed in the evolution of open-market operations came in the second half of the nineteenth century with the easing of the establishment of joint stock companies through the Companies Acts of the time. This expanded greatly the amount of non-government bonds that could be traded in open market operations. On the whole, central banks have avoided buying and selling shares in companies.[18] But corporate bonds have been more regularly used as collateral for central bank loans and even on occasion added through open market operations to central bank portfolios. Through such operations, the central bank was able to influence the liquidity of the secondary market for long-term securities, as well as influencing the liquidity of banks.

Open market operations were used through the first decades of the twentieth century up to the Second World War, with particular challenges during the inter-war decades when international debt hung over and depressed European economies. The Second World War was the fourth major watershed in the evolution of open market operations. Having experienced the difficulties of external debt management governments now tried to ensure that as much as possible of their debt was domestic, and central banks assisted with open market operations to facilitate the financing of the war effort through banking system, and at low rates of interest.

[16] c.f. Humphrey, 'The Real Bills Doctrine', 1982.

[17] Niebyl, *Studies in the Classical Theories of Money*, 1946, chapter 7.

[18] A major exception was the rescue of the Hong Kong Stock Exchange by the Hong Kong Monetary Authority in 1998. See Goodhart and Dai, *Intervention to Save Hong Kong*, 2003.

After the Second World War, the wartime debt overhang and the new era of the welfare state provided fresh challenges of government debt management. A particular innovation of this time was the tap stock, a government bond that was issued in Britain to the Bank of England. The Bank would then sell it on into the bond market to regulate liquidity in that market. As former colonies achieved independence, central banks were established, but with few opportunities for open market operations except in foreign currencies to maintain exchange rate pegs.[19]

The final (so far at least) watershed arose with the widespread abolition, by the countries in Europe, North America, and Japan, of foreign exchange controls in the final decade of the twentieth century. As under the gold standard, the major financial centres now operated in integrated cross-border markets. But, unlike under the gold standard, banking was no longer national, but increasingly cross-border. In these circumstances, any central bank undertaking open market operations is in effect operating in global markets. This watershed marks the beginning of the withdrawal of central banks from their previous regulation of liquidity in capital markets. At this point it is helpful to consider more systematically the policy that guides open market operations.

11.3 The Policy Framework

The academic discussion of open market operations is heavily tilted towards the monetary implications of open market operations, that is their effects on the supply of money or bank reserves, or the rate of interest on borrowing money.[20] This has been reinforced by the statutory frameworks adopted by central banks in Europe banning the buying of government stocks, on the grounds that this may be inflationary and certainly contrary to the central bank's chief goal of maintaining the value of the currency unit for which it bears an unique responsibility. This may be contrasted with an earlier, but no less authoritative view at that time that '...it is important that the central bank should be, from the start, the government's banker. In highly developed systems, the importance of coordinating debt management and credit policy is universally recognized, and this state of affairs will come more naturally if the central bank always handles all (or nearly all) the government's financial

[19] See Allen, *Monetary Policy and Financial Repression 1951–1959*, 2014, chapters 6 and 12, and the same author's *The Bank of England and the Government Debt Operations in the Gilt-Edged Markets, 1928–1972*, 2018.

[20] See, for example, Allen, 'The Scope and Significance of Open Market Operations', 2007.

business. This is not merely a matter of technical arrangements; it is at least as importantly a question of the direction from which the government seeks financial advice...'[21]

The monetary consequences of particular operations therefore dictate the kind of open market operations that are undertaken. The **reserve position doctrine** (that the central bank should operate its monetary policy in order to control the amount of reserves of commercial banks) would indicate that open market operations should be:

Either conducted using short-term paper, because the buying of, for example, a short-term bill, will reverse itself when the bill matures, and is repaid by its issuer, to its current owner, the central bank, by a transfer of bank reserves to the central bank.[22] On the other hand, if the central bank wishes to effect a lasting increase or decrease in the quantity of bank reserves, then the central bank should buy or sell longer term securities. A lasting increase or decrease in commercial bank reserves may be obtained by using short-term paper, but this may require a higher turnover in the portfolio of discount bills which may be costly and unnecessary;

Or conducted using repurchase/resale agreements. These allow the central bank to 'inject' or reserves into the inter-bank markets, or take reserves out regardless of the maturity of the securities bought and sold in operations which are reversed by the central bank by agreement with its counterparty but at a term that the central bank can set.

However, in the case of emerging markets, that is countries outside the OECD that have open capital accounts, the reserve position of commercial banks is heavily affected capital inflows and outflows. Capital inflows expand commercial bank reserves either as claims on foreign currency deposits that a commercial bank acquires, or as reserves at the central bank if the central bank buys in the foreign currency reserves (usually to stabilize the exchange rate). These inflows and outflows of reserves caused by exogenous factors may then require open market *sterilization* operations in order to stabilize the quantity of commercial bank reserves.

There is, however, an additional complication in using open market operations in order to regulate the amount of bank reserves. This complication

[21] Sayers, *Central Banking after Bagehot*, 1957, p. 119.

[22] This is the principle of reflux behind the Real Bills Doctrine that a note issue to discount trade bills could not be inflationary.

arises from an implicit assumption in the reserve position doctrine that open market operations do not affect the liquidity of markets for longer-term securities and, hence, the velocity of circulation of commercial bank reserves.[23] If indeed that velocity is affected by the open market operations undertaken to *stabilize* the commercial bank reserves, then the possibility arises that stabilizing commercial bank reserves may destabilize the capital market and other forms of credit, as in fact happened during the 1980s.

These contradictions between a set target for bank reserves and the impact of open market operations on the financial system became apparent in the 'overfunding' episode of the early 1980s. Between the fiscal years 1982–1983 and 1983–1984, the Bank of England increased its net sales of gilt-edged stocks (conventional and index-linked) by 70 per cent from £7,927m to £13,442m, well in excess of the public sector borrowing requirement at that time, which was £8.9bn in 1982–1983, and £9.8m in the following year. This drained liquidity out of the banking system. In order to maintain that liquidity, the Bank was obliged to intervene and, to maintain consistency, had to do so at shorter maturities, buying commercial bills. In this way the Bank built up a large holding of bills that reached £15.1bn, or 4.75 per cent of GDP, and came to be known as the 'bill mountain'. The striking anomaly, however, was that it had little impact on the growth rate of the broad money aggregate, M3, that the government was trying to limit. This reached 12 per cent (against a target of 6–10 per cent) in 1984–1985 before it was finally abandoned in October 1985.[24] The government moved to targeting narrow money, which proved more tractable but excludes most of the bank credit that is used as means of payment in the modern capitalist economy.

The episode played its part in discrediting monetarism by demonstrating the ineffectiveness of using funding operations to control monetary aggregates. The alternative that emerged was a return to Wicksell, with the use by central banks of **the rate of interest as its key policy instrument**. Most central banks have been doing this since the end of the 1980s. However, if monetary policy is only concerned with the rate of interest, then open market operations may be wholly unnecessary: The monetary transmission mechanism is usually presumed to operate through the inter-bank market and that can be kept on target simply by keeping a suitable 'corridor' of interest rates for deposits and loans of reserves at the central bank. Open

[23] See Toporowski, 'Open Market Operations: Beyond the New Consensus', 2006.
[24] Allen, 'Government Debt Management and Monetary Policy in Britain since 1919', 2012.

market operations may then be undertaken in order supply or reduce the liquidity in the financial markets.

Finally, it should be mentioned that, a central bank is a government agency and that, traditionally, open market operations have been undertaken using government bonds. Such bonds held in the central bank portfolio have therefore, in a financial sense at least, been bought back by the government. The interest paid on them adds to the profits of the central bank and those profits are an income to the government sector. So, for example, the bonds issued by the Japanese government amount to over three times the Gross Domestic Product of Japan. However, in massive open market operations since 2001,[25] the Bank of Japan has acquired half of those bonds, so that the net debt of the Japanese Government is really only half of the total gross debt.

Open market operations therefore have fiscal implications, as well as monetary and liquidity effects. Insofar as it contains government bonds, the portfolio that the central bank holds reduces net government borrowing. Insofar as it contains private sector securities, that portfolio consists of claims by the central bank on the private sector. The exception here is the European Central Bank and the central banks in the Franc Zone, which belong to groups of governments. The latter do not engage in open market operations using government paper, while the ECB uses a wide range of private sector bonds in its open market operations and its operations in government securities are controversial and carefully scrutinized.

In considering the intrinsic link between open market operations and fiscal policy, it is worth mentioning the respective views of two rival monetary theorists who reflected on this link with not altogether dissimilar conclusions. Henry Simons is well known for advocating 100 per cent reserves in the Chicago Plan for Banking Reform that he drew up. But he also drew the logical conclusion from this position, that the Federal Reserve, whose loose credit policies he blamed for the speculative 'bubble' in the stock market before 1929, should be abolished. This would allow the concentration of responsibility for monetary policy which '...must focus on fiscal policy as its mode of implementation'. He went on '...The Treasury might be given freedom within wide limits to alter the form of public debt (which would be the means, through public expenditure, or inserting money into the economy—JT)—to shift from long-term to short-term borrowing or vice versa, to issue and retire demand obligations in a legal-tender form. It might be granted

[25] See Sandilands, 'Hawtreyan "Credit Deadlock" or "Keynesian Liquidity Trap"?', 2010; Doi, Ihori, and Mitsui, 'Sustainability, Inflation and Public Debt Policy in Japan', 2007.

some control over the timing of expenditures. It might be given limited power to alter tax rates by decree and to make refunds of taxes previously collected...'[26]

John Maynard Keynes also reflected on the role and principles by which open market operations should be conducted. In his *Treatise on Money* he commended the use of open market operations: 'The new post-war element of "management" consists in the habitual employment of an "open market policy" by which the Bank of England buys and sells investment with a view keeping the reserve resources of the member banks at the level which it desires. This method—regarded as a method—seems to me to be the ideal one.'[27]

Subsequently, Keynes came to the conclusion that open market operations held the key to managing the liquidity of the market in long-term securities. This liquidity determines the long-term rate of interest (rather than the official central bank rate of interest) that, for Keynes, is the rate of interest that is relevant to the fixed capital investment which determines output and employment. This played a key part in his advice to the government on debt management.[28] Thus open market operations became central in his view to maintaining the liquidity of corporate and government bonds, and keeping down the cost of long-term finance for business. Keynes's view was echoed in the 'stable bond market' policy of the post-war period. This was justified by the high proportion of commercial bank assets that was held in the form of medium- and long-term government securities. Open market sales of such securities could therefore squeeze the balance sheets of commercial banks more effectively than changes in the discount rate.[29] As noted above, Keynes's associate, Richard Kahn, urged the extension of the scope of monetary policy and open market operations to include the whole yield curve, rather than short or long-term rates of interest, or the reserve position of banks.[30]

11.4 Conclusion

Kalecki, and Keynes, saw monetary circulation as intrinsically linked to fiscal policy and the debt management, with a policy framework around the

[26] Simons, 'Rules versus Authorities in Monetary Policy', 1936, p. 175.

[27] Keynes, *Treatise on Money Volume 2* 1930/1971b, p. 206.

[28] Keynes, 'National Debt Enquiry', 1945/1980, pp. 396–400; see also Tily, *Keynes's* **General Theory**, 2007, chapter 7.

[29] Sayers, *The American Banking System*, 1948, pp. 121–2.

[30] Kahn, 'Memorandum of Evidence submitted to the Radcliffe Committee', 1972.

management of government debt to regulate the financial circulation of money and support government expenditure. Monetarism reversed this policy framework from the support of government expenditure to having fiscal policy and debt management support targets for monetary expansion. Making central banks independent of governments did not rupture the structural connections between monetary policy, debt management and fiscal policy. But this did not become apparent until after the 2008 financial crisis, when it became clear that the Neo-Wicksellian reliance on short-term interest rates had little purchase on the financial system, let alone the economy at large. Quantitative easing and the resumption of open market operations was the first public recognition since the rise of monetarism that central banks operate within a structured financial system, whose liquidity varied in different segments of that system. Financial systems have not been homogenized by international financial integration. Nor has such integration rendered open market operations marginal to the liquidity of banking and financial markets. That liquidity, rather than the amount of money in the economy, or the short-term rate of interest, is what underpins business activity in the modern capitalist economy.

Open market operations are the oldest activity of central banks, predating the use the discount or interest rate as an instrument of policy. The use of such operations is essential in times of banking 'panic' or crisis, and they have been used at other times to manage the reserve position or liquidity of banks, or to support the official rate of interest in the money market, or even to regulate the liquidity of the market in longer-term securities. Thus the effectiveness of such operations depends not only on the state of the economy, but also on the complexity and liquidity of the financial system. Recent open market operations under the form of repurchase agreements or 'quantitative easing' has not altered these fundamental characteristics of such operations.

12
Kalecki Vindicated
The Endogeneity of Monetary Policy

12.1 Introduction

In the state money, or bank credit approach, monetary policy is conducted by governments, or by central banks on governments' behalf, in the belief that it affects economic outcomes, such as output, employment or inflation; in other words that a change in monetary policy causes those target variables in the economy to be different to what they would otherwise be; that is that monetary policy acts as an *exogenous* influence on the economy that is outside the institution(s) conducting that policy. Monetary policy is therefore commonly set with a view to some future desired change in the target variable(s). The relationship between the change in the target variable and the monetary policy setting (a change in the central bank rate of interest, or a change in the money supply) is usually given by modelling past monetary policy against past changes in target variables. The monetary policy setting is supposed to operate through channels that make up the monetary transmission mechanism which transmits the effect of monetary policy to the economy at large.

In the simplest exposition of monetary policy setting, the desired level of the target variable is measured directly or indirectly against its current level, which provides the most recent data on the state of the economy. If, for example, the current level of inflation is above the target level then monetary policy may be 'tightened' in order to bring down the rate of inflation. In 'forward-looking' models, the current rate of change of the target variable is also taken into consideration: Current inflation may be above its target rate but, if it is falling, then it may be that no further change in monetary policy is necessary. In this way, monetary policy is *pragmatic* and based on the latest available information about current economic circumstances. Monetary policy may be said to be *endogenous* when it merely reflects or is driven by

Interest and Capital: The Monetary Economics of Michał Kalecki. Jan Toporowski, Oxford University Press.
© Jan Toporowski 2022. DOI: 10.1093/oso/9780198816232.003.0013

current circumstances, rather than influencing those circumstances and their evolution.

When targeting economic variables, the effectiveness of monetary policy depends on the influence that monetary policy has on future economic outcomes. This effect is not obvious, like, say, the force of a nut-cracker on the shell of a nut. In the first place, the future cannot be immediately observed and, by the time that it arrives, has itself been influenced by many factors other than monetary policy: including developments outside the economy in which the monetary policy operates, and seasonal and other cyclical changes. What is called 'the monetary transmission mechanism' is itself a synthesis of possible influences of monetary policy, rather than a direct mechanism linking monetary policy to its outcomes. Furthermore, in a situation in which the lead time between a given monetary policy setting and its effects may be over one, and possibly two years long, monetary policy activism is much more likely to be discounted in economic decision-making, because any current policy is likely to be superseded by a different policy.

In practice, the belief in the effectiveness of monetary policy arises from the logic of the situation in which a central bank finds itself, what the philosopher Karl Popper called its 'situational logic': central banks conduct operations in banking and financial markets on instruction from the governments that own central banks. If told by their owners to pursue a particular target, a central bank will conduct its operations by reference to that target, because the profession of the central banker is to make reference to government policy in the conduct of their business.[1] But this does not mean that central bankers can *effect* that policy. The tools of monetary policy, official interest rates, open market operations and credit regulation, have a direct effect on banking, but only an indirect effect on the private economic transactions that determine economic outcomes. It is those private economic transactions, in particular those of capitalist businesses, that are at the heart of Kalecki's monetary analysis.

[1] Hicks as much as admitted this in observing that, under the Gold Standard, the Banking Department, which was not supposed to conduct monetary policy operations, '...became a Central Bank, which, at least to a limited extent, did exercise monetary policy. It had to be cautious about it, since it was not in accordance with official doctrine that it should do so. I think nevertheless that there is no doubt that this is what it did.' Hicks cited as evidence Sayers' classic work on the operations of the Bank of England in the period preceding the First World War (Hicks, 'Monetary Theory and History, 1967, p. 168).

12.2 Policy Endogeneity and Structure of Financial Markets

By examining the structure of banking and financial markets it is possible to identify circumstances in which monetary policy may be completely ineffective, just as it is possible to suggest situations in which monetary policy is very effective. In financially-advanced economies, the endogeneity of monetary policy is intimately linked to the complexity of financial systems in such economies. Complexity here means having a variety of banking institutions, but also markets for longer-term financial securities whose liquidity is maintained by specialist banking institutions (investment banks, hedge funds) as well as central bank open market operations intermediating along the yield curve. In such an economy it is possible to identify two systems. One is the system of real resources, production and exchange and the monetary circulation that facilitates the exchange part of that economic activity. These are the flow variables of output, employment, consumption, and investment that make up national income in a given period. The second system is the financing of those real resources and transactions in them. In a complex financial economy, a given real resource, such as a building, a mine, or a factory (also a hospital or a university) may be financed in various ways with financial instruments of differing maturity, from short-term bank loans, through bonds to equity.

This second system is therefore a set of evolving stocks of financial assets and liabilities, returns on, or the cost of, which constitute the yield curve of the financial system. Monetary policy may be said to be endogenous when such policy changes with the evolution of the business cycle in the real economy, but affects only the composition of the second system (of financing real resources), without affecting the real economy, that is the flow variables that make up the system of national income and output.

This endogeneity arises because the tools of monetary policy affect the terms on which one form of financing may substituted for another in the banking and financial markets in which the central operates, that is the slope of the yield curve. For example, the official rate of interest is a short-term one. Changes in that rate of interest clearly will affect the terms on which short-term financing may be substituted by longer-term financing, for example in the 'funding' of investment projects, or refinancing of existing debt. Open market operations, such as the recent 'quantitative easing' policies of buying, bonds affect the liquidity of portfolios and the secondary market for bonds. Such operations would therefore influence the rate of substitution of long-term financing for short-term financing.[2] Changes in monetary policy in the first instance affect the type of financing that is used in an economy, transforming the shape of the yield curve that summarizes the rates at which different kinds of financing may be substituted for each other. However, to affect national income variables that may be the target of monetary policy, those terms of financial substitution need to change output, employment, and price decisions. Such decisions are determined in the first instance by current orders for goods and services and then by estimations of future orders for goods and services. Changes in the terms of financing will only affect the financing of such orders, that is the composition of the financing structures that accompany a given composition of output. The *frisson* in the markets that accompanies changes in monetary policy is in anticipation of shifts in financing rather than in the variables that make up national income.

There are two reasons why monetary policy may fail to influence economic, as opposed financing, decisions. On the one hand current expenditure largely depends on current income. On the other hand, expenditure commitments for the future, such as fixed investment, depend on expectations much more than on *current* financing terms. One of the strong claims of monetarism and any kind of monetary policy activism has always been that public estimations of future national income variables, in particular pricing (inflationary expectations), would depend on monetary policy settings. However, this claim always depended on the conviction of the public in projecting those policy settings into the future. With active monetary policy such projection is much less likely. After nearly half a century of monetary policy activism (roughly from the release of monetary policy from its obligation to maintain the Bretton Woods system of fixed exchange rates), the one thing that business and finance, if not the consumer, has learned is that monetary policy, however stable in recent months, is unlikely to be the same next year as it is today.

Thus monetarism and the use of monetary policy to influence the business cycle always tacitly assumed a public that did not learn from its experience of monetary policy activism to discount changes in monetary policy. For the public to make monetary policy a factor in future output, employment, and pricing decisions, that monetary policy has to be inactive so that the public can come to rely on it in the future.[3] With learning, what has been called the

[2] There are hints of this in Keynes, 'National Debt Enquiry' in Keynes, *Collected Writings*, 1980b, pp. 395–9 and Kalecki, 'Essay on the Business Cycle Theory', 1933, pp. 93–8.

[3] Initially, at least, it was observed that an 'inflation forecast is based on (i.e., conditional on) the assumption that interest rates are held constant thereafter over the remaining two years'. Goodhart,

'credibility' of monetary policy really depends on the durability of a given monetary policy setting, rather than any history of achieving inflation or employment targets. Thus, only an inactive monetary may be completely exogenous both because it offers a stable anchor for future economic decision-making (this is the essential rationale for the 'forward guidance' that central banks in the UK and US have issued since 2010) but also because it does not respond to the changing economic circumstances of the business cycle.[4]

The second reason why active monetary policy may fail to influence economic decisions is because a complex financial system offers a growing number of ways of insulating economic decisions from changes in monetary conditions, from funding (refinancing short-term debt into bonds with fixed interest payments, or even equity, with discretionary payments, both of which are independent of central bank monetary policy), to interest rate futures and swaps. These derivative instruments allow businesses to 'hedge' their economic decisions in ways that allow firms to have their cash flow unaffected by changes in monetary policy.

This complexity provides the link between Kalecki's analysis of corporate finance and the argument in this chapter. Central banks today model the monetary transmission mechanism, linking their interest rate policy to economic decision-making, on the assumption that the business sector responds in much the same way to changes in its interest rates and that, if they do not, there is something wrong with the mechanism in the financial system. So, for example, when economies failed to recover after the 2008 crisis, this was blamed on the breakdown of the monetary transmission mechanism as evidenced by the failure of the inter-bank money market.[5] But, as Kalecki knew, the business sector is not all the same, but is polarized into two segments. The part of it that does depend on borrowing at rates fixed by central bank policy rates, are small and medium-sized enterprises. In virtually all countries of the world they employ the bulk of private sector workers. But precisely because they have little money, they can borrow little, their investments are therefore insignificant, and they mostly passively

'Monetary Transmission Lags and the Formulation of the Policy Decision on Interest Rates', 2001. It should be pointed out that after approaching zero, following the financial crisis of 2008, policy interest rates have not moved very much.

[4] See Romer and Romer, 'Does Monetary Policy Matter', 1989. Kothari, Lewellen, and Warner provide evidence that the rate of interest does not affect business investment in the way predicted by the textbook theory in 'The Behavior of Aggregate Corporate Investment', 2014.

[5] Subsequently, as central bank interest rates approached zero, the argument turned neo-Wicksellian with suggestions that the 'natural' or 'equilibrium' rate of interest (or the rate of return on new investments, or the rate of interest that secures the inflation target) was also approaching zero or had turned negative. In order to stimulate investment, or raise inflation, the money rate of interest had to be even more significantly negative.

accommodate changes in monetary policy into their cash flows because they have few financing options.

The other segment consists of the much smaller number of corporations with access to the full range of financial markets. They may employ fewer private sector workers than small and medium-sized enterprises. But they undertake the bulk of private business investment that, in Keynes's and Kalecki's macroeconomics, determines output, employment and, crucially, the business cycle that is supposed by the currently ruling Neo-Wicksellian doctrine to be regulated by monetary policy. Their access to the full range of financial markets allows corporate managers to insulate their businesses from monetary policy by hedging monetary policy changes in the cash and derivatives markets. They are able to do this through two features of corporate structure designed to manage the liquidity of corporate balance sheets. The first of these is overcapitalization: the issue of long-term capital stocks in excess of the financing needs of a given corporation. Excess capital is typically held in the form of liquid assets or employed in merger and acquisition activity, thereby effectively 'internalizing' a portion of the capital market into the balance sheet of the corporation.[6] The second feature of corporate organization is the holding company structure, organizing associated businesses in web of cross-holdings that include businesses with varying cash flow and liquidity, which can then be averaged out by means of internal transfers. The web may even include a bank or credit subsidiary, making the credit policy of its owners, rather than the central bank, the effective monetary policy affecting any given corporation.

This business structure is itself the outcome of the rise of institutional investors, over the course of the twentieth century, from investment trusts to today's pension funds and insurance companies. While the monetary transmission mechanisms of central banks postulate portfolio rebalancing in response to changes in monetary policy, institutional investors are much more driven by liquidity and cash flow considerations than by monetary policy.[7] With long-term liabilities, frequent changes of interest rates fade in significance.

In short, active monetary policy follows the business cycle but typically is undertaken with a view to influencing that cycle. Insofar as it influences that cycle, monetary policy may be said to be *exogenous*. Insofar as monetary policy is adjusted to changing economic circumstances, but has no influence on that cycle, monetary policy is *endogenous*. In any given situation, monetary

[6] Toporowski, 'Overcapitalisation', 2012.

[7] Toporowski, *The End of Finance*, 2000, Part II.

policy may be more or less endogenous, as it is less or more exogenous. This is merely another way of saying that the effectiveness of the monetary transmission mechanism is not predetermined and constant, but depends on the degree to which monetary policy affects financing structures as opposed to output, employment, and prices. When monetary policy is endogenous, the monetary transmission mechanism merely serves to adapt financing structures to the current phase of the business cycle, rather than changing that cycle. When that policy follows the business cycle, financing structures cease to be a mechanism for transmitting monetary policy to the business cycle. Rather, monetary policy becomes part of the mechanism for transmitting the business cycle to financing structures.

12.3 Monetary Policy and the Real Economy

Endogeneity of monetary policy suggests the following statistical relationship between a given monetary policy setting and macroeconomic variables:

$$M_t = (m.Y_t)^\alpha$$

where:

M_t is the monetary policy setting (the money supply, or the central bank rate of interest, or changes in those variables);

Y_t is the vector of current national income variables (output, output gap, inflation etc.) that are taken into account in setting the central bank's monetary policy;

m is a vector of coefficients relating the national income variables to the central bank's monetary policy, indicating the proportion of monetary policy that may be attributed to a given national income variable, or the central bank's reaction function;

α is a coefficient indicating the degree of monetary policy activism. Thus, an inactive monetary policy would be shown as $\alpha = 0$. A linear relationship between monetary policy and the current state of the economy would make $\alpha = 1$. A weak monetary policy would be indicated by $\alpha < 1$; a robustly active monetary policy would make $\alpha > 1$.

It is obvious that this is a generalized relationship in which a Taylor Rule becomes a special case where the vector Y_t is reduced to a linear relationship with two independent variables (Y_t), the output gap, and the difference between the target rate of inflation and the actual rate of inflation, with coefficients m that sum to 1, in a linear relationship ($\alpha = 1$).

Charles Goodhart has pointed out to me that monetary policy decision-making consists of forecasting the state of the economy at some point in the future (Y^f), estimating the monetary policy (money supply, central bank rate of interest) implied by this state of the economy, say M^f, and then setting $M - M^f$ at such a level as to *change* a given target element (output gap, or inflation) of that future state of the economy, Y^f. We may leave aside the question here of whether the setting of monetary policy by committee allows for some future *implied* official rate of interest (or money supply), M^f, rather than the current rate or money supply, M_t, to be the benchmark from which changes in monetary policy are instituted. Insofar as the current state of the economy, Y_t, is the best estimate of the future state of the economy, Y^f (and the current monetary policy setting, M_t, is the best estimate of future *implied* monetary policy, M^f) the above equation still holds. If, however, the future state of the economy and its implied monetary policy is estimated in a non-linear way from current states, then this would be incorporated in the α coefficient, since non-linear projection amounts to a non-linear treatment of the reaction function of a central bank.[8]

12.4 Monetary Policy and Neutrality and the Scope of Policy Effectiveness

Endogeneity of monetary policy implies monetary neutrality. But this is not neutrality in the monetarist sense, restricting neutrality to quantities in the economy, but assuming a direct relationship between the money supply and the price level. Endogeneity of monetary policy suggests a rather broader neutrality in relation to nominal as well as real variables. In an economy with a complex financial system, monetary policy affects the terms of financing: current and future economic variables are determined by the business cycle, rather than the financing of economic activity at any point in the cycle.[9]

Finally, endogeneity does not mean central banking and monetary operations are wholly ineffective. Since the nineteenth century central banks have played a prominent part in dealing with banking crises and assuring financial stability. As has been apparent since 2008, the task of monetizing

[8] See also Goodhart, 'Monetary Transmission Lags and the Formulation of the Policy Decision on Interest Rates', 2001; Svensson, 'The Inflation Forecast and the Loss Function', 2003.

[9] See Dow and Saville, *A Critique of Monetary Policy Theory and British Experience*, 1988, chapter 12, although those authors recognize a limited function for monetary policy in exchange rate management.

financial assets is one that only a central bank can do. Precisely because monetary policy has its primary effect on financing structures, it may be directly effective in alleviating financial instability. Those structural connections between financing and monetary policy that make monetary policy endogenous are exactly the ones that are relied upon in alleviating instability. By implication, the more effective is monetary policy in dealing with financial crisis, the less effective it is in achieving employment or inflation targets.

Such endogeneity of policy is signalled in Kalecki's first exercise in monetary theory in 1933, where he stated that 'changes in the rate of interest are determined by the mechanism of the business cycle…[but] the rate of interest is of secondary importance for the "will to invest", the factor of prime importance being unquestionably the gross profitability of existing plant…'. But he went on to say that this endogeneity of the rate of interest was only correct if a 'crisis of confidence' is excluded. Then the rate of interest may be a factor.[10]

With inflation-targeting, Wicksellianism, the doctrine that economic and business affairs can be regulated by means of the central bank's policy rate of interest, reached the pinnacle of its influence. In Keynes's and Kalecki's lifetimes that influence had been limited by the failure of monetary policy, and the suppression of interest rates to keep down the costs of government debt; in the 1970s and 1980s it was devotion to the control of monetary aggregates that kept Wicksellianism on the margins of academic and political economics. From the 1990s, Neo-Wicksellianism ruled in central banks and the corridors of government advisers, until the low prices brought about by the industrialization of East Asia proved the doctrine incontrovertible. The financial crisis of 2008 showed that Neo-Wicksellianism had been following inflation rather than controlling it, and vindicated Keynes's emphasis on liquidity, and Kalecki's insistence that, in a capitalist economy, the money that counts is the money of capitalists.

But Wicksellianism is not only wrong in the power that it attributes to interest rate policy. It is also wrong in its diagnosis of inflation as a monetary phenomenon. This is not altogether surprising. From their beginnings in the twilight of mercantile capitalism, central banks have been concerned with the value of the paper money that they issue. From this has come the myopic conviction that this value, in a mercantile world, is an attribute of the scarcity of that paper money, or its price in the form of the rate of interest on that

[10] Kalecki, 'Essay on the Business Cycle Theory', 1933.

money. By contrast, Kalecki argued that inflation is a phenomenon rooted in the labour market, where the cost of labour is determined; the commodity markets, where the costs of raw materials are decided; and the exchange rate that fixes the costs of imports.[11] At best, and only in limited circumstances, central banks have been able to influence that exchange rate. It is the monetary policy of business that matters, rather than that of the state or banking. Attempts to influence the conduct of business in a non-catastrophic way by varying the terms on which business is financed inevitably lead to the subordination of banking to business conditions. 'The events which I thought I was controlling were in fact controlling me.'[12]

[11] Kalecki, 'The Lesson of the Blum Experiment', 1938/1990.
[12] Kyril Bonfiglioli, *Don't Point That Thing At Me*, 1972.

Bibliography

Works by Kalecki

Kalecki, M. (1928) 'The Swedish Match Trust', in J. Osiatyński (ed.), *Collected Works of Michał Kalecki, Volume VI. Studies in Applied Economics 1927–1941*. London: The Clarendon Press, 1996.

Kalecki, M. (1932/1990) 'The Business Cycle and Investment', in J. Osiatyński (ed.), *Collected Works of Michał Kalecki, Volume I. Capitalism: Business Cycles and Full Employment*. Oxford: Clarendon Press, 1990.

Kalecki, M. (1932/1996) 'Ivar Kreuger', in J. Osiatyński (ed.), *Collected Works of Michał Kalecki, Volume VI. Studies in Applied Economics 1927–1941*. Oxford: The Clarendon Press, 1996.

Kalecki, M. (1933) 'Essay on the Business Cycle Theory', in J. Osiatyński (ed.), *Collected Works of Michał Kalecki, Volume I. Capitalism: Business Cycles and Full Employment*. Oxford: The Clarendon Press, 1990, pp. 65–108.

Kalecki, M. (1933/1990) 'Stimulating the Business Upswing', in J. Osiatyński (ed.), *Collected Works of Michał Kalecki, Volume I. Capitalism: Business Cycles and Full Employment*. Oxford: The Clarendon Press, 1990.

Kalecki, M. (1936) 'Some Remarks on Keynes's Theory', translated by F. Targetti and B. Kinda-Hass in J. Osiatyński (ed.), *Collected Works of Michał Kalecki, Volume I. Capitalism: Business Cycles and Full Employment*. Oxford: The Clarendon Press, 1990.

Kalecki, M. (1937) 'A Theory of Commodity, Income and Capital Taxation', *Economic Journal*, Vol. 47, No. 3, pp. 444–50.

Kalecki, M. (1937/1990) 'The Principle of Increasing Risk', *Economica*, Vol. 4, No. 16, Nov. 1937 pp. 440–6, in J. Osiatyński (ed.), *Collected Works of Michał Kalecki, Volume I. Capitalism: Business Cycles and Full Employment*. Oxford: The Clarendon Press, 1990, pp. 285–93.

Kalecki, M. (1938) 'A Comment on the "Principle of Increasing Risk": A Reply', *Economica*, Vol. 5, No. 20, pp. 459–60.

Kalecki, M. (1938/1990) 'The Lesson of the Blum Experiment', *Economic Journal*, Vol. 48, No. 1, pp. 26–41, in J. Osiatyński (ed.), *Collected Works of Michał Kalecki, Volume I. Capitalism: Business Cycles and Full Employment*. Oxford: The Clarendon Press, 1990, pp. 326–41.

Kalecki, M. (1939a) *Essays in the Theory of Economic Fluctuations*. London: George Allen and Unwin.

Kalecki, M. (1939b) 'The Long-Term Rate of Interest', in *Essays in the Theory of Economic Fluctuations*. London: George Allen and Unwin.

Kalecki, M. (1940a) 'The "Mysteries" of the Money Market', *Bulletin of the Institute of Statistics Oxford*, Vol. 2, No. 8, pp. 2–5, in J. Osiatyński (ed.). *Collected Works of Michał Kalecki, Volume VII. Studies in Applied Economics 1940–1967, Miscellanea*. Oxford: The Clarendon Press, 1997.

Kalecki, M. (1940b) 'Wage Bill and Cash Circulation' *Bulletin of the Institute of Statistics Oxford* Vol. 2, No. 5, pp. 2–6, in J. Osiatyński (ed.) *Collected Works of Michał Kalecki Volume VII Studies in Applied Economics 1940–1967, Miscellanea* Oxford: The Clarendon Press, 1997.

Kalecki, M. (1940c) 'Wage Bill and Cash Circulation: A Supplement', *Bulletin of the Institute of Statistics Oxford*, Vol. 2, No. 6, pp. 10–13, in J. Osiatyński (ed.), *Collected Works of Michał Kalecki, Volume VII. Studies in Applied Economics 1940–1967, Miscellanea.* Oxford: The Clarendon Press, 1997.

Kalecki, M. (1941a) 'What is Inflation', *Bulletin of the Institute of Statistics Oxford*, Vol. 3, No. 8, pp. 159–64, in J. Osiatyński (ed.), *Collected Works of Michał Kalecki, Volume VII. Studies in Applied Economics 1940–1967, Miscellanea.* Oxford: The Clarendon Press, 1997.

Kalecki, M. (1941b) 'The Short-Term Rate of Interest and Velocity of Cash Circulation', *Review of Economics and Statistics*, Vol. 23, No. 2, May, pp. 97–9.

Kalecki, M. (1942a) 'Employment, Wage Bill and Cash Circulation', *Bulletin of the Institute of Statistics Oxford*, Vol. 4, No. 3, pp. 67–70, in J. Osiatyński (ed.), *Collected Works of Michał Kalecki, Volume VII. Studies in Applied Economics 1940–1967, Miscellanea.* Oxford: The Clarendon Press, 1997.

Kalecki, M. (1942b) 'A Theory of Profits', *Economic Journal*, Vol. 52, No. 2, pp. 258–67.

Kalecki, M. (1943a) 'The Burden of the National Debt', *Bulletin of the Institute of Statistics Oxford*, Vol. 5, No. 5, pp. 76–80, in J. Osiatyński (ed.), *Collected Works of Michał Kalecki, Volume VII. Studies in Applied Economics 1940–1967, Miscellanea.* Oxford: The Clarendon Press, 1997.

Kalecki, M. (1943b) *Studies in Economic Dynamics.* London: George Allen and Unwin.

Kalecki, M. (1943/1990) 'Political Aspects of Full Employment', *Political Quarterly*, Vol. 14, No. 4, pp. 322–31, and in J. Osiatyński (ed.), *Collected Works of Michał Kalecki, Volume I. Capitalism: Business Cycles and Full Employment.* Oxford: The Clarendon Press, 1990, pp. 347–56.

Kalecki, M. (1943/1997) 'The War-time Trend of Deposits', *Bulletin of the Institute of Statistics Oxford*, Vol. 5, No. 4, pp. 63–6, in J. Osiatyński (ed.), *Collected Works of Michał Kalecki, Volume VII. Studies in Applied Economics 1940–1967, Miscellanea.* Oxford: The Clarendon Press, 1997.

Kalecki, M. (1943/1991) *Studies in Economic Dynamics.* London: George Allen and Unwin, in J. Osiatyński (ed.), *Collected Works of Michał Kalecki, Volume II. Capitalism: Economic Dynamics.* Oxford: The Clarendon Press, 1991.

Kalecki, M., and Schumacher, E. F. (1943) 'International Clearing and Long-Term Lending', *Bulletin of the Institute of Statistics Oxford Supplement No. 5*, Vol. 5, 7 August, pp. 29–33, in J. Osiatyński (ed.), *Collected Works of Michał Kalecki, Volume VII. Studies in Applied Economics 1940–1967, Miscellanea.* Oxford: The Clarendon Press, 1997.

Kalecki, M. (1944) 'Professor Pigou on "The Classical Stationary State": A Comment', *Economic Journal*, Vol. 54, No. 213, April, pp. 131–2, in J. Osiatyński (ed.), *Collected Works of Michał Kalecki, Volume I. Capitalism: Business Cycles and Full Employment.* Oxford: The Clarendon Press, 1990.

Kalecki, M. (1944/1990) 'Three Ways to Full Employment', in The Oxford University Institute of Statistics, *The Economics of Full Employment.* Oxford: Basil Blackwell, in J. Osiatyński, (ed.) *Collected Works of Michał Kalecki, Volume I. Capitalism: Business Cycles and Full Employment.* Oxford: The Clarendon Press, 1990.

Kalecki, M. (1945) 'The Maintenance of Full Employment after the Transition Period: A Comparison of the Problem in the USA and the UK', *International Labour Review* Vol. 52, No. 5, pp. 449–64, in J. Osiatyński, (ed.) *Collected Works of Michał Kalecki,*

Volume I. Capitalism: Business Cycles and Full Employment. Oxford: The Clarendon Press, 1990.

Kalecki, M. (1946/1990a) 'A Comment on "Monetary Policy"', *Review of Economics and Statistics*, Vol. 28, No. 2, May, pp. 81–4, in J. Osiatyński (ed.), *Collected Works of Michał Kalecki, Volume I. Capitalism: Business Cycles and Full Employment.* Oxford: The Clarendon Press, 1990.

Kalecki, M. (1946/1990b) 'Multilateralism and Full Employment', *Canadian Journal of Economics and Political Science*, Vol. 12, No. 3, pp. 322–7, in J. Osiatyński (ed.), *Collected Works of Michał Kalecki, Volume I. Capitalism: Business Cycles and Full Employment.* Oxford: The Clarendon Press, 1990.

Kalecki, M. (1949) 'Introductory Remarks on Inflationary and Deflationary Processes', in *Inflationary and Deflationary Tendencies, 1946–1948*. New York: United Nations, republished in J. Osiatyński (ed.), *Collected Works of Michał Kalecki, Volume VII. Studies in Applied Economics 1940–1967, Miscellanea.* Oxford: The Clarendon Press, 1997.

Kalecki, M. (1950) 'A New Approach to the Problem of Business Cycles', *Review of Economic Studies*, Vol. 17, No. 1, 1949–1950; also in J. Osiatyński (ed.) *Collected Works of Michał Kalecki, Volume II Capitalism: Economic Dynamics.* Oxford: The Clarendon Press, 1991.

Kalecki, M. (1954a) *Theory of Economic Dynamics An Essay on Cyclical and Long-Run Changes in Capitalist Economy.* London: George Allen and Unwin.

Kalecki, M. (1954b) 'The Problem of Financing Economic Development', in J. Osiatyński. (ed.), *Collected Works of Michał Kalecki, Volume V. Developing Countries.* Oxford: The Clarendon Press.

Kalecki, M. (1962) 'A Model of Hyper-inflation', *The Manchester School*, Vol. 32, No. 3, pp. 31–41, in J. Osiatyński (ed.) ,*Collected Works of Michał Kalecki, Volume II. Capitalism: Economic Dynamics.* Oxford: The Clarendon Press, 1991.

Kalecki, M. (1964) 'Ludwik Landau – Economist and Statistician', in J. Osiatyński (ed.), *Collected Works of Michał Kalecki, Volume VII. Studies in Applied Economics 1940–1967, Miscellanea.* Oxford: The Clarendon Press, 1997.

Kalecki, M. (1966) 'Money and Real Wages', in *Studies in the Theory of Business Cycles 1933–1939.* Oxford: Basil Blackwell, pp. 40–71.

Kalecki, M. (1968) 'Trend and the Business Cycle', in J. Osiatyński (ed.), *Collected Works of Michał Kalecki, Volume II. Capitalism: Economic Dynamics.* Oxford: The Clarendon Press, 1991.

Kalecki, M. (1970) 'Theories of Growth in Different Social Systems', in J. Osiatyński (ed.), *Collected Works of Michał Kalecki, Volume IV. Socialism: Economic Growth and Efficiency of Investment.* Oxford: The Clarendon Press, 1993.

Other Works Cited

Allen, F. (1995) 'Stock Markets and Resource Allocation', in C. Mayer and X. Vives (eds), *Capital Markets and Financial Intermediation.* Cambridge: Cambridge University Press, 1995.

Allen, W. A. (2007) 'The Scope and Significance of Open Market Operations', in D. G. Mayes and J. Toporowski (eds), *Open Market Operations and Financial Markets.* London: Routledge.

Allen, W. A. (2012) 'Government Debt Management and Monetary Policy in Britain since 1919', in Bank for International Settlements, 'The Threat of Fiscal Dominance', *BIS Papers*, No. 65, May 2012, pp. 135–7.

Allen, W. A. (2014) *Monetary Policy and Financial Repression 1951–1959.* Basingstoke: Palgrave.

Allen, W. A. (2019) *The Bank of England and the Government Debt Operations in the Gilt-Edged Markets, 1928–1972.* Cambridge: Cambridge University Press.

Andrews, P. W. S. (1940) 'A Further Inquiry into the Effects of the Rate of Interest', *Oxford Economic Papers*, Vol. 3, No. 1, pp. 32–73.

Anonymous (1943) 'Lessons of the Past', *Bulletin of the Institute of Statistics Oxford Supplement No. 5*, Vol. 5, 7 August.

Arthmar, R., and McLure, M. (2017) 'Pigou on War Finance and Welfare', *History of Economics Review*, Vol. 66, No. 1, pp. 2–18.

Bagehot, W. (1873) *Lombard Street A Description of the Money Market.* London: Henry S. King and Co.

Balogh, T. (1943) 'The Foreign Balance and Full Employment', *Bulletin of the Oxford Institute of Statistics*, Vol. 5, Supplement No. 5, 7 August, pp. 33–9.

Balogh, T. (1944) 'The Unimportance of a Capital Levy', *Bulletin of the Oxford Institute of Statistics*, Vol. 6, No. 3, 26 February, pp. 44–8.

Bank of England (1971) *Competition and Credit Control.* London, May.

Bank of England (1983) 'The Bank of England's Operational Procedures for Meeting Monetary Objectives'. *Bank of England Quarterly Bulletin*, June.

Bank of England (2004) 'Reform of the Bank of England's Operations in the Sterling Money Markets', *Bank of England Quarterly Bulletin*, Summer, pp. 217–27.

Bank of England (2015) *The Bank of England's Sterling Monetary Framework.* London, June.

Barro, R. J. (1974) 'Are Government Bonds Net Wealth?', *Journal of Political Economy*, Vol. 82, No. 6, Nov.–Dec., pp. 1095–1117.

Bellofiore, R. (2005) 'Monetary Economics after Wicksell: Alternative Perspectives within the Theory of the Monetary Circuit', in G. Fontana and R. Realfonzo (eds), *The Monetary Theory of Production Tradition and Perspectives.* Basingstoke: Palgrave Macmillan, 2005.

Bellofiore, R. (2014) 'Luxemburg and Kalecki: The Actuality of Tadeusz Kowalik's Reading of the *Accumulation of Capital*', in R. Bellofiore, E. Karwowski, and J. Toporowski (eds), *The Legacy of Rosa Luxemburg, Oskar Lange and Michał Kalecki. Volume 1 of Essays in Honour of Tadeusz Kowalik.* Basingstoke: Palgrave, 2014.

Bernanke, B., and Gertler, M. (1989) 'Agency Costs, Net Worth and Business Fluctuations', *American Economic Review*, Vol. 79, No. 1, pp. 14–31.

Bindseil, U. (2004a) 'The Operational Target of Monetary Policy and the Rise and Fall of the Reserve Position Doctrine', *Working Paper*, No. 372, Frankfurt: The European Central Bank.

Bindseil, U. (2004b) *Monetary Policy Implementation, Theory, Past and Present.* Oxford: Oxford University Press.

Bindseil, U., and Würtz, F. (2007) 'Open Market Operations – Their Role and Specification Today', in D. G. Mayes and J. Toporowski (eds), *Open Market Operations and Financial Markets.* London: Routledge.

Bőhm-Bawerk, E. von (1922) *Capital and Interest: A Critical History of Economical Theory.* New York: Brentano's.

Breit, M. (1935a) 'Problemy rynku pieniężnego i kapitałowego na tle depresji', *Prace Instytutu Koniunktur Gospodarczych i* Cen, 4/2, pp. 39–50.

Breit, M. (1935b) 'Ein Beitrag zur Theorie des Geld- und Kapitalmarktes', in *Zeitschrift für Nationalőkonomie* Vol. 6, No. 5, 1935.

Buchanan, N. S. and Calkins, R. D. (1938) 'A Comment on Mr. Kalecki's "Principle of Increasing Risk"', Economica, Vol. 5, No. 20.

Burgess, W. R. (1964) 'Reflections on the Early Development of Open Market Policy', *Monthly Review*. New York: Federal Reserve Bank of New York, November, pp. 219–26.

Cecchetti, S. (2012) 'Comment' in Bank for International Settlements 'The Threat of Fiscal Dominance', *BIS Papers*, No. 65, May 2012, pp. 135–7.

Chick, V. (1986) 'The Evolution of the Banking System and the Theory of Saving, Investment and Interest', in S. C. Dow and P. Arestis (eds), *On Money, Method and Keynes Selected Essays*. London: Macmillan, 1992.

Chick, V. (2005) 'Lost and Found: Some History of Endogenous Money in the Twentieth Century', in G. Fontana and R. Realfonzo (eds), *The Monetary Theory of Production Tradition and Perspectives*. Basingstoke: Palgrave Macmillan, 2005.

Chick, V., and Dow, S. C. (2002) 'Monetary Policy with Endogenous Money and Liquidity Preference: A Nondualistic Treatment', *Journal of Post Keynesian Economics*, Vol. 24 No. 4, pp. 587–607.

Chilosi, A. (1982) 'Breit, Kalecki and Hicks on the Term Structure of Interest Rates, Risk and the Theory of Investment', in M. Baranzini (ed.), *Advances in Economic Theory*. Oxford: Basil Blackwell.

Corry, B. A. (1962) *Money, Saving and Investment in English Economics 1800–1850*. New York: St. Martin's Press.

Curdia, V., and Woodford, M. (2011) 'The Central-Bank Balance Sheet as an Instrument of Monetary Policy', *Journal of Monetary Economics*, Vol. 58, Issue 1, pp. 54–79.

Davidson, P. (1978) *Money and the Real World*, Basingstoke: Macmillan.

Davidson, P. (2002) *Financial Markets, Money and the Real World*, Cheltenham, UK and Northampton, MA, USA: Edward Elgar.

De Cecco, M. (1984) *Money and Empire: The International Gold Standard 1890–1914*, New York: St. Martin's Press.

de Walque, G., Pierrard, O., and Rouabah, A. (2010) 'Financial (In)Stability, Supervision and Liquidity Injections: A Dynamic General Equilibrium Approach', *Economic Journal*, Vol. 120, No. 549, December 2010, pp. 1234–61.

Dodig, N., Hein, E., and Detzer, D. (2016) 'Financialisation and the Financial and Economic Crises: Theoretical Framework and Empirical Analysis 15 Countries', in *Financialisation and the Financial and Economic CrisesCountry Studies*. Cheltenham: Edward Elgar.

Doi, T., Ihori, T., and Mitsui K. (2007) 'Sustainability, Inflation and Public Debt Policy in Japan', in D.G. Mayes and J. Toporowski (eds), *Open Market Operations and Financial Markets*. London: Routledge.

Dow, J. C. R., and Saville, I. D. (1988) *A Critique of Monetary Policy Theory and British Experience*. Oxford: The Clarendon Press.

Dymski, G. A. (1996) 'Kalecki's Monetary Economics', in J. E. King, *An Alternative Macroeconomic Theory*. Boston/Dordrecht/London: Kluwer Academic Publishers.

Eggertsson, G. B., and Woodford, M. (2003) 'The Zero Bound on Interest Rates and Optimal Monetary Policy', Brookings Papers on Economic Activity 1:2003.

Ehlers, T. (2012) 'The Effectiveness of the Federal Reserve's Maturity Extension Program – Operation Twist 2: The Portfolio Rebalancing Channel and Public Debt Management' in Bank for International Settlements 'The Threat of Fiscal Dominance', *BIS Papers*, No. 65, May 2012, pp. 245–55.

Fawley, B. W., and Neely, C. J. (2013) 'Four Stories of Quantitative Easing', *Federal Reserve Bank of St. Louis Review*, January/February (95)1, pp. 51–88.

Fisher, I. (1911) *The Purchasing Power of Money*. New York: Macmillan.

Fisher, I. (1933) 'The Debt Deflation Theory of Great Depressions', *Econometrica*, Vol. 1, No. 4, October, pp. 337–57.

Friedman, M. (1948) 'A Monetary and Fiscal Framework for Economic Stability', *American Economic Review*, Vol. 38, No. 3, June, pp. 245–64.

Friedman, M. (1959) *A Program for Monetary Stability*. New York: Fordham University Press.

Friedman, M., and Schwartz, A. J. (1963) *A Monetary History of the United States 1867–1930*. Princeton NJ: Princeton University Press for the National Bureau of Economic Research.

Godley, W. (2000) 'Seven Unsustainable Processes', *Special Report*. New York: Jerome Levy Economics Institute at Bard College.

Goodfriend, M. (2003) 'The Phases of US Monetary Policy 1987–2003', in P. Mizen (ed.), *Central Banking, Monetary Theory and Practice, Essays in Honour of Charles Goodhart Volume One*. Cheltenham: Edward Elgar.

Goodfriend, M., and R. G. King (1988) 'Financial Deregulation, Monetary Policy, and Central Banking'. *Federal Reserve Bank of Richmond Economic Review*, Vol. 74, No. 3, May–June, pp. 216–53.

Goodhart, C. A. E. (1975) *Money, Information and Uncertainty*. Basingstoke: Macmillan.

Goodhart, C. A. E. (2001) 'Monetary Transmission Lags and the Formulation of the Policy Decision on Interest Rates', *Federal Reserve Bank of St. Louis Review*, July/August, pp. 165–81.

Goodhart, C. A. E. (2014) 'Competition and Credit Control', *Special Paper*, No. 229, The London School of Economics Financial Markets Group.

Goodhart, C. A. E., and Dai, L. (2003) *Intervention to Save Hong Kong: The Authorities' Counter-Speculation in Financial Markets*. Oxford: Oxford University Press.

Goodhart, C. A. E., Sunirand, P., and Tsocomos, D. (2005) 'A Risk Assessment Model for Banks', *Annals of Finance*, Vol. 1(2), pp. 197–224.

Goodhart, C. A. E., Sunirand, P., and Tsocomos, D. (2006) 'A Model to Analyse Financial Fragility', *Economic Theory*, Vol. 27, pp. 107–42.

Goodhart, C. A. E., Romanidis, N., Shubik, M., and Tsocomos, D. (2019) 'Macromodeling, Default and Money', in D. G. Mayes, P. L. Siklos, and J-E. Sturm (eds), *The Oxford Handbook of the Economics of Central Banking*. New York: Oxford University Press.

Górecki, R. (1935) *Poland and Her Economic Development*. London: George Allen and Unwin.

Graziani, A. (1965) 'Equilibro generale ed accumulazione di capitale nel sistema Paretiano', *Cahiers Vilfredo Pareto*, 3, n. 5, pp. 75–88, *Études sur Pareto et les doctrines économiques, politiques et sociologiques de son époque offertes à M. Georges-H Bousquet*.

Graziani, A. (1989) 'The Theory of the Monetary Circuit', *Thames Papers in Political Economy*. London: Thames Polytechnic.

Graziani, A. (2002) 'The Investment Decision in Keynes's Thought', in P. Arestis, M. Desai, and S. C. Dow (eds), *Money Macroeconomics and Keynes Essays in Honour of Victoria Chick, Volume One*. London: Routledge.

Graziani, A. (2003a) 'Finance Motive', in J. E. King (ed.), *The Elgar Companion to Post Keynesian Economics*. Cheltenham: Edward Elgar.

Graziani, A. (2003b) *The Monetary Theory of Production, the Federico Caffè Lectures*. Cambridge: Cambridge University Press.

Halevi, J. (2016) 'Luigi Pasinetti and the Political Economy of Growth and Distribution', *Working Paper* No. 40, Institute for New Economic Thinking.

Halevi, J., and Taouil, R. (2002) 'On a Post-Keynesian stream from France and Italy: the *Circuit Approach*', in P. Arestis, M. Desai, and S. C. Dow (eds), *Money Macroeconomics and Keynes Essays in Honour of Victoria Chick, Volume One*. London: Routledge.

Harcourt, G. C., and Kerr, P. (2009) *Joan Robinson*. Basingstoke: Palgrave.

Hasbrouk, J. (2007) *Empirical Market Microstructure: The Institutions, Economics and Econometrics of Securities Trading*. London: Oxford University Press.

Hawtrey, R. G. (1926) *Monetary Reconstruction*. London: Longmans Green and Co.

Hawtrey, R. G. (1933) *The Art of Central Banking*. London: Longmans Green and Co.

Hawtrey, R. G. (1934) *Currency and Credit*. London: Longmans Green and Co.

Hawtrey, R. G. (1938) *A Century of Bank Rate*. London: Longmans, Green and Co.

Hayek, F. A. (1933) *Monetary Theory and the Trade Cycle*, translated by N. Kaldor and H. Croome. London: Routledge and Kegan Paul.

Hein, E. (2012a) *The Macroeconomics of Finance-Dominated Capitalism—And Its Crisis*. Cheltenham, UK: Edward Elgar.

Hein, E. (2012b) 'The Crisis of Finance-Dominated Capitalism in the Euro Area, Deficiencies in the Economic Policy Architecture, and Deflationary Stagnation Policies', *Working Paper* No. 734, The Levy Economics Institute of Bard College, New York.

Hicks, J. (1935) 'A Suggestion for Simplifying the Theory of Money', *Economica*, New Series, No. 2, pp. 1–19, reprinted in *Critical Essays in Monetary Theory*. Oxford: The Clarendon Press, 1967.

Hicks, J. (1967) 'Monetary Theory and History – An Attempt at Perspective', in *Critical Essays in Monetary Theory*. Oxford: The Clarendon Press.

Hicks, J. R. (1939) *Value and Capital An Inquiry into Some Fundamental Principles of Economic Theory*. Oxford: The Clarendon Press.

Hobson, J. A. (1913) *Gold, Prices and Wages with an Examination of the Quantity Theory*, London: Methuen.

Hőrman, M, and Schabert, A. (2015) 'A Monetary Analysis of Balance Sheet Policies', *The Economic Journal*, Vol. 125, No. 589, December 2015, pp. 1888–1917.

Humphrey, T. M. (1982) 'The Real Bills Doctrine', *Quarterly Review*, Federal Reserve Bank of Richmond, September/October.

Johnson, E. S., and Johnson, H. G. (1979) *The Shadow of Keynes: Understanding Keynes, Cambridge and Keynesian Economics*. Oxford: Basil Blackwell.

Kahn, R. F. (1954/1972) 'Some Notes on Liquidity Preference', *Manchester School* September 1954, in *Essays on Employment and Growth*. Cambridge: Cambridge University Press, 1972.

Kahn, R. F. (1971) 'Notes on the Rate of Interest and the Growth of Firms', in *Essays in Employment and Growth*. Cambridge: Cambridge University Press, 1972.

Kahn, R. F. (1972) 'Memorandum of Evidence Submitted to the Radcliffe Committee', in R. F. Kahn, *Selected Essays on Employment and Growth*. Cambridge: Cambridge University Press, pp. 124–52.

Kahn, R. F. (1976) 'Historical Origins of the International Monetary Fund', in A. P. Thirlwall (ed.), *Keynes and International Monetary Relations: The Second Keynes Seminar Held at the University of Kent at Canterbury*. Basingstoke: Macmillan.

Kaldor, N. (1982) *The Scourge of Monetarism*. Oxford: Oxford University Press.

Keynes, J. M. (1920) *The Economic Consequences of the Peace*. London: Macmillan.

Keynes, J. M. (1922) *A Revision of the Treaty being a sequel to The Economic Consequences of the Peace*. London: Macmillan.

Keynes, J. M. (1923) *A Tract on Monetary Reform*. London: Macmillan.

Keynes, J. M. (1930/1971a) *A Treatise on Money, Volume 1. The Pure Theory of Money.* Basingstoke: Macmillan for the Royal Economic Society.

Keynes, J. M. (1930/1971b) *A Treatise on Money, Volume 2. The Applied Theory of Money.* Basingstoke: Macmillan for the Royal Economic Society.

Keynes, J. M. (1934) 'Poverty in Plenty: Is the Economic System Self-Adjusting?', *The Listener,* 21 November, in *The Collected Writings of John Maynard Keynes, Volume XIII. The General Theory and After Part I: Preparation.* London: Macmillan, 1973, pp. 485–92.

Keynes, J. M. (1936) *The General Theory of Employment, Interest and Money.* London: Macmillan.

Keynes, J. M. (1945/1980) 'National Debt Enquiry: A Summary by Lord Keynes of His Proposals', in D. Moggridge (ed.), *The Collected Writings of John Maynard Keynes, Volume XXVII, Activities 1940–1946. Shaping the Post-War World: Employment and Commodities.* Cambridge: Macmillan and Cambridge University Press for the Royal Economic Society.

Keynes, J. M. (1973) *The Collected Writings of John Maynard Keynes, Volume XIV. The General Theory and After, Part II: Defence and* Development, edited by D. E. Moggridge. London: Macmillan.

Keynes, J. M. (1978) *The Collected Writings of John Maynard Keynes, Volume XVIII, Activities 1922–1932. The End of Reparations,* edited by Elizabeth Johnson. London: Macmillan for the Royal Economic Society.

Keynes, J. M. (1980a) *The Collected Writings of John Maynard Keynes, Volume XXV, Activities 1940–1944. Shaping the Post-War World: The Clearing Union,* edited by D. E. Moggridge. London: Macmillan/Cambridge University Press.

Keynes, J. M. (1980b) *The Collected Writings of John Maynard Keynes, Volume XXVII, Activities 1940–1946. Shaping the Post-War World Employment and Commodities,* edited by D. E. Moggridge. London: Macmillan/Cambridge University Press.

Keynes, J. M. (1983) *The Collected Writings of John Maynard Keynes, Volume XI, Economic Articles and Correspondence: Academic,* edited by D. E. Moggridge. Cambridge: Cambridge University Press.

Kiyotaki, N., and Moore, J. (1997) 'Credit Cycles', *Journal of Political Economy,* Vol. 105, No. 2, April, pp. 211–48.

Kothari, S. P., Lewellen, J., and Warner, J. B. (2014) 'The Behavior of Aggregate Corporate Investment', *Working Paper* No. 5112–14. MIT Sloan School of Management.

Kregel, J. A. (1986) 'Shylock or Hamlet: Are There Bulls and Bears in the Circuit?', *Économies et Sociétés,* Série Monnaie et Production, 3, 11–22.

Laidler, D. (1991) *The Golden Age of the Quantity Theory.* Princeton NJ: Princeton University Press.

Landau, L. (1957) *Wybór Pism.* Warszawa: Państwowe Wydawnictwo Naukowe.

Lange, O. (1941) 'Review of M. Kalecki *Essays in the Theory of Economic Fluctuations*', *Review of Political Economy,* No. 2, pp. 279–85.

Lange, O. (1986) *Dzieła tom 8 działalność naukowa i społeczna.* Warszawa: Państwowe Wydawnictwo Naukowe.

Lapavitsas, C. (2013) *Profiting without Producing: How Finance Exploits Us All.* London: Verso Press.

Łaski, K. (2019) *Lectures in Macroeconomics A Capitalist Economy Without Unemployment.* Oxford: Oxford University Press.

Lavington, F. (1921) *The English Capital Markets.* London: Methuen.

League of Nations (1930) *First Interim Report of the Gold Delegation of the Financial Committee.* Geneva: League of Nations.

Lee, F. S. (1998) *Post-Keynesian Price Theory.* Cambridge: Cambridge University Press.

Leontief, W. (1937) 'Implicit Theorizing: A Methodological Critique of the Neo-Cambridge School', *Quarterly Journal of Economics*, Vol. 51, No. 2, pp. 337–51.

Levy-Orlik, N., and Toporowski, J. (2007) 'Open Market Operations in Emerging Markets: The Case of Mexico', in D. G. Mayes and J. Toporowski (eds), *Open Market Operations and Financial Markets.* London: Routledge.

López, G. J., and Assous, M. (2010) *Michał Kalecki.* Basingstoke: Palgrave Macmillan.

MacLachlan, F. (1993) *Keynes's General Theory of Interest: A Reconsideration.* London: Routledge.

Marshall, A. (1887) 'Minutes of Evidence' to the Royal Commission on the Values of Gold and Silver, in *Official Papers by Alfred Marshall.* London: Macmillan, 1926.

Marx, K. H. (1970) *Capital: A Critique of Political Economy, Volume III: The Process of Capitalist Production as a Whole.* London: Lawrence and Wishart.

Marx, K. H. (1974) *Capital: A Critique of Political Economy, Volume II: The Process of Circulation of Capital.* London: Lawrence and Wishart.

Mayer, C., and Vives, X. (1995) 'Introduction', in C. Mayer and X. Vives (eds), *Capital Markets and Financial Intermediation.* Cambridge: Cambridge University Press.

Meade, J. E., and Andrews, P. W. S. (1938) 'Summary of Replies to Questions on Effects of Interest Rates', *Oxford Economic Papers*, Vol. 1, No. 1, pp. 14–31.

Michell, J., and Toporowski, J. (2012) 'The Stock-flow Consistent Approach with Active Financial Markets', in D. B. Papadimitriou and G. Zezza (eds), *Contributions in Stock-flow Modelling.* New York: Palgrave Macmillan, pp. 173–96.

Minsky, H. P. (1986) 'Conflict and Interdependence in a Multipolar World', *Studies in Banking and Finance*, Vol. 4, pp. 3–22.

Minsky, H. P. (2008) 'Securitization', *Policy Note* 2008/2. New York: The Levy Economics Institute of Bard College.

Mints, L. W. (1946) 'Monetary Policy', *Review of Economics and Statistics*, Vol. 28, No. 2, May, pp. 60–9.

Modigliani, F., and Miller, M. (1958) 'The Cost of Capital, Corporation Finance and the Theory of Investment', *American Economic Review*, Vol. 48, No. 3, pp. 261–97.

Modigliani, F., and Sutch R. (1966) 'Innovations in Interest Rate Policy', *American Economic Review*, Vol. 56, No. 1/2, pp. 178–97.

Modigliani, F., and Sutch, R. (1967) 'Debt Management and the Term Structure of Interest Rates: An Empirical Analysis of Recent Experience', *Journal of Political Economy*, Vol. 75, No. 4, Part 2, pp. 569–89.

Moore, B. J. (1988) *Horizontalists and Verticalists: The Macroeconomics of Credit Money.* Cambridge: Cambridge University Press.

Mott, T. (1982) *'Kalecki's Principle of Increasing Risk: The Role of Finance in the Post-Keynesian Theory of Investment Fluctuations'*. Ph.D. dissertation, Stanford University.

Mott, T. (1985–1986) 'Kalecki's Principle of Increasing Risk and the Relation Among Mark-up Pricing, Investment Fluctuations, and Liquidity Preference', *Economic Forum*, Vol. XV, Winter, pp. 65–76.

Mott, T. (2010) *Kalecki's Principle of Increasing Risk and Keynesian Economics.* Abingdon: Routledge.

Niebyl, K. H. (1946) *Studies in the Classical Theories of Money.* New York: Columbia University Press.

Osiatyński, J.(ed.) (1990) *Collected Works of Michał Kalecki Volume I Capitalism: Business Cycles and Full Employment.* Oxford: The Clarendon Press.

Osiński, J., and Sławiński, A. (1995) *National Bank of Poland and Open Market Operations.* Warsaw: Narodowy Bank Polski.

Pasinetti, L. L. (1997) 'The Social "Burden" of High Interest Rates', in: P. Arestis, G. Palma, and M. Sawyer (eds), *Capital Controversy, Post-Keynesian Economics and the History of Economic Thought*, Volume I. London & New York: Routledge, pp. 161–8.

Pasinetti, L. L. (1998) 'The Myth (or Folly) of the 3% Deficit/GDP Maastricht Parameter', *Cambridge Journal of Economics,* Vol. 22 (1), pp. 103–16.

Patinkin, D. (1982) *Anticipations of the General Theory? And Other Essays on Keynes.* Oxford: Basil Blackwell.

Pigou, A. C. (1912) *Wealth and Welfare.* London: Macmillan.

Pigou, A. C. (1916) *The Economy and Finance of the War, Being a Discussion of the Real Costs of the War and the Way in Which They Should Be Met.* London: J. M. Dent and Sons.

Pigou, A. C. (1943) 'The Classical Stationary State', *Economic Journal,* Vol. 53, No. 212, December, pp. 343–51.

Piketty, T. (2013) *Capital in the Twenty-First Century.* Cambridge Mass: Harvard University Press.

Reinhart, C. M., and Rogoff, K. S. (2008) *This Time Is Different: Eight Centuries of Financial Folly.* Princeton NJ: Princeton University Press.

Reynolds, P. J. (1987) *Political Economy: A Synthesis of Kaleckian and Post-Keynesian Economics.* Brighton: Wheatsheaf.

Ricardo, D. (1810) *The High Price of Bullion: A Proof of the Depreciation of Bank Notes.* London: Murray, in Sraffa, P. (ed.), *The Works and Correspondence of David Ricardo, Volume III, Pamphlets and Papers, 1809–1811.* Cambridge: Cambridge University Press, 1951.

Ricardo, D. (1816) *Proposals for an Economical and Secure Currency with Observations on the Profits of the Bank of England as the Regard the Public and the Proprietors of Bank Stock*, in P. Sraffa with M. H. Dobb (eds), *The Works and Correspondence of David Ricardo, Volume IV: Pamphlets and Papers, 1815–1823.* Cambridge: Cambridge University Press.

Ricardo, D. (1817) *On the Principles of Political Economy and Taxation*, in P. Sraffa with M. Dobb (eds), *The Works and Correspondence of David Ricardo, Volume I.* Cambridge: Cambridge University Press.

Robertson, D. H. (1926) *Banking Policy and the Price Level.* London: Macmillan.

Robertson, D. H. (1928) 'Theories of Banking Policy', in *Essays in Monetary Theory.* London: P. S. King, 1940.

Robertson, D. H. (1954/1966) 'Thoughts on Meeting Some Important Persons', *Quarterly Journal of Economics*, Vol. 68, No. 2, May, pp. 181–90, in *Essays on Money and Interest.* Glasgow: Collins.

Robinson, J. V. (1936) 'The Long-Period Theory of Employment', *Zeitschrift für* Nationalökonomie, March, reprinted in *Essays in the Theory of Employment.* London: Macmillan, 1937.

Robinson, J. V. (1945) 'Review of *The Economics of Full Employment*', *Economic Journal,* April, reprinted in *Collected Economic Papers Volume One.* Oxford: Basil Blackwell, 1966, pp. 99–104.

Robinson, J. V. (1951) 'The Rate of Interest', *Econometrica*, Vol. 19, No. 1, pp. 92–111.

Robinson, J. V. (1952) *The Rate of Interest and Other Essays.* London: Macmillan.

Robinson, J. V. (1966) 'Kalecki and Keynes', in *Problems of Economic Dynamics and Planning Essays in Honour of Michał Kalecki.* Warszawa: Państwowe Wydawnictwo Naukowe.

Robinson, J. V. (1976) 'Michał Kalecki, A Neglected Prophet', *New York Review of Books*, 4 March.

Romer, C. D., and Romer, D. H. (1989) 'Does Monetary Policy Matter? A New Test in the Spirit of Friedman and Schwarz', National Bureau of Economic Research *Macroeconomics Annual*, pp. 121–84.

Samuelson, P. A. (1964) 'Theoretical Notes on Trade Problems', *Review of Economics and Statistics*, Vol. 46, No. 2, pp. 145–54.

Sandilands, R. J. (2010) 'Hawtreyan "Credit Deadlock" or "Keynesian Liquidity Trap"? Lessons for Japan from the Great Depression', in R. Leeson (ed.), *David Laidler's Contributions to Economics.* Basingstoke: Palgrave Macmillan.

Sawyer, M. (2001) 'Kalecki on Money and Finance', *European Journal of the History of Economic Thought*, Vol. 8, No. 4, pp. 481–508.

Sawyer, M. (2004) 'Money and Finance in Kalecki's Analysis', in Z. L. Sadowski and A. Szeworski (eds), *Kalecki's Economics Today.* London: Routledge.

Sayers, R. S. (1936) *Bank of England Operations 1890–1914.* London: P. S. King and Sons.

Sayers, R. S. (1948) *The American Banking System: A Sketch.* Oxford: The Clarendon Press.

Sayers, R. S. (1957) *Central Banking after Bagehot.* Oxford: The Clarendon Press.

Schumacher, E. F. (1943a) 'Multilateral Clearing', *Economica*, New Series, Vol. 10, No. 38, May, pp. 150–65.

Schumacher, E. F. (1943b) 'The New Currency Plans', *Bulletin of the Institute of Statistics Oxford Supplement No. 5*, Vol. 5, 7 August, pp. 8–29.

Schumacher, E. F., and Balogh, T. (1944) 'An International Monetary Fund', *Bulletin of the Institute of Statistics Oxford*, Vol. 6, No. 6, 29 April, pp. 81–93.

Schumpeter, J. A. (1954) *History of Economic Analysis,* London: Allen and Unwin.

Shabani, M., and Toporowski, J. (2015) 'A Nobel Prize for the Empirical Analysis of Asset Prices', *Review of Political Economy*, Vol. 27, No. 1, January, pp. 62–85.

Shaikh, A. (2016) *Capitalism Competition, Conflict, Crises.* Oxford University Press.

Simons, H. C. (1934) 'A Positive Program for Laisez-Faire Some Proposals for a Liberal Economic Policy', in *Economic Policy for a Free Society.* Chicago: University of Chicago Press, 1948.

Simons, H. C. (1936) 'Rules versus Authorities in Monetary Policy', in *Economic Policy for a Free Society.* Chicago: Chicago University Press1948.

Skidelsky, R. (2001) *John Maynard Keynes Volume Three Fighting for Freedom, 1937–1946.* New York: Viking.

Sławiński, A., and Osiński, J. (1994) 'National Bank of Poland and Open Market Operations', Paper No. 11, Warszawa: Narodowy Bank Polski.

Smithin, J. (2003) *Controversies in Monetary Economics.* Cheltenham: Edward Elgar.

Steindl, J. (1945) 'Capitalist Enterprise and Risk', *Oxford Economic* Papers, March, in J. Steindl, *Economic Papers 1941–1988.* Basingstoke: Macmillan, 1990.

Steindl, J. (1965) *Random Processes and the Growth of Firms: A Study of the Pareto Law.* London: Charles Griffin & Co.

Steindl, J. (1982) 'The Role of Household Saving in the Modern Economy', *Banca Nazionale del Lavoro Quarterly* Review, March 1982, No. 140, in J. Steindl, *Economic Papers 1941–1988.* Basingstoke: Macmillan, 1990.

Steindl, J. (1989a) 'Saving and Debt', in A. Barrère (ed.), *Money, Credit and Prices in Keynesian Perspective.* London: Macmillan, pp. 71–89.

Steindl, J. (1989b) 'Reflections on Kalecki's Dynamics', in M. Sebastiani (ed.), *Kalecki's Relevance Today.* New York: St Martin's Press.

Stenfors, A., and Toporowski, J. (2020) *Unconventional Monetary Policy and Financial Stability: The Case of Japan.* Abingdon: Routledge.

Stockhammer, E. (2012) 'Financialization', in J. Toporowski and J. Michell (eds), *Handbook of Critical Issues in Finance.* Cheltenham: Edward Elgar.

Svensson, L. E. O. (2003) 'The Inflation Forecast and the Loss Function', in P. Mizen (ed.), *Central Banking, Monetary Theory and Practice Essays in Honour of Charles Goodhart.* Cheltenham: Edward Elgar.

Thirlwall, A. P. (1980) *Balance-of-Payments Theory and Export-led Growth: The United Kingdom Experience.* Basingstoke: Palgrave.

Tily, G. (2007) *Keynes's **General Theory**, the Rate of Interest and 'Keynesian' Economics.* Basingstoke: Palgrave Macmillan.

Tobin, J. (1963) 'An Essay on the Principles of Debt Management', in Commission on Money and Credit, *Fiscal and Debt Management Policies.* Englewood Cliffs: Prentice Hall, reprinted in J. Tobin, *Essays in Economics, Volume 1.* Amsterdam: North-Holland, 1971.

Tobin, J. (1969) 'A General Equilibrium Approach to Monetary Theory', *Journal of Money Credit and Banking*, No. 1, February, pp. 15–29.

Toporowski, J. (2000) *The End of Finance: The Theory of Capital Market Inflation, Financial Derivatives and Pension Fund Capitalism.* London: Routledge.

Toporowski, J. (2006) 'Open Market Operations: Beyond the New Consensus', *Bank of Finland Research Discussion Papers* 14/2006.

Toporowski, J. (2008) 'Notes on Excess Capital and Liquidity Management', *Working Paper* No. 549, Annandale-on-Hudson, New York: The Jerome Levy Economics Institute of Bard College, November, pp. 1–10.

Toporowski, J. (2010) *'Why the World Economy Needs a Financial Crash' and Other Critical Essays on Finance and Financial Economics.* London: Anthem Press.

Toporowski, J. (2012) 'Overcapitalisation', in J. Toporowski and J. Michell (eds), *Handbook of Critical Issues in Finance.* Cheltenham: Edward Elgar.

Toporowski, J. (2013) *Michał Kalecki: An Intellectual Biography, Volume 1: Rendezvous in Cambridge 1899–1939.* Basingstoke: Palgrave.

Toporowski, J. (2015) 'A Kalecki Fable on Debt and the Monetary Transmission Mechanism', London School of Economics, Financial Markets Group *Special Paper* No. 239, August.

Toporowski, J. (2016a) 'Microfoundations, Minsky and Classical Political Economy', *Review of Political Economy*, Vol. 28, No. 1, January, pp. 92–7.

Toporowski, J. (2016b) 'Multilateralism and Military Keynesianism: Completing the Analysis', *Journal of Post-Keynesian Economics*, Vol. 39, No. 4, pp. 437–43.

Toporowski, J. (2016c) 'The Crisis of Finance and the Crisis of Accumulation: It Was Not a Lehman Brothers Moment', in T. Subasat (ed.), *The Great Financial Meltdown Systemic, Conjunctural or Policy Created?* Cheltenham: Edward Elgar, pp. 236–47.

Toporowski, J. (2018) *Michał Kalecki: An Intellectual Biography, Volume II: By Intellect Alone, 1939–1970.* Basingstoke: Palgrave.

Toporowski, J. (2020) 'Anwar Shaikh and the Classical Theory of Interest: A Critical Note', *Cambridge Journal of Economics*, Vol. 44, No. 2, March 2020, pp. 465–74.

United Nations (1950) 'Growth, Disequilibrium and Disparities: Interpretation of the Process of Economic Development', in *Economic Survey of Latin America 1949.* New York: United Nations.

US Treasury (1943) *Preliminary Draft Outline of a Proposal for an International Stabilisation Fund of the United and Associated Nations made public by the Secretary of the Treasury on April 17, 1943.* Washington DC.: US Treasury.

White Paper (1943) *Proposals for an International Clearing Union,* Cmd 6437. London: HM Stationery Office Cmd 6437.

White Paper (1944) *Joint Statement by Experts on the Establishment of an International Monetary Fund.* London: HM Stationery Office Cmd 6519.

Wicksell, K. (1936) *Interest and Prices: A Study of the Causes Regulating the Value of Money,* translated by R. Kahn. London: Macmillan for the Royal Economic Society.

Williams, J. C. (2016) 'Monetary Policy in a Low R-star World', *Economic* Letter, 2016–23, 15 August, Federal Reserve Bank of San Francisco.

Williams, J. H. (1943) 'Problems of Post-War International Monetary Stabilization', *Proceedings of the American Philosophical Society,* Vol. 87, No. 2, 16 August, pp. 133–8.

Wilson, J. S. G. (1962a) 'France', in R. S. Sayers (ed.), *Banking in Western Europe.* Oxford: The Clarendon Press.

Wilson, J. S. G. (1962b) 'The Netherlands', in R. S. Sayers (ed.), *Banking in Western Europe.* Oxford: The Clarendon Press.

Withers, H. (1909) *The Meaning of Money.* London; Smith Elder and Co.

Withers, H. (1917) *Our Money and the State.* London: John Murray.

Wolff, E. N. (2010) 'Recent Trends in Household Wealth in the United States: Rising Debt and the Middle Class Squeeze – An Update to 2007', *Working Paper* No. 502. Annandale-on-Hudson, NY: The Levy Economics Institute of Bard College.

Woodford, M. (2003) *Interest and Prices: Foundations of a Theory of Monetary Policy.* Princeton NJ: Princeton University Press.

Wray, L. R. (2013) 'Money', in G. C. Harcourt and Peter Kriesler (eds), *The Oxford Handbook of Post-Keynesian Economics, Volume 1: Theory and Origins.* Oxford: Oxford University Press.

Zampolli, F. (2012) 'Sovereign Debt Management as an Instrument of Monetary Policy: An Overview', in Bank for International Settlements, 'The Threat of Fiscal Dominance', *BIS Papers,* No. 65, May 2012 pp. 97–118.

Index

For the benefit of digital users, indexed terms that span two pages (e.g., 52–53) may, on occasion, appear on only one of those pages.